THE TRIAL OF CIVILIANS BY MILITARY COURTS
IRELAND 1921

THE TRIAL OF CIVILIANS BY MILITARY COURTS
IRELAND 1921

SEÁN ENRIGHT

IRISH ACADEMIC PRESS
DUBLIN • PORTLAND, OR

First published in 2012 by Irish Academic Press

2 Brookside,
Dundrum Road,
Dublin 14, Ireland

920 NE 58th Avenue, Suite 300
Portland, Oregon,
97213-3786, USA

www.iap.ie

British Library Cataloguing in Publication Data

Enright, Sean.
The trial of civilians by military courts : Ireland 1921.
1. Martial law—Ireland—History—20th century.
2. Military courts—Ireland—History—20th century.
3. Trials (Military offenses)—Ireland—History—20th century. 4. Justice, Administration of—Ireland—History—20th century. 5. Ireland—History—War of Independence, 1919-1921.
I. Title
345.4'1507'09042-dc22

978 0 7165 3133 3 (cloth)
978 0 7165 3134 0 (paper)

Library of Congress Cataloging-in-Publication Data
An entry can be found on request

Printed and bound by CPI Group (UK) Ltd, Croydon, CR0 4YY

For Jack, Will, Jonjo and Lorna

Contents

Acknowledgements		x
Abbreviations		xii
List of Illustrations		xiv
Preface		xvii
Chapter 1	Overview	1
	PART I	
Chapter 2	History and Law	7
Chapter 3	Ireland 1920	21
Chapter 4	Vernon Hart, Auxiliary Division, RIC	29
Chapter 5	The Military Court	34
	PART II	
Chapter 6	Cornelius Murphy, Ballydaly, County Kerry	47
Chapter 7	John Allen, Tipperary Town	53
Chapter 8	Dripsey	60
Chapter 9	Mourne Abbey	72
Chapter 10	Clonmult	80
Chapter 11	Patrick Casey, Ballybricken, County Limerick	92
Chapter 12	Daniel O'Brien, Liscarroll, County Cork	96
Chapter 13	Clifford and Sullivan	100
Chapter 14	Thomas Keane, Limerick	104
Chapter 15	John Joseph Egan, Ennis	108

Chapter 16 Egan v Macready And All That 112

PART III

Chapter 17 Thomas Malone, Tyrrell's Pass, County Westmeath 123

Chapter 18 Gabbett and Fenton, Mount Rivers, Newport, County Tipperary 126

Chapter 19 Rahanisky House 128

Chapter 20 John McBride, Knockmoylan, County Kilkenny 134

Chapter 21 Michael Kelleher and James Keogh, Youghal, County Cork 137

Chapter 22 Denis Murphy, Godfrey's Cross, County Cork 138

Chapter 23 Patrick Coakley, Lissanisky, Near Upton, County Cork 140

Chapter 24 Laurence Medlar, Paulstown, County Kilkenny 145

Chapter 25 O'Brien's Castle, County Clare 148

Chapter 26 John Duane, Ballina Cross, County Cork 153

Chapter 27 Timothy Dennehy, Clash, Kilbrin, County Cork; Cornelius Cunningham, Drominagh, County Cork 154

Chapter 28 Michael Casey, Newmarket on Fergus, County Clare 159

Chapter 29 Edward Punch and Timothy Murphy, Limerick 161

Chapter 30 John O'Sullivan, Abbeyfeale, County Limerick 165

Chapter 31 Jack Shine, Athea, County Limerick 168

Chapter 32 O'Connell and Cregan, Limerick 169

Chapter 33 Mallow Barracks 171

Chapter 34 Seán Moylan, Newmarket, County Cork 182

Chapter 35 Patrick Loughlin, Cashel, County Tipperary 188

Chapter 36 Patrick Cronin, Finuge, County Kerry 189

Chapter 37 Jones Bridge 191

Chapter 38	Garryricken House, County Kilkenny	194
Chapter 39	James O'Connell, Ballinleenty, County Tipperary	201
Chapter 40	Patrick Higgins, Ardra, Rostellan, County Cork	204
Chapter 41	Patrick Casey, Milford, County Cork	206
Chapter 42	Adam Jones, Rosslare Strand, County Wexford	208
Chapter 43	Thomas Looby, Irishtown, Clonmel, County Tipperary	211
Chapter 44	Michael Purcell, Kildringagh, County Kilkenny	213
Chapter 45	Michael O'Callaghan, Ballyhone, Emly, County Tipperary	215
Chapter 46	Waterfall, County Cork	217
Chapter 47	Denis Driscoll, Coolgarriv, Killarney, County Kerry	222
Chapter 48	Grenagh House, Killarney, County Kerry	224
Chapter 49	William Ryan, Ballinroe, County Tipperary	229
Chapter 50	Lieutenant Hanley Hunt, RNVR	231
Chapter 51	Father Noonan, Ballina and Boher, County Tipperary	233

PART IV

Chapter 52	Analysis of Trials by Military Court	239
Chapter 53	Postscript	256
Appendix 1	Proclamation of Martial Law, 10 December 1920	258
Appendix 2	Proclamation No. 1, 12 December 1920	259
Appendix 3	Proclamation No. 3	261
Appendix 4	Military Court Trials Not Covered in this Work	262

Select Bibliography 264

Notes 271

Index 298

Acknowledgements

I acknowledge research by Matt Dempsey, Tom Carroll, David Purcell and Will Enright. I acknowledge the resolute and generous help given by Aideen Carroll. I am also grateful to Michael Birnbaum, David Foxton, Jack Enright, D.J. Enright, David Gilbody, Jack Browne and Catherine O'Callaghan for reviewing extracts from the text and making many helpful suggestions. Also to Dr John Hayes, Miko O'Grady, William Sheehan (Sunday's Well), Tim Horgan, Pádraig Óg Ó Ruairc and Thomas Toomey for directing my attention to important source material.

I express my gratitude to the staff of the Imperial War Museum, the Public Record Office and also to the National Library of Ireland for assistance given. I also express my thanks to the staff at the Parliamentary Archives, Westminster and also to the Judge Advocate General for providing access to the archives to study the role of the Judge Advocate General.

The photographs of Chief Justice Molony, Tim Healy and Henry Hanna are reproduced by kind permission of the Council of King's Inns, Dublin. The photograph of Michael Comyn KC is reproduced with the consent of Michelle Comyn. The photographs of Patrick Lynch KC and John O'Byrne are reproduced from the Superior Courts of Law with the permission of Dr Eamonn Hall and the Office of the Attorney General of Ireland. My thanks also to Timothy Cassel QC for permission to use the photograph of Sir Felix Cassel. The photograph of the portrait of Colonel C.B. Vandeleur (by Archibald Haswell Miller, 1924) is reproduced courtesy of South Lanarkshire Council. The photograph of F.E. Young is reproduced with the kind consent of the trustees of the Black Watch Museum. The photograph of Chief Justice Hugh Kennedy and the First Judiciary of the Irish Free State is by permission of the *Irish Times*. The photograph of Lord Simon KC is by kind permission of Viscount Simon. The photograph of Albert and Edythe Wood is by permission of Chris Wood and the photograph of Barry Sullivan with the consent of Helen Sullivan. The following images are included courtesy of the Imperial War Museum: Q107743, Q107753, Q113489, Q71685, Q71694.

Permission has been given by the *Irish Examiner* to quote extracts from a number of trials reported by the *Cork Examiner*. I acknowledge the gracious assistance of the *Irish Examiner* in this respect. I also acknowledge permission given by the *Clare Champion*, the *Limerick Leader* and the *Waterford News and Star* to quote various reports. I have taken all possible steps to identify copyright holders for the *Clonmel Chronicle* and the *Cork Constitution*. Many of the newspaper accounts have been accessed via the National Library of Ireland and where such material is reproduced this is by courtesy of the National Library of Ireland. My thanks also to Irene Stevenson of the *Irish Times*.

Extracts from statements compiled by the Bureau of Military History are included in this work and in that respect I am indebted to the Irish Military Archives, Cathal Brugha Barracks, Dublin, my thanks especially to Lisa Dolan for assistance given.

Extracts from the diaries of Sir Henry Wilson are by kind permission of the trustees of the Imperial War Museum. I should add that the trustees would like to make contact with the copyright holder of the Strickland Papers. I have taken all reasonable steps to trace the copyright holders, without success. Extracts from the diary of R.M. Grazebrook are reproduced courtesy of the trustees of the Soldiers of the Gloucestershire Museum. Extracts from the archives of the Lancers are reproduced courtesy of the Queen's Royal Lancers Museum. I also acknowledge and thank the trustees of the Manchester Regiment Archive and Museum, Tameside, with regard to the extracts from the Manchester Regiment Arrest Register and the Manchester Regiment Record of Service. My thanks also to J.P. Kelleher of the Museum of the Royal Fusiliers for permission to use extracts from the archives.

From time to time I have looked to Kenneth Ferguson's *King's Inns Barristers*, which has proved a useful starting point for research, and I acknowledge that debt.

Any opinions expressed are mine alone.

Abbreviations

ADRIC	Auxiliary Division, Royal Irish Constabulary
BMH	Bureau of Military History
CO	Colonial Office
Circular Memoranda	The full title of this document is the *Circular Memoranda on Martial Law* which came to govern the procedures of the Military Court
DORA	Defence of the Realm Act
DORR	Defence of the Realm Regulations
FGCM	Field General Court Martial
GOC	General Officer Commanding
ILTR	*Irish Law Times Reports*
IR	Irish Reports
IWM	Imperial War Museum
JAG	Judge Advocate General
NLI	National Library of Ireland
PRO	Public Record Office, Kew, London
RAMC	Royal Army Medical Corps
Record of the Rebellion:	*The Record of the Rebellion and the Part Played by the Army in Dealing with it*. Compiled by the general staff at GHQ Parkgate, Dublin.
6th Division	The 6th Division of the British Army commanded by Major General Sir E.P. Strickland, which occupied what became known as the Martial Law Area.
Sixth Division Record of the Rebellion:	Compiled by staff officers of the Sixth Division. The full title is *The Irish Rebellion in the Sixth Divisional Area From After 1916 Rebellion to December 1921*
ROIA	Restoration of Order in Ireland Act 1920
ROIR	Restoration of Order in Ireland Regulations 1920
RIC	Royal Irish Constabulary

RM	Resident Magistrate
The Register	The Register of Trials by Military Courts, PRO/WO/35/208
Summary of Evidence	Where a court martial was envisaged under the Army Act or the Restoration of Order in Ireland Act, there was a hearing in which the witnesses related their evidence which was written down. The accused was present and was permitted to cross-examine and make a statement, if he so desired. The presence of the accused was regarded as an important protection against prosecutorial misconduct. In military court trials this protection was dispensed with.
TLR	*Times Law Reports*
WO	War Office

List of Illustrations

5.1 Captain F.E. Young, courts martial officer of the Sixth Division, second row, far left. Courtesy of the Trustees of the Black Watch Museum. 35

5.2 Lt Colonel Vandeleur, who presided over many of the trials by military court. Courtesy of the South Lanarkshire Council. 38

5.3 Victory Arch and Guardroom, Victoria Barracks. Courtesy of the Commanding Officer, Collins Barracks. 42

5.4 The Square, Victoria Barracks. Courtesy of the National Library of Ireland. 44

6.1 Sir Felix Cassel, KC, Judge Advocate General. Courtesy of Timothy Cassel QC. 51

7.1 Lord Chief Justice Molony. Reproduced by permission of the Council of King's Inns. 54

7.2 Henry Hanna KC, counsel for the Crown in Clifford and Sullivan and other cases. Reproduced by permission of the Council of King's Inns. 55

7.3 Tim Healy KC, counsel for John Allen. Healy was later Governor-General of the Irish Free State. Reproduced by permission of the Council of King's Inns. 56

8.1 General Macready. Reproduced courtesy of the Trustees of the Imperial War Museum. 64

8.2 Mrs Mary Lindsay of Leemount. Courtesy of the Trustees of the Imperial War Museum. 71

9.1 Albert Wood KC and his wife Edythe. Albert Wood was counsel for a number of the prisoners. Courtesy of Chris Wood. 73

10.1 John O'Byrne, counsel for Adam Jones. O'Byrne was later Attorney General and a Judge of the Supreme Court. Courtesy of Dr Eamonn Hall and the Office of the Attorney General. 81

10.2 Patrick Lynch KC, counsel for J.J. Egan and other prisoners. Courtesy of Dr Eamonn Hall and the Office of the Attorney General. 81

10.3 Michael Comyn KC on his elevation to KC, in 1914. Courtesy of Michelle Comyn. 84

10.4 Sir John Simon, a principled and articulate critic of the Lloyd George government and counsel for Clifford and Sullivan. Courtesy of the Palace of Westminster Collection. 87

10.5 The house at Clonmult. Courtesy of the Trustees of the Imperial War Museum. 90

16.1 The Emerging Judiciary of the Supreme Court and the High Court. 114

Standing (left to right): Thomas Lopdell O'Shauhnessy, William Wylie (who prosecuted most of the leaders of the 1916 Rebellion), William Johnston and James Murnaghan.

Sitting (left to right): Gerald Fitzgibbon, Timothy Sullivan, Chief Justice Kennedy, Charles O'Connor (who gave the judgment in Egan v Macready) and James Creed Meredith. Courtesy of the *Irish Times*.

16.2 Chief Justice Kennedy. By permission of the *Irish Times*. 116

23.1 Royal Fusiliers near Killarney. Courtesy of the Royal Fusiliers Museum. 142

23.2 Soldiers inspect bullet holes following a train ambush. Courtesy of the Royal Fusiliers Museum. 144

33.1 Barry Sullivan, solicitor for many of the prisoners tried by military court including Ronayne and Mulcahy, Moylan, and also those tried in connection with the Mallow Barracks Raid. Courtesy of Helen Sullivan. 172

46.1 Round up of suspects, Martial Law Area 1921. Courtesy of the Trustees of the Imperial War Museum. 219

46.2 Officers of the Auxiliary Division RIC (ADRIC). Courtesy of the Trustees of the Imperial War Museum. 221

Preface

This is an account of the trials by military court during the martial law era in Ireland, 1921. Bound up in this drama is an analysis of the lawfulness of the detention and trial of the prisoners which have an enduring importance and which reach out from history. The nature of the relationship between the state and those it seeks to govern is fundamental in any country which subscribes to the rule of law. One of the great dilemmas faced by every state is the extent to which it affords the protection of due process to those bent on its destruction by force of arms. The events of 1920–21 illustrate this tension all too well. Martial law represented the most extreme response.

The consequences of the conflict were profound: the partition of Ireland, the creation of Stormont and the process by which the twenty-six counties severed connections with Britain and the Empire. It is an emotive subject but if one strips away the dynamics of this conflict – Empire versus nationalism – it is easier to recognise the constitutional and libertarian implications of martial law. The army created their own courts to try civilians. Offences not punishable by death were converted into capital offences: trials and executions followed. As the months passed, the army sought greater powers to try and punish suspects, to control the civil courts and to suspend habeas corpus – the most ancient protection of liberty.

The rule of law is one of the cornerstones of the democratic process. In times of peace it is easy to uphold. Paradoxically, it is at times of great crisis that the rule of law is most needed but always threatened. It is in such circumstances that the constitutional arrangements in a democratic state may be undermined. This book provides a reminder of what those arrangements are and why they continue to be important.

There are upheavals in every age which may emerge in any part of the globe – the triggers may be ethnic or religious tensions, a desire for equality or self-determination or a complex mix of these issues. The important questions, however, tend to be the same. They relate in general, to the maintenance of due process and in particular, to the legality of detention and trial.

In recent years the United States Supreme Court has wrestled with the legality of interrogation techniques, internment and trial by military tribunals.[1] In the United Kingdom the debate has focused on detention without trial, extraordinary rendition, the Special Immigration Appeals Commission, pre-charge detention and control orders.[2] It is not necessary to express a view about any of these issues, simply to observe that this is the ambit of the current debate about due process. The precise nature of the issues will change from generation to generation but the tension between political imperatives and the rule of law is always present. History simply provides a broader perspective.

Which brings us back to Ireland in 1920. This book analyses a neglected episode of Anglo-Irish legal history. It charts the rebellion and the slide to martial law as one abrogation of due process followed another. The most significant feature of the martial law era was the Military Court, and this is the focus of this study.

There has never been an in-depth study of the Military Court in Ireland during this period.[3] Perhaps as a consequence a number of myths have grown up around the subject. The Military Court was created to deal swiftly with those who were thought to pose the greatest threat and there remains a perception that all or most of the prisoners tried were, to use the terminology of the time, rebels. The evidence will show that the process of identifying those to be tried by the Military Court was unfocused, to put it neutrally. The prisoners included one Auxiliary, three RIC men, three domestic servants, a housewife, a parish priest, an officer of the Royal Naval Volunteer Reserve, a Unionist landowner, and two men with learning difficulties, one of whom was severely disabled.[4] A careful analysis suggests that a significant number of other prisoners who stood trial were not involved in the rebellion and were simply caught up because they were on the periphery of events.

There are other myths. It has been said by more than one historian that the trials were rushed; sometimes completed in just fifteen minutes.[5] There are many criticisms that can be made of the military courts but this one cannot be sustained. It has been suggested that a significant number of prisoners may not have been legally represented: that was also not so.[6] It was widely reported that the landmark constitutional case of Clifford and Sullivan was won by the prisoners.[7] It was not. It has been said that when the case of Clifford and Sullivan went to the House of Lords there were forty-two other men being held under sentence of death by the Military Court.[8] None of these assertions are correct but the bare facts, which this book seeks to establish, are just as dramatic, disquieting and became in the years that followed an obstacle to reconciliation.

CHAPTER ONE

Overview

In 1920 the War of Independence reached a critical stage and the criminal justice system collapsed under the strain. In response, Parliament at Westminster passed the Restoration of Order in Ireland Act (ROIA). This Act extended the power of the army to courts martial civilians with power to impose the death penalty for offences so punishable under civil law. This measure did not suppress the crisis and in December 1920 martial law was declared in Cork, Kerry, Limerick and Tipperary. Soon after, four more counties were added to the Martial Law Area: Clare, Kilkenny, Wexford and Waterford. The army instituted a range of counter-measures in the Martial Law Area. As part of this process the army created the Military Court to try those contravening the provisions of martial law. The Military Court functioned alongside the trial of civilians by courts martial under the Restoration of Order in Ireland Act.

The Military Court had two tiers. First, the Summary Court which tried less serious infractions of martial law. It dealt with 2,296 people and imposed 549 sentences of imprisonment. Then there was the upper tier of the Military Court which tried just 128 people, a tiny fraction of those interned or tried under the ROIA in the Martial Law Area.[9] The Military Court enjoys an importance that far outweighs the number of cases it tried, because it was created by the army, not by any recognised process of law. Between late December 1920 and the advent of the Truce in July 1921, the Military Court sentenced thirty-seven men to death. Fourteen of these men were executed.[10] Many others received long sentences of imprisonment. During this time there were a series of challenges to the legality of this process which gave rise to judgments of enduring importance.[11]

The focus of this study is on trials by the Military Court heard under the provisions of martial law. We are also concerned with the pre-trial procedures and the process of review and confirmation of sentence and the legal challenges to the Military Court. In general terms this study does not address events outside the Martial Law Area, nor does it deal with the courts martial of civilians under the Restoration of Order in Ireland Act, because these were outside the ambit of martial law. For that reason some of the major trials of this era, such as Knocklong and Caherguillamore House,[12] are outside the scope of this study.

A central problem in this research has been to identify a reliable record of trials by the Military Court. Record-keeping was not at that time a priority. The most complete record of these trials can be found in a register at the National Archive at Kew.[13] The Register appears to have been compiled in the following way. After a trial by military court, and following acquittal or confirmation where there was a conviction, the case papers went to the office of the Judge Advocate General who held responsibility for overseeing the conduct of all trials conducted by the army. It is clear from the Register that the staff at the Judge Advocate General's office had sight of the case papers and the Military Court trials were logged as such. These case papers were then sent to storage at the National Archive. Many of the case papers were 'not selected for preservation' or simply did not survive. The Register, however, and a significant number of case papers did survive.

The Register provides a significant amount of detail and it is likely that it is as complete a record as can be found of the trials by the Military Court. This proposition can be tested in a number of ways. First, by reference to a letter written by General Macready, commander in chief in Ireland, dated 1 November 1921, to the War Office. General Macready, faced with yet another legal challenge and the prospect of the imminent collapse of martial law, observed that sixteen men were then under sentence of death by the Military Court, a further 133 were serving sentences of imprisonment and a further 790 were interned under martial law.[14] Given the position occupied by General Macready, his figures are likely to be accurate.

The Register at the National Archive at Kew records the trials of 128 men and women. It shows that thirty-seven men were sentenced to death by the Military Court, and, of this number, five had their sentences commuted to life imprisonment. It is a matter of public record that fourteen were executed.[15] This leaves a figure of eighteen. If one removes the names of the two men who were released at the end of July 1921 by order of the Master of the Rolls in Egan v Macready,[16] we are left a figure of sixteen which agrees with General Macready's figure for those under sentence of death.[17] It should be acknowledged that the Macready letter writes of 133 men serving sentences of imprisonment imposed under martial law, whereas the Register records the trials of only 128 individuals, some of whom were acquitted. It is clear, however, that Macready's calculation includes those tried by both the upper tier of the Military Court and also the Summary Court and that would account for the discrepancy.[18]

This analysis is corroborated by a review of other sources. In the first place, all those cases which came to be reported in the law reports appear in the Register. Secondly, the Bureau of Military History, which was set up to collate personal accounts of the conflict provides another source of reference. The Bureau took statements from eight men who were tried by the Military Court. The names of each of these men also appear in the Register.[19] Finally, the press coverage at the time, which was very full, does not suggest that there are other military court trials which do not appear in the Register. This process of cross-referencing suggests that the Register provides a complete record of those tried by the Military Court.

There have been other difficulties identifying records of trials. Although many of the case papers survive at the National Archive in Kew, many others were not selected for preservation.[20] Therefore, a number of these trials have been pieced together by using a variety of sources. A number of trials were reported in the *Cork Examiner*, *Clare Champion*, *Waterford News and Star*, *Limerick Leader*, *Limerick Chronicle* and *Cork Constitution*. This is an unsatisfactory basis on which to proceed. However, in the high-profile cases the accounts are a verbatim record of what took place. A hallmark of these reports is that they are factual and free from editorial comment. Some of these reports are brief and therefore need to be treated with considerable caution. Even in these reports there is sufficient detail to provide answers to some important questions: whether there was evidence to support the charge; whether the accused was represented and had an adequate opportunity to make out his case and call witnesses.

In rare instances where, for instance, the case has been adjourned or on one occasion the reporter had to leave court to avoid being in breach of curfew, the reports are incomplete. A small number of reports suggest that the press refrained from relating allegations detrimental to the army or the RIC. This self-censorship operated as a means of avoiding the fate of a number of newspapers, notably the *Freeman's Journal* which was suppressed in January 1920[21] and again in November of 1920 when the editor and owners of the paper were court martialled for sedition.[22] The owners were sentenced to prison terms, while the editor, Hooper, was also imprisoned, although no conviction was recorded. He was subsequently released by a writ of habeas corpus. It is hardly surprising, therefore, that newspapers were circumspect about reporting matters to the discredit of the military. In a small number of trials it is evident that reports have been redacted for this reason.[23] Using these reports raises a question as to accuracy, but comparison with surviving case papers and law reports suggests that the reporters, particularly at the *Cork Examiner*, were working to a high standard. These reports have been drawn on subject to these qualifications.

The question of terminology requires mention. Courts martial is a term that can be applied to the trial of soldiers under the Army Act. It may also be applied to describe the trial of civilians under the Restoration of Order in Ireland Act because the scheme of the Act was to treat civilians as soldiers. One sometimes sees a trial by military court referred to as a court martial. That is not an accurate description. The military courts of 1921 were created by the army. They had no legal status and were simply a collection of officers who advised the commander in chief.[24]

We turn then to the content of this study. Part I sets out a brief history of martial law. It provides the historical context and the legal justification asserted by the government of Lloyd George for the declaration of martial law in December 1920. It deals with the first trial under martial law (Vernon Hart) and the regulations which underpinned the Military Court. Part II reviews the key trials: those that led to execution and/or a concluded legal challenge in the civil courts. Part III records all those military court trials that did not result in execution or a concluded challenge before the High Court. This section also is confined to trials by the Military Court save that an exception is made in respect of the Mallow Barracks raid. This was a court martial under the ROIA which by a side wind casts some light on trials by the Military Court and is of interest for that reason. Part IV sets out an analysis of the trials by the Military Court.

PART I

CHAPTER TWO

History and Law

Martial law last existed in England in 1685 when the Duke of Monmouth landed at Lyme Regis with a small army. Monmouth was defeated at Sedgemoor and in the weeks that followed many rebels were tried by military court, the names of the men being noted on the regimental drum. There were no recorded acquittals and execution followed immediately. Colonel Kirke, the military commander, was famously rebuked by the Bishop of Wells: 'This is murder ... Now that the battle is over, these Rogues must be tried before they can be put to death.'[25] The Bishop, of course, meant tried by their peers according to due process of law. The executions ceased soon after and the remaining prisoners were sent for trial at the Western Assizes.[26] The central question raised by this episode is an enduring one: whether insurgents may lawfully be tried and punished by military courts.

The focus of this study is limited to Ireland in 1920–1921 but in order to understand the controversy that surrounded the proclamation of martial law, it may help to consider what was then recognised as the law and the historical context. We are concerned with the process by which insurrection, which could not be dealt with by the military acting in support of civil authority, was suppressed.[27] The power to act could only be invoked when war raged and the courts were unable to sit.[28] The power was limited only by necessity. This was the core of the matter although there were a number of divergent and respectable legal perspectives on the scope and nature of martial law[29] and when it might be deployed. The Duke of Wellington offered his own prosaic analysis: that martial law was merely 'the will of the commander' and it was 'no law at all'.[30]

In Britain the use of martial law became strictly confined by the end of the seventeenth century. This turbulent century was marked by a series of events; the Petition of Right,[31] the Civil War and the Monmouth Rebellion, which marked a growing revulsion against the use of arbitrary power by the sovereign or the army. There were, even so, still powerful social tensions which had to be reconciled before reform could come about. The Habeas Corpus Act of 1679[32] strengthened protection against arbitrary imprisonment by the sovereign. There was, however, a more fundamental barrier to the liberty of the subject and political stability: the power of the army. It was recognised that while a standing army was necessary for the defence of the realm, it carried with it a threat of dictatorship, either by a king who claimed rule by divine right or a man such as Cromwell. The argument was resolved in 1689 with the Bill of Rights, which created an army which was authorised and financed each year by Parliament and therefore under close control.[33] The Mutiny Act of the same year gave the army the powers to try and punish soldiers and sailors for breaches of discipline, but as the preamble to the Mutiny Act made clear, this did not permit the trial of civilians by military courts: '... no man may be prejudged of life or limb or subjected to any kind of punishment by martial law or in any other manner than by the judgment of his peers'.[34] In this way the power of the military was defined, curbed and the concept of trial by due process of law strengthened. The reforms coincided with a period of relative stability and prosperity in the United Kingdom and were therefore never tested in court but acquired the status of settled law.

While the power of the military was curbed, the political classes sought less extreme methods of control, which they reserved for themselves. This was one of the purposes of passing the Riot Act of 1714[35] which allowed magistrates to put down rioting and to call on troops to act at their direction and under their control. The Riot Act has often been portrayed as an instrument of oppression and it often was, but it also strengthened the civil authorities and for that reason was also a check on the military. From time to time the army was called out in support, and under the direction of the civil authorities. Sometimes the mere threat was sufficient to disperse a riot, but on other occasions force was used with fatal consequences, notably during the Gordon Riots, at Peterloo,[36] Featherstone[37] and with regularity in Ireland and the colonies.

But if martial law was avoided in England, the position was different in a growing and sometimes turbulent Empire. It is not necessary to be drawn into an argument about the merits and demerits of Empire. Simply to observe that the establishment of trade routes, the subjugation of indigenous peoples, the settlement of new lands and the defence of strategic interests carried with it the need to offer protection and enforce order. There were many flashpoints: inter-ethnic rivalries, religion, exploitation and slavery. As colonies grew and aspired to social change or independence, the potential for conflict loomed large and careful management was required. A thin leavening of English soldiers garrisoned the Empire. Irish and Scottish troops served with distinction in Canada, India and Africa. Hessian mercenaries were deployed to subdue the American colonies and later Australian, New Zealand and Canadian troops were used to defeat the Boers. The formula had many permutations and only rarely did the tactic wear thin.[38] The ordinary process of law was usually sufficient but these garrisons were the means by which martial law was enforced if all else failed. The arrangement was recognised by law and it is inconceivable that a structure of this magnitude could be sustained in any other way. Martial law was invoked by proclamation whenever the necessity arose: in Jamaica in 1760, in Lexington and Concord in 1775, in Ireland in 1798 where the suppression of the rebellion was conducted with particular cruelty, in Barbados,[39] Demerara,[40] Jamaica,[41] Canada,[42] Ceylon,[43] Cephalonia,[44] Cape of Good Hope,[45] Hong Kong and St Vincent.[46] Where necessary an Act of Indemnity was passed to protect those who had assisted the forces of the Crown.

The relationship between martial law and civil law needs examination. They could not stand together, they were mutually exclusive but the point at which martial law might be invoked or extinguished was a vexed one as the 1798 rebellion shows. One trial captures the tension between martial law and the civil law: that of Wolfe Tone. In October 1798 a bloody encounter took place off the Irish coast between a French fleet and a squadron commanded by Sir John Warren. Tone, who held a commission in the French army, was captured aboard *La Hoche*, a French ship of the line. Bad weather meant that some weeks elapsed before Tone was brought to Dublin for trial before a military court. The last of the fighting had taken place some weeks before. Civil law again prevailed and the Assizes sat without difficulty. Despite this, Tone was tried by a military court at Dublin Barracks under martial law. He appeared before the court in the uniform of a French officer: 'a large and fiercely cocked hat, with broad gold lace and the tricoloured cockade and blue uniform coat'.[47]

Although 'a natural born subject of the King', he had taken a commission with the French army and he was therefore charged with treason. He did not dispute the charges and after an eloquent address which was tragic and theatrical by turns, Tone asked 'to be shot by a file of grenadiers'.

The following day the Lord Lieutenant confirmed sentence of death but ordered that he should be hanged 'in the most public manner'. Tone's father instructed John Philpot Curran, the leading advocate of his generation, to apply for a writ of habeas corpus which he made to the Lord Chief Justice of Ireland in these terms:

> Mr Tone had no commission under his Majesty and therefore no court martial could have cognisance of any crime imputed to him ... I stand upon this sacred and immutable principle that martial law and civil law are incompatible, and that the former must cease with the existence of the latter. This is not the time for deciding that momentous question. My client must appear in this court. He is cast for death this day. He may be ordered for execution while I address you.[48]

The Lord Chief Justice issued a writ without further argument but Wolfe Tone cut his throat the same day and died from the wound. The supremacy of civil law over martial law was not definitively decided and the crisis ebbed away gradually.[49]

The notion that martial law had to give way to civil law remained a fundamental part of the common law. Once the crisis was over, however, it was not always easy to wrest control from the military. The Demerara Slave Rebellion of 1823 was a case in point. The rebellion was crushed in a few days, about 250 slaves were killed or executed and for those fortunate enough to have the benefit of a trial, no record survives. Martial law was retained for over five months and the last man to be tried by a military court was the Reverend John Smith of Rothwell Northamptonshire, a young Methodist preacher serving his first mission abroad. Smith had attracted the ire of the authorities by trying to ensure that slaves did not work on Sunday and he became despised for teaching slaves to read the Bible. This was objected to on the grounds that if the slaves could read the Bible they might also read other more controversial tracts. After the rebellion was crushed Reverend Smith was arrested and held for many weeks before being tried by a military court on charges of fomenting disaffection and assisting one of the rebels. Smith's trial remains an all-but-forgotten landmark in legal history. The charges for the most part related to acts done before martial law was imposed and the trial took place eight weeks after the insurrection had ceased. It could not be argued that necessity required trial by military court. He was denied counsel until he entered his plea and therefore lost any real opportunity of challenging the jurisdiction of the court. His defence, such as it was, was buried under an avalanche of hearsay and leading questions before a tribunal eager for conviction.

This naive young preacher died in jail while a ship carrying an order for release was still some weeks out of port. These events gave rise to a motion of censure at Westminster and a famous debate on the ambit of martial law[50] which helped shape future policy but came too late for Reverend Smith.

Although the politicians wrung their hands after the fact, events in Demerara simply echoed what was done elsewhere. The brutal reality was that the implementation of martial law was often associated with cruelty and excess, notably in 1798,[51] the Indian Mutiny, the Jamaica Rebellion and the Boer War. It is not constructive to linger over every instance of martial law but it is necessary to look briefly at some of these episodes.

We start with the Great Indian Mutiny in 1857. Suspicions were fostered that the cartridge for the new Lee Enfield rifle had been greased with beef or pig fat. The cartridge came in a paper wrapping and the rumour about pig and beef fat also attached itself to the wrapping. Despite efforts to meet the concerns of the soldiers, the idea took hold and many sepoys refused to use the new cartridges. And in these circumstances a small and apparently spontaneous mutiny broke out.

With adept and sensitive leadership the worst of what followed might yet have been avoided but the trial and execution of the first mutineer, Mangal Pande, was a turning point and anarchy spread. Officers were hacked down by their men. The slaughter was unconfined and civilians, and women and children, were massacred without mercy. The worst and most shocking series of massacres took place at Cawnpore where the Nana Sahib orchestrated the brutal slaying of settler women and children. Most were slashed to death with cleavers and the bodies were tipped into a well.

The response by the army was swift. There was no proclamation of martial law, nor did the law require one.[52] In the months that followed, a great slaughter ensued. There are aspects of the British campaign which compare with the greatest feats of arms by British soldiers – the defence of Lucknow; General Havelock's relief of Lucknow and the storming of Delhi – but the campaign was also marked by the most savage brutality. Mutineers or suspected mutineers were often bayoneted or shot on sight. Those fortunate enough to be held were accorded the most summary form of trial. There are examples of magistrates who strived for fair trials but these are rare[53] and many men were summarily hanged or blown from the mouth of the cannon – a method of execution not prescribed by law.

This was the scene in Delhi after the recapture of the city:

> Multiple gallows were erected in the squares of the city, where British officers and soldiers watched – officers puffing cigars,

> soldiers their pipes – while the victims danced the 'Pandies' hornpipe. Martial law proved no better than the anarchy it replaced.[54]

At home in England the public supported what was done and few urged moderation. Governor Canning was one of those who urged restraint and he was quickly dubbed by the press 'Clemency Canning'. After order was restored no Act of Indemnity was passed by Parliament excusing what was done. There was no desire to subject the conduct of the army to the scrutiny of law. Less than a decade later there was a rebellion in another distant colony, with very different consequences.

The Jamaica Rebellion of 1865 was triggered by a land dispute which resulted in a group of tenant farmers descending on the police station at Morant Bay. They seized what arms they could find and went to the courthouse. The magistrates, forewarned of their approach, had the local militia drawn up in front of the courthouse. The Riot Act was read to the growing crowd. Stones were thrown and the magistrate called upon the militia to open fire into the crowd. This they did and bodies were seen to fall.

The crowd attacked the militia and set the courthouse ablaze. The magistrate and seventeen others, mostly white settlers, were hacked to death. Thirty-one others were wounded with machetes. The rebels gathered in numbers and looted freely and there was a great deal of talk about ridding the country of 'the Buckra' – the white farming community.

While these events were taking place, Governor Eyre and the Privy Council had met in Kingston. The Council declared martial law in the south-east corner of Jamaica and troops were despatched to meet the rebels and restore order. Before the soldiers arrived the rebellion simply melted away and the army suffered not a single casualty. Military courts convened the next day, many of the rebels being hanged from the scorched stone archway which was all that remained of the courthouse.

The Royal Commission that reported the following year found that about 439 people were killed during the suppression of the rebellion. Some 354 of these were executed after trial by military court. The remainder were shot or hanged without trial. About 1,000 homes were burned and 600 people were flogged.[55]

But of all the deaths that took place, one excited political interest back in England – that of George Gordon, the illegitimate son of a white plantation owner and a slave.[56] He was also a British citizen. By his own efforts he had educated himself, acquired land and become a magistrate.

A tall, gaunt, prickly and sometimes troublesome man, Gordon had espoused the cause of the poorest natives and hopes of prosperity and greater political freedom.

Governor Eyre had formed the view that the rebellion had been whipped up by Gordon, who was then in Kingston outside the Martial Law Area. According to Eyre's account he duped Gordon into accompanying him into custody. Gordon was transported in HMS *Wolverine* to Morant Bay on 17 October. He arrived in the Martial Law Area on the 20th and was tried by a military court the following day.

Gordon was tried in a small timbered house down by the wharf on Morant Bay. The living room of the house was 'full and hot' as men crowded around the table. From time to time the President stopped to tell onlookers to 'lean off' to allow the record to be written. As evening came candles were bought. Gordon, like the other prisoners, was not represented. His request to adjourn to secure a witness was refused. He was 'rather nervous', a witness told the Royal Commission. 'He kept hemming and hawing.' As he made out his evidence, he would ask his captors: 'Am I not keeping you?'

Thirty-six hours later Gordon was hanged from the archway of the ruined courthouse at Morant Bay. The executions continued for days until Governor Eyre declared the emergency over. Some prisoners secured their release by writs of habeas corpus but all this came too late for George Gordon. The Royal Commission found that the evidence brought against George Gordon was 'wholly insufficient to establish the charge'.[57]

Back in England a small circle of liberals led by John Stuart Mill formed the Jamaica Committee and seized on this moment to establish new standards in the colonies. They lacked the influence to bring about legislation and so focused on the possibility of a prosecution to effect reform. It must be obvious that prosecutions for acts done under martial law were rare if only because those who might have cause for complaint were often dead, or too cowed to take action. The number of cases in which redress was secured for acts done under martial law were very few, perhaps only one – Wright v Fitzgerald – an action arising out of the 1798 rebellion in which the sheriff, known locally as 'Flogger', was found to have subjected a man to 500 lashes without reason.[58]

Mill and his adherents brought a private prosecution for murder against the officers who had conduct of the trial of Gordon. The case was heard by Chief Justice Cockburn and a grand jury. Cockburn's directions to the grand jury were followed by nearly every man and woman in Britain and Ireland who could read a newspaper. It was learned, florid, moving and rambling by turns. He criticised the duration during which civil law was suspended and railed against the injustices that might occur in such circumstances. Gordon, he intimated had been unlawfully brought into the Martial Law Area and convicted on insufficient evidence and 'hurried to his end'.

Lord Chief Justice Cockburn finished this epic summing up by inviting the jury to return an indictment against the officers but declaring himself in 'some doubt' about the state of the law. This was hardly helpful to the jury, who must have been a little dumbfounded. They declined to return a bill against the officers but suggested that Parliament might legislate so that the law was 'more clearly defined'.

The matter did not rest there. Governor Eyre had been turned out of office, abandoned by the government. Pilloried in some papers and praised in others, he was brought close to financial ruin. The Jamaica Committee brought repeated prosecutions against Governor Eyre for murder and for being an accessory to the murder of Gordon, and it seemed that he might suffer the fate of other governors who had gone too far.[59] Eyre was fortunate to have a skilful counsel, Hardinge Giffard QC. Giffard, who was not beyond shedding a few tears for the grand jury, fought off all prosecutions.

Yet another prosecution was brought against Eyre for high crimes and misdemeanours under the Colonial Governors Act.[60] In this case Mr Justice Blackburn directed the grand jury that a colonial governor would not be criminally liable for acts done which he perceived to be reasonably necessary in times of crisis. This prosecution also foundered on the obstinacy of a jury and the law remained uncertain.[61]

But we see here a debate about the rights of indigenous peoples in the colonies: whether those rights were unqualified, and from what did they derive – was it British citizenship or a shared humanity?[62] Once the concept that rights derived from humanity gained currency the Empire was mortally weakened, but that was still far off.

The Jamaica Rebellion did give rise to some modest reforms. In 1867 the Colonial Office issued a circular to all colonial governors on martial law.[63] It acknowledged earlier excesses. The guidance emphasised the 'exceptional' nature of martial law and the pre-condition of insurrection which could not be dealt with by the military acting in support of civil authority. The guidance stipulated that the duration and geographical extent of martial law should be limited by necessity and laid down the most basic rules governing trial and punishment under martial law: prisoners should not be punished without trial 'unless military reasons do not admit of a trial'. Trials by military court required at least three officers and hearsay should not be admitted. Prisoners were to be afforded 'every reasonable facility for making their defence'. The court was required to keep a detailed record which, in the event of conviction, would be sent to the convening officer to confirm or not. The death sentence was not to be passed save with the agreement of two-thirds of the court. The Guidance also cautioned against 'unnecessary severity'.

Those parts of the Guidance suggesting that the power to suppress rebellion extended to the trial and punishment of rebels after capture were of doubtful legality,[64] and the precise ambit of the law remained uncertain. This goes to the heart of this study in respect of Ireland in 1921. The point at issue is whether these prisoners were tried by due process of law. Military courts come into existence when the institutions of society are under strain or in a state of collapse. They are often called into being too readily, they have a disposition towards extreme penalties and they represent a failure of the rule of law.

The Guidance issued by the Colonial Office enjoyed a status akin to law and remained in force throughout the Empire until well into the twentieth century.[65] Although it must also be said that the Guidance was soon flouted. In 1872 the suppression of the Kooka Sect in India was achieved by wholesale executions and a return to blowing prisoners from the cannon.[66]

There is no doubt, however, that the Colonial Office circular edged a small step closer towards the establishment of the rule of law in the colonies, although it left much to the conscience and discretion of colonial governors. The picture that emerges in the latter half of the nineteenth century is a mixed one. We see the Empire, skilfully and without loss of blood, renegotiate relations with a number of emerging nation states: New Zealand, Australia and Canada. Elsewhere, other considerations dictated the maintenance of rule by force of arms: Egypt occupied a strategically important location by the Suez Canal; India and South Africa had large expatriate settlements and were a source of wealth and prestige; Ireland, had become part of the Union and although Home Rule was contemplated, secession was unthinkable.

Martial law was again imposed during the Boer War. During this conflict military courts were extensively used against insurgents and others. Forty-eight men were shot by firing squads for treason, spying, carrying arms and wearing British uniforms and other offences. Many of these men were not legally represented and a significant number were tried and executed within days of capture.[67]

In this conflict, and for the first time, we see not quite a concerted legal challenge to martial law but something close to it. Here the mechanism was a challenge to martial law by asserting private rights before the Privy Council. These efforts were poorly coordinated and under-resourced but this was a significant moment because the Privy Council was then the Supreme Court of Appeal from the courts of the Indian Empire and of all Crown dominions.

Challenges to special courts,[68] freedom of movement[69] and internment all foundered on the reluctance of the courts to question acts done by the army or the executive.

In the case of David Marais,[70] the challenge was to internment under martial law. The importance of this case should not be underestimated. A successful outcome for the prisoner might have put an end to the concentration camps and the misery and suffering of Boer women and children. In this case the Privy Council laid down a general rule that while 'war is raging, acts done by the military authorities are not justiciable' and added the rider that the fact that some courts were allowed to sit 'was not conclusive'.

The Boer War came to an exhausting, bitter end. The next test of martial law arose out of Zulu unrest a few years later. A poll tax riot took place in which an inspector of police and a trooper were killed. Martial law was declared the next day and although the proclamation declared that the civil courts would continue to sit, the accused were tried by a military court flanked by a massive parade of the Cameron Highlanders and the Natal Field Artillery. Twelve Zulus were convicted and sentenced to death in these circumstances. It is clear that this trial took place despite the fact that all the civil courts were sitting and there was no obstacle to trial by due process of law. The Privy Council declined to intervene. The leading judgment was delivered by Lord Loreburn, who tersely described what was done as 'the act of the Executive'.[71]

In the case of Tilonko,[72] a Zulu tribal leader was tried and convicted by a military court convened under martial law for sedition and raising an army. His challenge to the jurisdiction of the Military Court failed because of an Act of Indemnity. In this case the Privy Council went much further than was necessary to decide the case, observing that: 'It is found convenient and decorous, from time to time, to authorise what are called "courts" to administer punishments, and to restrain by acts of repression the violence that is committed in time of war.'

We see in this line of cases not just a retreat from the position taken by Lord Chief Justice Cockburn but a confirmation and extension of the scope of the marital law doctrine without full argument or reference to precedent.[73] There is a revealing irony here, because the judgment of the Privy Council in this last case was delivered by Lord Halsbury, who, many years before, had been Governor Eyre's defence counsel. Appointed Lord Chancellor, Halsbury had become the pre-eminent judicial figure of his generation and he carried with him onto the bench a readiness to support martial law in the colonies.

Leaving Africa, therefore, we turn to the Great War, in which nearly 3,000 British soldiers were sentenced to death, of whom 304 were executed.[74] To which should be added forty-seven sepoy soldiers publicly executed after the Singapore Mutiny. Nearly all of these men were tried by field general court martial – the model used for the trial of civilians under martial law – and are of passing interest for that reason.

A significant number of civilians were also tried by military courts during the Great War and of these, one hundred and twenty-nine were sentenced to death. Most were reprieved, including a west African labourer whose name is recorded only as 'Jumbo' who was sentenced to death for theft.[75] His sentence was commuted to three months' imprisonment. These trials were convened in the United Kingdom, Macedonia, Egypt, Salonika, Ireland, Russia, east Africa and Turkey to try civilians for espionage, treason, insurrection, murder and other offences.[76] In total thirty-seven men were executed by order of military courts.[77] Many of these trials were convened under military law, some under martial law or in a twilight area where jurisdiction remains opaque.

The Irish trials in 1916 resulted in ninety-three death sentences, of which fifteen were carried out. In the aftermath of martial law, a test case[78] was brought to challenge the legality of these trials on the ground, among others, that they were conducted in camera. The fact that this challenge could be brought at all was possible because the Crown asserted for tactical reasons that the trials had been conducted under statutory powers granted by the Defence of the Realm Act, not martial law. When this action was brought, Britain was still locked in the Great War and it is entirely unsurprising that the challenge failed. Although, according to William Wylie, King's Counsel, who prosecuted the trials arising from the Easter Rising, there were more compelling grounds for concern than secrecy: in the early trials there was a failure to permit the prisoners to be represented or to make provision for defence witnesses.[79] In the trial of Éamonn Ceannt the prisoner applied to call Thomas McDonagh only to learn that he was not available, having been shot earlier that day.[80] What was done and, perhaps just as important, the manner in which it was done laid the seeds of further conflict.

Martial law was again declared in 1919 in India. The Amritsar Massacre is the best-known episode although it should also be remembered that special courts were convened to try offenders under martial law: 108 death sentences were passed, and eighteen of the offenders were executed.[81] Martial law was also proclaimed in Egypt the same year in response to a widespread revolt that was mainly non-violent, and it is clear, ironically, that the machinery of martial law found non-violent protest the most difficult to combat. This turbulent era comes to a natural break in 1920 when Parliament passed an Act of Indemnity validating trials by military courts during the Great War and other emergencies.[82]

It should not be thought that this brief review of trials under martial law gives rise to any direct inference that the military courts in Ireland in 1921 were fair or not, although in fact they were rather better than their predecessors. Some lessons had been learned. What this review does show, however, is the historical context. It demonstrates the tension that exists in times of crisis between non-legal imperatives and the rule of law. It also demonstrates how readily due process was set aside in favour of what was pragmatic and convenient.

This review shows how the law stood in 1920, and the uncertainties attaching to the concept of martial law. There was some doubt whether martial law might be invoked within the Union of Britain and Ireland without legislation.[83] In the colonies the exercise of martial law was still governed by the internal guidance issued by the Colonial Office. Martial law might be invoked by proclamation, although it was settled law that it was not the proclamation that brought martial law into being but the circumstances that rendered it necessary. The practical effect of the proclamation was that it put the population on notice that martial law was in force and that there were drastic consequences for failing to render obedience.

There was also a growing legal debate as to whether martial law was a function of the royal prerogative or the common law doctrine of necessity. As we shall see, this apparently arcane debate would become a critical issue in Ireland in 1921. Whichever of the two theories was correct, the law permitted any measures reasonably necessary for the purpose of suppressing rebellion, invasion, riot or disorder. The duty rested most heavily on the army, the magistracy and later the police who had the resources to keep order. But the common law also stipulated that every citizen owed a duty to put down disorder, riot, rebellion or invasion and support the Crown. Therefore citizens might also be prosecuted for inaction.[84] This principle would also prove significant in Ireland in 1921.

The area of greatest controversy and ambiguity related to the claim of the army to try and execute insurgents where the emergency was over or where there was no driving necessity for such action. Although the existence of such a power was denied by Dicey, the greatest of constitutional lawyers,[85] the army sometimes took a different course.

It was settled law, however, that when war or rebellion raged, the courts had no jurisdiction to interfere in the acts of the military. The acid test of whether war raged was whether the courts were able to sit, although following the case of Marais, the Privy Council recognised that this principle was no longer decisive.[86] The question, however, as to whether the country was in a state of war was a factual one, which the courts retained power to decide.[87]

There were other limitations on the powers to contain rebellion: if a prisoner was moved out of the Martial Law Area there was no legal power to hold him. These factors influenced army policy in Ireland in 1921 because there was a physical limit on the number of prisoners that could be held within the Martial Law Area.

When the emergency was over the military were obliged to immediately hand over control to the civil authorities, although, as we have seen, the precise point at which martial law might be invoked or relinquished was always uncertain.[88]

After the crisis was over, acts done under martial law were justiciable by the courts. The only defence that might be advanced to a charge of excesses committed in time of martial law was that of necessity or an Act of Indemnity.

Also, in the absence of an Act passed to validate prison sentences imposed during martial law, the prisoners were entitled to release when the emergency was over.

These, in summary, were the legal principles which underpinned the declaration of martial law in Ireland in 1920 and the creation of military courts and other measures to suppress the rebellion.[89] It can be seen that the area of greatest importance and ambiguity related to the trial of prisoners by military courts. Where the prisoner was at risk of execution by the military his only remedy was a writ of habeas corpus to challenge the legality of detention. In the usual course of events the legal hurdles were almost insurmountable and there were practical difficulties in securing access to a lawyer or a court.

Each instance of martial law brought excesses to a greater or lesser degree and every episode was followed by an inquiry at the Colonial Office, a motion of censure at Westminster[90] or more rarely a Royal Commission,[91] public outcry,[92] the resignation of a governor or recall of a commander[93] or the prosecution of an officer who had demonstrably gone too far.[94] In this way events were managed and occasionally modest improvements were made. But there was no effective legal redress for civilians in a Martial Law Area.

In Ireland, in 1921, such a challenge was made possible by an unusual combination of circumstances. First, martial law was confined to south-west Ireland but the civil courts in Dublin continued to scrutinise writs of habeas corpus for prisoners in the Martial Law Area. Second, the presence of an active legal profession and good communications allowed the possibility of an immediate and effective legal challenge. And third, the politicians and administrators who ran the Empire were, for once, uncharacteristically hesitant. The reasons for this are difficult to evaluate. It may have a great deal to do with the personalities involved and it may be that what might be done in a distant colony was less easy in Ireland, where events were reported in London the very next day.

This concludes the review of the legal and historical context of martial law. It is now necessary to look at the circumstances in which a large part of south-west Ireland came to be placed under martial law.

CHAPTER THREE

Ireland 1920

The main thrust of the rebellion, and the response to it, centred on the criminal justice system. The RIC were in the front line and by late spring 1920, 277 RIC barracks and police huts had been destroyed by fire.[95] Most of these were quite small buildings which had been abandoned following a decision by the army that it could no longer provide the RIC with protection in outlying areas.[96] The RIC concentrated their forces in larger, less remote barracks which were loopholed and reinforced with steel shutters, but as the conflict escalated these too were attacked.

By the end of March 1920, two soldiers and twenty-four policemen had been killed and there had been another eighty-two attempts to kill police officers.[97] The shooting of RIC men was accompanied by a policy of harassment and ostracism which diminished morale, brought early resignations and dented recruitment.[98] The result of this campaign was that the effectiveness of the RIC was greatly diminished. In this environment the new Republican courts and the rebellion flourished.

As to the courts established under British rule, no less than forty-seven were destroyed by fire in the spring of 1920.[99] Much of the records which underpinned the criminal justice system went up in smoke and could not be replaced. Courts were fortified with 'sandbags, barbed wire and garrisons'[100] but the burnings continued and by December of the following year the number of courthouses destroyed by fire or explosives had risen to eighty-nine.[101]

Defending the magistrates proved less easy. Hundreds of lay magistrates resigned[102] – some out of choice but many were compelled to resign by threats.[103] There is evidence of a campaign against the magistracy which lasted until the end of the war. At least one lay magistrate was shot and killed[104] and others were intimidated.[105] A few were kidnapped,[106] while others simply failed to attend the petty sessions.[107]

The Resident Magistrates were also targeted. Three were killed during the War of Independence. RM Milling was shot through the window of his house in Westport. RM Lendrum was ambushed at a level crossing. He drew a handgun but was shot down before he could fire. Another resident magistrate, Alan Bell, was dragged off a tram at

Ballsbridge and shot dead. Yet another escaped unhurt when his assailant's gun blew up in his face.[108] At Causeway in Kerry RM Edward Wynne fought off an armed attack[109] and in Bandon RM Brady was kidnapped and held for some days.[110]

The most acute problems lay with reluctant witnesses and jurors. Witnesses and jurors were vulnerable to intimidation, particularly since the RIC had abandoned the outlying barracks. Even where jurors and witnesses came to court they were often hostile to the Crown.

Finally, the prisons. There was what was quaintly termed 'a refusal to accept prison discipline'.[111] This translated into a refusal by many prisoners to work or follow orders, hunger strikes, riots and escapes.

This was the emerging challenge posed by the rebellion in the first half of 1920. It was against this febrile atmosphere that a conference of influential cabinet ministers met at the end of May. Those attending included Lloyd George, Bonar Law, Churchill and Birkenhead. They were joined by the Attorney General for Ireland, Sir Denis Henry, Sir John Anderson, the senior civil servant at Dublin Castle, a man of legendary intellect, and his political chief, Sir Hamar Greenwood, described as a man who was incapable of holding more than one thought in his head at any one time.[112]

Also at the meeting was the new commander in chief of the army in Ireland, Sir Neville Macready, who had made his reputation at the siege of Ladysmith. He had served as adjutant general of the British Expeditionary Force and on promotion to adjutant general of the forces immediately abolished the rule that required all soldiers to wear a moustache. His own was the first to go and somehow this small act contributed to his reputation as a liberal. Macready had been a successful commissioner of the Metropolitan Police and he was also an able professional soldier. Although he was married to an Irish woman, he did not welcome the posting: 'I loathe the country.'[113]

The political strategy being pursued by the Cabinet was to push through the Government of Ireland Bill which would allow a Home Rule Parliament in Belfast and Dublin. The strategy could not be implemented without quelling the rebellion or negotiating a truce.

There was a consensus that convictions for politically motivated crimes were almost impossible.[114] The difficulties of seizing arms were also discussed. The country was awash with firearms, mainly handguns. As the Attorney General put it: 'We made ten thousand raids in six months, we did not get hold of the revolvers.'[115]

Martial law was discussed. General Macready posed the question: 'Can martial law be brought into operation in any part of the United

Kingdom without legislation?' As a matter of law the answer was uncertain and there were also practical difficulties. We have seen that a general who declared martial law was sometimes later abandoned by the politicians. Only days before, Macready had asked for and received advice from the chief Crown Solicitor on this very issue. The substance of the advice was that once the emergency was over, army officers might be prosecuted for acts done under martial law, and that the army could only be protected if martial law was declared by statute.[116] It may be surmised that Macready wanted Westminster to take responsibility for this momentous decision. He developed the advantages for the Cabinet: 'Under martial law you surround Limerick and get the whole place searched effectively. All civil courts of the area would cease ...'[117]

Lloyd George favoured strong measures but urged caution: 'We do not want racial enmity raised nor have the name of drumhead martial law.' Churchill agreed and made an oblique reference to recent events at Amritsar. These words read well on the Cabinet record but they do not sit comfortably with the policy of reprisals. In any event the moment passed: the martial law proposal was shelved.

The Assizes were the next major test to be faced by the government in the summer of 1920. And in fact, the Assizes ground to a halt in the south and west, where 1,068 jurors were fined for non-attendance.[118] The Cabinet record shows: 'Intimidation extends to all officers concerned in the administration of justice, Clerks of the Crown, Magistrates, Petty Sessions Clerks, Sheriffs, Process Servers and Bailiffs. Court houses are burnt down and court records are destroyed. The administrative machinery of the Courts has been brought to a standstill.'[119]

RIC barracks were still being attacked by large parties of rebels and police casualties continued to rise but even by mid-July there had still not been a single conviction for murder. Outside of the North and Dublin the justice system was nearly at a standstill. A further difficulty for the authorities was that there was no power for a court martial convened under the Defence of the Realm Act to impose a sentence of death except for offences committed with the intention of assisting the enemy – Germany – a legacy of the Great War.[120] The options for the administration were stark: negotiate, invoke special powers or impose martial law. The Judge Advocate General (JAG), Felix Cassel, was called on to advise on whether martial law might be imposed: it could be done, the JAG advised; military courts modelled on field general courts martial could be set up to proceed in 'the most summary manner'. But the advice was hedged with prescient warnings that the introduction of martial law might engender great bitterness and prove counterproductive.[121]

The government opted to pursue special legislation and in early August pushed the Restoration of Order in Ireland Act through Parliament. This Act extended the power of the army to try civilians by courts of summary jurisdiction or by courts martial with power to impose the death penalty where the offence was so punishable under civil law. It permitted the creation of new offences by order in council. It also permitted military courts of inquiry to sit in lieu of inquests. The following month Parliament put in place the last part of Westminster's response to the rebellion by passing the Firearms Act, increasing the maximum penalty for possession of arms.

As the new ROIA courts martial process began to yield convictions, there were efforts to disrupt the system. In one case a group of Cork prisoners swapped identities with a group of Volunteers from Roscommon, derailing their court martial.[122] Other prisoners fell back on the well-tried tactic of declining to recognise the court. Although, as one magistrate pointed out: 'Unfortunately, the Court recognises *you*.'[123] This tactic became increasingly rare in capital trials. But it was not the government legal strategy which claimed headlines, it was the policy of reprisal.

The latter half of 1920 developed into a grim war of ambush and reprisal against property and people.[124] The signs had been only too visible for months: the killing of Lord Mayor MacCurtain, for example, where the verdict of the inquest jury could hardly be ignored. Then there was the Listowel Mutiny[125] in which a number of RIC men rebelled over a speech by Divisional Commissioner Smyth which they regarded as incitement to murder. These events brought reprisals out in the open and although the government showed a united front in public, in private and on the fringe of Cabinet there were dissenting voices. The government senior law officer William Wylie KC met with Greenwood and produced a memo urging the government to stamp out reprisals.[126] It was ripped up. Wylie later wrote that the failure to curb reprisals was the pivotal moment in the war.[127]

Another critic was the Chief of the Imperial General Staff, Sir Henry Wilson. His diary entry for 29 September 1920 shows a meeting with Lloyd George and Bonar Law: 'I told them both what I thought of these indiscriminate reprisals by the Black and Tans and how this must lead to chaos and ruin. Lloyd George danced about and was angry but I never budged. I pointed out that these reprisals were carried out without anyone being responsible, men were murdered, houses burned, villages wrecked (such as Balbriggan, Ennistymon, Trim, Mallow, etc) … I said this was due to want of discipline, and must be stopped.'[128]

Lloyd George and his inner coterie were not persuaded and the government continued to turn a blind eye to reprisals. While this argument was being played out in private, there were other successes for the government. The system of courts martial of civilians under the ROIA was functioning: whether it was just or not is a different matter but by the end of October there had been 219 convictions under the Act.[129] Events acquired an unrelenting and tragic momentum: the hunger strikes reached a grim conclusion and the first execution took place: a medical student who had taken part in a raid on Monks' Bakery in which three young soldiers were killed.

Martial law was considered by the Cabinet in October[130] and shelved again in November.[131] The Cabinet discussions show that the argument for martial law hinged on a growing perception that reprisals had the effect of reducing rebel activity.

The Cabinet record shows that an argument was made that as part of martial law, reprisals could be undertaken officially: 'The war of 1870 and the recent war afforded many instances of the success of reprisals in this form.'[132]

According to Thomas Jones, the Whitehall diarist, Churchill circulated a memo around Cabinet in early November. The memo advocated official reprisals. The argument was tersely summarised by Jones: 'The troops are said to be getting out of control, drinking and thieving, and destroying indiscriminately. Courts martial are being held but increasingly difficult to restrain soldiers when outrages occur near them.' And so the argument ran: 'Strictly defined policy of reprisals are less discreditable and more effective than what is going on.'[133]

The policy of official reprisals could only be implemented as part of martial law. So far as the military was concerned, the other attraction of martial law was the prospect of unified command.[134]

The turning point came about with the Kilmichael ambush at the end of November in which seventeen Auxiliaries lost their lives. This triggered the decision in Cabinet to finally implement martial law.

On 10 December the Lord Lieutenant General and Governor General, Viscount French, proclaimed martial law in Cork, Kerry, Limerick and Tipperary. After representations from the army[135] four more counties were soon added to the Martial Law Area: Clare, Kilkenny, Wexford and Waterford. The result was that the Martial Law Area coincided with the operational area of the 6th Division under General Strickland.

General Macready, stationed in Dublin, was appointed Military Governor-General of the Martial Law Area. In Cork the Military

Governor was Major General Strickland,[136] or 'Old Hungry Face' as the troops called him, who was respected by his men but never loved. A tall, thin, fair-haired man with a pencil moustache, his manner always reserved and quietly spoken. He lived for the army, his new wife and lawn tennis: 'Rain ruined tennis' was a frequent and solitary diary entry.[137]

Strickland's preparations for martial law were hindered by unofficial reprisals committed by the RIC or less often by his own troops slipping out of barracks while others dined or slept.[138] While the army was gearing up for martial law, Bishop Cohalan intervened dramatically and publicly. He denounced with equal vigour the Volunteers for the 'murder campaign' and the government for using the curfew to pursue 'a campaign of murder and destruction'.[139] The Bishop excommunicated those who took part in ambushes and killings. Most of his parish priests followed his lead, at least in public.

As the army and the church struggled to assert authority over their own people, the civilian death toll continued to rise. A spate of ambushes also took place at this time: at Dillon's Cross, at Leary's Cross, Kilcommon Cross, Nine Mile House and at Glencurrane.

It was the ambush of K Company of the Auxiliaries at Dillon's Cross which had the most far-reaching repercussions. K Company had been posted to Cork in early December. They were billeted in Victoria Barracks with most of the men sleeping on the floor of the gym.[140] Their commander, Colonel Latimer, lodged at the Imperial Hotel. The formation of the Auxiliaries had been bitterly opposed by Sir Henry Wilson, the Chief of the Imperial General Staff: 'no discipline, no espirit de corps, no cohesion, no training'. Sir Henry's reservations were fully borne out by autumn 1920: the record of the Auxiliaries is well documented, and their service was also marked by a high rate of desertion, dismissals for indiscipline[141] and a culture of heavy drinking.

All of this came to a head on 11 December when a routine patrol of two lorry loads of Auxiliaries left Victoria Barracks and were ambushed after only a few hundred yards. The Auxiliaries sustained serious casualties and carried one of their men into Sullivan's Public House. This man, Spencer Chapman, was in great pain and was given first aid by a local woman. Within just over an hour reprisals began. According to the police report, fifty-seven buildings were burned to the ground, including City Hall and Carnegie Library. Twenty other properties were partially destroyed by fire and about a dozen others ruined and looted.[142] Fire hoses were cut and Auxiliaries shot at fire crews. Two men known to be Volunteers were dragged from their beds and shot dead.[143] At 3 am General Strickland ordered all police units off the streets[144] and later the same morning made his view plain by ejecting K Company out of barracks and out of Cork city.[145]

Later that morning, with a pall of smoke still drifting over the city centre, Proclamation No. 1[146] was issued by General Macready which brought about the creation of military governors. All persons were required to 'render obedience to their orders in all matters whatsoever'. The proclamation subordinated the civil courts and all civil authorities to the military governors, and also declared the following conduct to be punishable by death:

- Taking part in the rebellion, aiding and abetting or harbouring rebels.
- Possessing arms, ammunition or explosives.
- The unauthorised wearing of a uniform or equipment of His Majesty's Army, Navy, Air Force or Police.

Arrangements were put in place to allow a surrender of arms by the cut off date of 27 December.

As part of the martial law regime the army created military courts to try those contravening the provisions of martial law. The military courts did not replace the courts martial system created by the ROIA; it was an addition, crudely bolted on in a matter of days. There were two attractions for the army: first, the courts martial procedure under the ROIA was regarded as too cumbersome and slow. Second, the new military courts were created by the army and were not susceptible to review by the civil courts. That at least was the theory.[147] It was thought that after overcoming initial opposition, the Military Court would be free from interference by the civil courts[148] and the army could bring about trial and execution expeditiously. The strategy was worked out at the office of the Judge Advocate General in early December 1920. The JAG, Cassel, had advised that execution should follow swiftly on conviction 'to minimise trouble with the civil courts over Habeas Corpus'.[149]

The first trial by military court would soon come about. K Company, having been ejected from Cork city, found a new billet in the RIC barracks at Dunmanway. On the morning of 15 December, a party from K Company were travelling back to Cork for the funeral of Cadet Spencer Chapman killed at Dillon's Cross. The convoy chanced upon an elderly priest, Canon Magner, and a young man by the name of Crowley who were helping Resident Magistrate Brady to fix his car by the roadside. Cadet Hart emerged from the second lorry and shot Crowley and Canon Magner dead.[150]

It was in these circumstances that on 21 December 1920, Hart became the first prisoner to be tried by military court. His counsel argued that the prisoner was insane and his trial was put back some days while medical reports were prepared.

In this turbulent month, it is necessary to relate only two other events which capture the spirit of the times. First, the arms amnesty was not a success. There is anecdotal evidence that a handful of shotguns, antique firearms and fowling pieces were surrendered, but as to revolvers and rifles, General Macready reported that not a single gun had been handed in.[151]

Second, General Macready issued a notice to the police and army that any of their number found guilty of reprisals were liable to suffer death under martial law.[152] As part of the same initiative General Strickland also sent a note to his officers calling for martial law to be implemented with 'humanity, common sense, restraint and discrimination'.[153] But the measures that General Strickland deemed necessary were extreme: censorship, internment,[154] restrictions on movement, carrying hostages on convoys,[155] curfew and the use of forced labour to repair bridges or trenched roads.[156] The most visible tactic was the destruction of homes of people who were thought to be supporters of the rebellion or to have failed to warn the police about impending ambushes.[157] The pill could hardly be sweetened. The Generals were optimistic, however, and reported to Cabinet that the rebellion would be sufficiently overcome by May, which would allow elections for devolved parliaments in the North and the South.[158]

Returning, therefore, to the narrative. Cadet Hart's trial stood adjourned over the new year. Other prisoners were also swiftly brought to trial, and the next military court was convened just before new year to try constables Lemon and Brown for robbery.[159] This new legal system came into being in a feverish atmosphere of ambush and reprisal. It was a legal system in miniature, created in a matter of days. It lasted until the Truce.

CHAPTER FOUR

Vernon Hart, Auxiliary Division, RIC

On 5 January 1921, the trial of Cadet Vernon Hart was reconvened. The accused did not speak during his trial and he remains an enigmatic figure, 'a well-built man turning grey'.[160]

Cadet Sergeant Vernon Hart was born in Lancashire. He married in 1907 and emigrated with his wife to Tasmania where he grew fruit. Late in 1915, with the war in Europe entering a new and desperate stage, he and his wife caught a boat to Melbourne where they picked up the SS *Mongolia* to make the trip home to England. Records[161] show that he was commissioned as a second lieutenant in the Manchester Regiment in 1917. He served on the Western Front, suffering trench fever and being injured in a shell blast.[162] After the war there were thousands of ex-officers looking for work, many of whom had difficulty re-adjusting to civilian life. Hart was probably one of these men and it may be that he was attracted to the Auxiliaries by the lucrative pay which might allow him to emigrate again. He joined the Auxiliary Division in September 1920[163] and was posted to Cork in December with K Company.

A military court of inquiry took place two days after the shootings at Dunmanway police barracks.[164] Medical evidence showed that Crowley had been shot in the face at very close range. Canon Magner had sustained two head wounds. The Auxiliaries who gave evidence suggested that Hart had been on a drinking binge. Cadet Milward described Hart as 'clean off his head', 'as mad as a hatter' and 'on the verge of delirium tremens'.[165] The inquiry closed without announcing the findings of the court.

A summary of evidence was taken on 20 December and the trial by military court[166] commenced at Victoria Barracks, Cork the following day. Hart was represented by James Reardon.[167] An issue arose immediately as to whether Hart was insane at the time of the killing and whether he was fit to plead and stand trial. Lieutenant Colonel Nicholls of the RAMC gave evidence that Hart had been under his care for a few days and he was unsure if the prisoner was fit to stand trial. A medical report was submitted from another expert. The case was stood out over the new year to give the prosecution and defence the opportunity of calling medical evidence.

The trial reconvened on 5 January. The prosecution called two neurologists who stated that Hart was now fit to plead and stand trial. This issue was conceded by the defence.

District Inspector Edgell of the Auxiliary Police gave evidence that on 15 December he was leading a convoy of Auxiliaries from Dunmanway to Cork. He was in the first Crossley tender and Hart was in charge of the second. However, the second tender soon dropped out of sight. After waiting a short while, Inspector Edgell turned his tender around and retraced his route. The other tender was stationary by the road. There were two bodies on the roadway. Hart was holding a revolver, which he pointed at the witness. The District Inspector gave evidence that after repeated orders Hart put his gun away. Hart 'did not recognise him'. Hart was taken back to Dunmanway. At the barracks, Hart refused to hand over his revolver. Inspector Edgell related the exchange set out below.

> 'The first man that tries to take my revolver I'll shoot him.'
> The inspector: 'I don't think your revolver is loaded.'
> Hart: 'It is.'
> 'Show it to me.'[168]

At this point Hart produced his revolver, which was snatched by the District Inspector, who ran from the room. The District Inspector recounted that he later conveyed Hart to the detention barracks at Cork. Hart did not appear to recall what had taken place. He appeared to think that he was still en route to the funeral of Cadet Spencer Chapman. The District Inspector saw Hart some days later when the summary of evidence was taken. Hart did not recognise him.

Cross-examined, the District Inspector related that Hart had been on good terms with Spencer Chapman, who had been badly wounded at Dillon's Cross on 11 December. Hart had spent some time at Chapman's bedside and Chapman had asked Hart to shoot him because of the pain. Chapman had died that morning. The District Inspector related that Hart had been greatly affected by the death of Chapman, more so than others in his unit. On the morning of 15 December, Hart had appeared better. He had been detailed to travel to Cork to escort the body of

Chapman to England for burial. He showed no signs of drink and 'was a temperate man'.

Another cadet gave evidence that he witnessed what had taken place from the tender. He saw Hart shoot the first man. After 'a couple of minutes' he saw Hart shoot the priest. Afterwards he had inspected the bodies. Both men had been shot in the head. This witness also stated that before they left the barracks Hart had said: 'Something ought to be done for Chapman. I should like to see Ireland swept with fire. And I should like to lead the boys.'[169]

In answers to questions put by the court, the witness said that Hart had been 'quiet and morose'. He told the court that Chapman and the accused were 'particular friends'. He added, in response to a question, that he had never seen Cadet Hart the worse for drink.

Resident Magistrate Brady gave evidence. He told the court that he had been driving from Bantry to Bandon. His car had broken down just outside Dunmanway. Canon Magner had passed by and came over to help. Crowley came by on a bike and Canon Magner had stopped Crowley so that he could help the Resident Magistrate. He saw the Crossley tender pass and then a second Crossley tender appeared and stopped. Hart got out and shouted:

> 'Who are you?' The witness replied that he was a resident magistrate. Hart replied: 'I don't care. I am going to shoot you.'[170]
> Hart was pointing a revolver at the witness.
> Brady: 'I am a government official. I am on duty now and on my way to the military barracks, Bandon.'
> Hart: 'I don't care. I am going to shoot you, you ———.'[171]
> A short interval passed before Hart spoke again.
> Hart: 'Have you any papers?'
> Resident Magistrate Brady: 'Yes, I have papers.'
> Hart: 'Don't talk to me you ———.'[172]
> Hart struck Resident Magistrate Brady and walked on towards Crowley.

Resident Magistrate Brady then went over to the Crossley tender and spoke to the cadets on board. He heard a revolver shot. He looked over and saw Crowley lying on the roadway by the ditch. Hart was 'refilling' his revolver. Two cadets got out of the tender and went over but returned to the tender. The Resident Magistrate looked over. He saw Canon Magner standing with his hat off with his hands in the air. Later he saw Canon Magner kneeling on the ground with his hands stretched out. Hart stood close by, covering the priest with his gun. About ten minutes later Hart shot Canon Magner.

> Resident Magistrate Brady turned to the men in the Crossley tender: 'He'll surely shoot me too.'
> 'You had better clear.'[173]
> The Resident Magistrate then took to the fields.

Cross-examined, the Resident Magistrate told the court that when he told Hart that he was a government official, this had no effect on Hart. He also told the court that Hart was not drunk but he smelled of drink. And he was suffering from 'a recent fit of drinking'.

Four specialists were called by the prosecution.[174] Two specialists were called by the defence.[175] All gave evidence that the accused had been insane at the time of the incident. It was rare for so many experts to be called on the question of insanity. The explanation appears to lie with the Cabinet at Westminster where there was concern at the developing parallels between the trial of Hart and that of Captain Bowen Colthurst in 1916 for the murder of Francis Sheehy-Skeffington;[176] the prospect of another insanity finding might have caused outrage. As a result, the Cabinet directed two forensic experts to examine Hart to ensure that the verdict was not tainted by allegations of a cover-up.[177] This intervention by the Cabinet probably makes Hart's case unique in the history of British jurisprudence.

The test for insanity was a high one. The standard direction at trial was as follows: 'Every man is presumed to be sane, and to possess a sufficient degree of reason to be responsible for his crimes, until the contrary is proved; and to establish a defence on the ground of insanity, it must be clearly proved that, at the time of the committing of the act, the party accused was labouring under such a defect of reason, from disease of the mind, as not to know the nature and quality of the act he was doing, or, if he did know it, that he did not know what he was doing was wrong.'[178]

What is striking about the medical evidence is that all the doctors were unequivocal and expressed a rare degree of certainty: Hart was insane at the time of the killings. It was described by one of the eminent doctors as 'confusional insanity' which arose from the stress of his work and the death of Chapman. According to one, the evidence was 'definite, distinct and clear'.

Verdict and Sentence

The verdict announced by the court was 'guilty but insane'. Hart was discharged from the Auxiliaries as 'medically unfit'.[179]

The verdict of guilty but insane was certainly a verdict known to law.[180] But there was another twist to come. Hamar Greenwood later informed the House of Commons that Hart had been sentenced to be detained during His Majesty's pleasure.[181] This was not accurate, although the implication of long-term imprisonment may have been intended to placate public outrage. Under the law as it stood then, a person found guilty by reason of insanity might be committed to an asylum but no sentence could be passed.[182] And no order for detention or restraint had any validity outside the Martial Law Area. In fact, however, Hart was taken to England where an undersecretary of state signed a warrant for his committal to Broadmoor Lunatic Asylum, as it was then known.[183] Hart was released the following year.

Some time later a revealing letter written by an Auxiliary of K Company came to light which described Hart as 'sodden with drink'. [184] In Cork there was a cursory internal inquiry into the question of whether Hart had been drinking. The inquiry, conducted by the Divisional Commissioner of police, proved inconclusive,[185] and it is unlikely that these issues will ever be definitively resolved.

This concludes the review of Hart's trial. It is necessary at this point to pause and take a wider look at the structures and procedures of the Military Court, which was developing quickly in a hand-to-mouth fashion.

CHAPTER FIVE

The Military Court

The Military Court had two tiers. First there was the Summary Court, which dealt with less serious breaches of proclamations and regulations under the Restoration of Order in Ireland Act.[186] Drunkenness and theft were to be tried by the Petty Sessions. The Summary Court also dealt with lesser civil disputes where the County Court could not sit on account of the rebellion.

The judge in the Summary Court was an army officer, usually either a major or captain, known as a summary court officer. Appointment was by nomination by the Military Governor. Fifty-five summary court officers were appointed and distributed throughout the Martial Law Area.[187]

The Summary Court could impose up to six months' imprisonment with or without hard labour and might also impose a fine of up to £100 or recommend an accused for internment or refer the case for trial by military court.[188]

Sentences took immediate effect. Confirmation of sentence was not required and there was no right of appeal, although an accused might make written representations to the Military Governor. The summary court officer was required to submit a brief note on each case to the Military Governor, who might make orders quashing, remitting or commuting sentence.[189]

Some 2,296 people were tried by the Summary Court, 549 sentences of imprisonment were imposed and fines totalling £3,777. 15s 2d were levied.[190]

Every battalion held a Summary Court as often as was required. The record kept by the 1st Battalion of the Manchester Regiment gives the flavour of events: Michael Ingleton was fined ten shillings for using a cycle during prohibited hours. John Kelleher of Inniscarra was charged with illegal assembly: six weeks' hard labour. Daniel Healy of Donoughmore: six months' hard labour for failing to halt and evading arrest. Richard Brown: for giving a false name on arrest, six months' hard labour. Another less typical case was that of Mrs Ryan of Wexford who refused to post a proclamation in the window of her home. She was fined £50 or three months. She declined to pay. Mrs Ryan was the wife of Dr Ryan, an MP then in jail. This fact, perhaps, provides the context in which the order was made and disobeyed.[191]

In Cork city the curfew was strictly enforced. Mobile search lights and fixed search lights high above the city on the walls of Victoria Barracks swept the streets. The curfew patrol walked the city each night. Within a few months the curfew officer also came to hold the post of summary court officer, although his powers were limited to either a fine or one month's imprisonment.[192] The curfew officer was a busy man and most nights brought a trickle of prisoners to the detention barracks, many with new and sometimes ingenious excuses for being out after dark. The results of each night's work was released to the press the following morning.

We turn now to the upper tier of the Military Court which dealt with the more serious trials. The prosecution of these trials fell on the 6th Division legal branch which was based at Victoria Barracks, Cork. The legal branch was run by a lieutenant colonel whose name was redacted from all contemporary documents and affidavits. He was Lieutenant Colonel Hugh Mobray Meyler. Colonel Meyler had qualified as a

5.1 Captain F.E. Young, courts martial officer of the Sixth Division, second row, far left. Courtesy of the Trustees of the Black Watch Museum.

solicitor but soon left legal practice to volunteer for service in the Boer War, where he served as a trooper. He was commissioned there and stayed on after the war; he ran a legal practice and became a member of the first Parliament of the Union of South Africa. He returned to England in 1914 and served throughout the Great War; he was decorated for dangerous reconnaissance work.[193] In 1920 he was transferred to Ireland and appointed legal officer in Cork. Meyler was like many officers with legal training in civilian life. He acquired courts martial experience in France during the Great War and later in Ireland. Although the best lawyers had returned to private practice,[194] there remained a significant pool of officers with relevant experience. However, the record of capital courts martial in the Great War does not inspire confidence;[195] it is one thing to prosecute a soldier for losing his rifle or deserting his post, it is quite another to conduct capital trials raising difficult issues of law.

Meyler ran a team of five officers in the legal branch at Victoria Barracks. The officers took summaries of evidence, drafted charges and prepared trials or acted as judge advocates. As far as can be established, all military court trials were prosecuted by officers of the legal branch. The officer who prosecuted or acted as judge advocate in the majority of the trials was probably Captain F.E. Young, a courts martial officer from a territorial battalion of the Black Watch.[196] Young was commissioned in 1915 and served in France and was fortunate to survive the war: he was wounded on the Somme in 1916 and again at the battle of Tardenois but made a full recovery. Young was a solicitor then in his late twenties. Having regard to the fact that he had spent most of the war on front line service, his experience in the law must have been slim. The question of the legal qualifications of those prosecuting or trying military court cases is one to which we will return in due course.

The centre of events was Victoria Barracks, built at the turn of the nineteenth century on the heights overlooking Cork city. Huge walls concealed a massive military complex. This was General Strickland's headquarters in the Martial Law Area. The administrative support was provided by three staff captains under the command of the new brigade major, B.L. Montgomery. The barrack square itself was a quarter of a mile across. Some prisoners were held on the edge of the square in wooden huts but most of those awaiting trial were detained close by at the military detention barracks. This facilitated pre-trial hearings and allowed the secure movement of prisoners to Victoria Barracks, which was the main trial venue. Most of the multi-defendant trials took place in the gymnasium, the smaller trials in the library. Other trial centres included Limerick's New Barracks, Fermoy and Waterford.

As the year wore on convicted prisoners and internees were moved to Bere or Spike Island or Kilkenny. Prisoners awaiting trial or execution were held at the detention barracks.

Those that wrote accounts of the detention barracks recalled, in the main, monotony and poor food.[197] There were sharper memories also. All the cells in Cork detention barracks were in earshot of the firing squads and it was possible for a number of prisoners to see executions from their cells.[198] Diarmuid O'Leary, captured at Clonmult, later wrote a sober account of the executions he witnessed.[199] The petition for the men tried for the Mallow Barracks raid describes the prisoners' 'agony of mind'[200] as the months passed and one execution followed another. This is a recurring theme in the accounts given by prisoners.[201]

The army was already running courts martial of civilians under the ROIA. In serious cases these were general courts martial which contained significant protections for an accused. Such a case was tried by a president of the rank of lieutenant colonel, at least five officers and a judge advocate. Once martial law was declared, different rules applied. Although general courts martial was retained for offences carrying the death penalty under civil law, for all other offences a field general court martial (FGCM) could be convened.[202] The FGCM was a much more rudimentary trial system. For instance, the right to call defence witnesses was limited to those who were 'available', having due regard to the public service.[203] A second point of distinction was that a FGCM did not carry an unqualified entitlement to representation or facilities to prepare a defence.[204] The military courts came to be modelled on FGCM but there were important differences.

Differences between Military Courts and Trial under the ROIA

A FGCM convened under the Restoration of Order in Ireland Act was cumbersome and slow. Proceedings before the Military Court were swifter and less complex. The army made arrests and quickly decided whether the arrestees would be tried by military court or not. For the army, this was the attraction of the Military Court. The High Command also believed that the Military Court was not subject to interference by the High Court.[205]

Under ROIA courts martial, where the charge was punishable by death, then the court was required to include a person certified to be a person of legal knowledge and experience.[206] This protection was not present in a trial before the Military Court.

5.2 Lt Colonel Vandeleur, who presided over many of the trials by military court. Courtesy of the South Lanarkshire Council.

In an ROIA court martial, the accused and his or her spouse were not competent witnesses for the defence,[207] which reflected the position under civil law in Ireland.[208] The army, unburdened by centuries of legal learning, concluded that this prevented the courts from returning a 'true verdict' and so in trials before the Military Court the accused and his spouse were able to give evidence for the defence.[209]

Under ROIA courts martial the court could only pass the sentence available under common law or statute. The Military Court was not so constrained. [210]

Under ROIA courts martial, the question of clemency was the preserve of the Lord Lieutenant and Governor General but in respect of military court trials the army reserved the question of clemency to the commander in chief.

The hand-written annotations on surviving trial notes show that the Military Court utilised the rules of procedure for FGCM in the *Manual of Military Law*.[211] Although an analysis of submissions in these trials suggests that trial procedure was evolving swiftly.[212] In May 1921 the emerging trial procedures were drawn together into a single document,[213] the *Circular Memoranda on Martial Law*.[214]

The *Circular Memoranda* asserted that the Military Court had jurisdiction to try all criminal offences and all offences contrary to the Restoration of Order in Ireland Act. It was also permitted to try all contraventions of any lawful order or regulation issued by any lawful authority or any act prejudicial to the safety, efficiency or well being of the forces of the Crown.[215] In short, the Military Court asserted the widest possible jurisdiction.

Referral to Military Court

Cases were referred to the Military Court by the Summary Court or any commanding officer.[216] The Regulations gave no guidance on the criteria for referral.

It should be remembered that this policy had its origin in the proclamation of martial law which converted a number of non-capital criminal offences into capital offences, most notably possession of arms. The proclamation also created the Military Court to try these cases and impose capital sentences. That in essence is how these cases came to be tried by military court. The broad rule laid down by General Strickland was that: 'Military courts are as a rule kept for those offences where a death sentence is likely to be awarded which cannot be awarded according to the ordinary law.' [217]

It was thought that after overcoming initial opposition, the Military Court would be free from interference by the civil courts[218] and that the army could bring about trial and execution expeditiously. As we have already seen, the JAG had advised that execution should follow quickly, 'to minimise trouble' over Habeas Corpus.[219]

Members of the Court

The court would be convened by the Military Governor, who would name the court members.[220] The officers comprising the court would usually include a field officer, a captain and a subaltern. There would never be fewer than three officers, and where a death sentence was likely a judge advocate would be appointed.[221]

The officers who tried these cases were drawn from a pool. One was Crofton Bury Vandeleur DSO of the Scottish Rifles. The surviving case papers show that Vandeleur sat as president in trials which resulted in eleven executions, and it may be inferred from the fact that he presided in so many of the high-profile trials that he also acted in many other cases where records do not survive.

Crofton Bury Vandeleur came from a military family steeped in service to the Crown and the Empire. His cousin had been Lord Lieutenant of Clare. His brother was a brigadier general, his father served as a captain in India. Two members of the Vandeleur family were killed in the Great War and another cousin in the Boer conflict. Crofton Bury Vandeleur had also served in South Africa where he gave the family name to an unclassified species of flower: Streptocarpus Vandeleurii. He later served in France and was wounded in 1914 and captured. He broke out, and travelling by night on foot he became the first British officer to escape from Germany. He rejoined his regiment and sustained machine-gun wounds in 1915 at the battle of Festaubert. Wounded in the hips, he lay out in no man's land for many hours before being rescued.

Vandeleur was shipped back to England and spent the remainder of the war on home service.[222] His wounds troubled him for the rest of his life, and though not fit for active duty this freed him for service on the military courts. In 1921 he was a 54-year-old 'half pay colonel on active service'. Of heavy build, with a full head of grey hair, he emerges as a formidable and unyielding man. Ireland was his last posting. He would have had significant courts martial experience during the Great War but, so far as one can see, no legal training.

Vandeleur was one of the officers at Victoria Barracks assigned to what was known as a standing court.[223] A review of the surviving case papers suggests a relatively large pool of officers.

Pre-trial Procedures

The most important pre-trial procedure was the taking of the summary of evidence. The term 'summary of evidence' simply meant that the witnesses related their evidence to an army officer. The evidence was written down. The accused had an opportunity to comment or cross-examine the witnesses. In courts martial under the Restoration of Order in Ireland Act the accused was usually present at the taking of the summary of evidence. This was recognised as a significant safeguard against prosecution malpractice. The Military Court soon dispensed with the presence of the accused at the taking of summaries of evidence.[224]

The Regulations required service of the summaries of evidence and charges on the accused prior to trial. The names of witnesses were withheld from the accused, who, if he had grounds, might apply to the Military Governor for an order.[225] This provision recognised the very real threat to witnesses. It also acknowledged that there might be circumstances in which an accused might need to know the identity of a witness to mount an effective challenge to the evidence. In fact in most of the trials by military court, the prosecution witnesses were exclusively RIC men and soldiers and so actual unfairness did not arise on this account.

Representation

If the accused wished to be represented, all reasonable steps were to be taken to facilitate this.[226] Where counsel was instructed they were required to appear wigged and robed. The rule was strictly enforced.[227] It might be thought there is a profound irony here, that a court not known to law should insist on all the trappings of normality and legality, but perhaps that was the point.

In cases carrying the death penalty, the accused could be assisted by an officer if he was not represented. If the accused declined to recognise the court, then an officer would be appointed to watch the interests of the accused. That officer would report to the Military Governor.[228]

The Regulations stipulated that the court had a duty to safeguard the interests of the accused, to elicit all facts in his favour[229] and take all reasonable steps to secure the attendance of witnesses.[230]

The Rules of Evidence

The Military Court was required to enforce the rules of evidence as strictly as any other court. Hearsay was not admissible[231] in support of the Crown case, except that a statement made as part of the summary of evidence where the accused was present could be put in evidence where the maker of the statement was dead, ill or had been kidnapped.[232] The Regulations further required the court to give the accused every latitude in cross-examination and to permit the accused to submit any documents in evidence.[233]

Pleas

In cases where the death penalty was likely, the court would not accept guilty pleas.[234] Not guilty pleas would be entered on behalf of the accused and evidence would therefore be called. The rationale of this rule appears to be a recognition that the accused may not be represented or well represented and the hearing of evidence might tease out any factors affecting culpability or mitigation. An accused who was jointly charged could insist on a separate trial.[235]

Trials

The Regulations required a detailed note of the proceedings to be kept.[236] Trials were to be conducted by no less than three officers and a judge advocate in capital cases.[237] The accused could maintain silence at trial or give evidence on his own behalf. The Regulations also permitted him to tender a sworn statement on which he could be cross-examined.[238] Alternatively, the accused could make an unsworn statement which would not expose him to cross-examination.

The accused was entitled to call evidence of his good character. The Regulations required the court to warn him that if he gave such evidence the prosecution could adduce evidence of bad character. Apart from this provision, the prosecution were not permitted to call evidence showing that the accused had a bad character or other convictions.[239]

5.3 Victory Arch and Guardroom, Victoria Barracks. The Victory Arch was built to welcome the Light Brigade returning from The Crimea. Courtesy of the Commanding Officer, Collins Barracks.

Finding

In the case of a death sentence, the court was required to be unanimous both as to finding and sentence.[240] This provision was later amended so that where there were five or more officers on the bench, a two-thirds majority was permissible.[241]

Punishment

The punishments available to the Military Court were death by hanging; death by shooting; a term of penal servitude from three years to life; imprisonment with or without hard labour for up to two years; a fine of up to £1,000.[242] The Military Court could also bind an accused over 'to be of good behaviour' or recommend the accused for internment.[243] Where sentence of death was imposed, the accused would be informed in closed court. The sentence would not be publicised until confirmed by the Military Governor.

There was no restriction on the sentence that might be imposed. Thus, subject to confirmation, the death sentence could be imposed for any offence, no matter how trivial.[244] It was never intended that the Military Court should have such a power. When the proclamations were made, the offences punishable by death were listed but by the late spring 1921, the *Circular Memoranda* asserted much wider powers.[245]

The members of the court and the Judge Advocate were required to swear an oath that they would not disclose the vote of any court member unless required by law. It is likely that this provision was intended to ensure that officers were able to vote freely without being the subject of peer pressure or adverse criticism from senior officers.

Conviction and sentence were subject to confirmation. The confirming officer would usually be the officer who convened the court. In a case where the death penalty was awarded, the confirming officer would be the Military Governor General.[246]

The Regulations made no provision for an appeal. But, as we shall see, within a few weeks there was a row between General Macready and the Judge Advocate General, who insisted on personally reviewing all death sentences by the Military Court.

These then were the Regulations and they were rather more generous than the rules for field general court martial. Much depended of course on how these regulations were applied. It should be emphasised that the Regulations continued to evolve as the months wore on and the army asserted greater powers.

The Regulations do not stipulate whether the public could attend these trials but they certainly did so. In practice the press were also admitted after the court was sworn and on the strict understanding that the names of prosecution witnesses and officers trying cases were not published.[247]

5.4 The Square, Victoria Barracks. Courtesy of the National Library of Ireland

PART II

CHAPTER SIX

Cornelius Murphy, Ballydaly, County Kerry

Cornelius Murphy was the first prisoner to be executed after trial by military court. He was captured during a raid on his family farm at Ballydaly near Rathmore in early January 1921. The army was still finalising the arrangements under which trial by military court would take place and there were unexpected wrinkles to iron out. One such difficulty culminated in a row between General Macready in Dublin and Felix Cassel KC, the Judge Advocate General, who had responsibility for reviewing all trials conducted by the military. Cassel, an unlikely JAG, was born in Germany of German parents but educated at Harrow. He was a Tory member of Parliament and served on the Western Front until 1915 when he was recalled to London to join the Judge Advocate General's office. His recall revived a rumour that he was the illegitimate son of the late Edward VII. Whether this was so cannot now be established but it is more likely that he was brought back to London because the caseload of the JAG's office had grown immensely after the Great War broke out. Cassel was undoubtedly an able lawyer and soon became Judge Advocate General despite public opposition on the ground of his German origin.

The shortcomings of the military justice system had been cruelly exposed during the Great War; a government committee under Mr Justice Darling had proposed the creation of a corps of legal officers but the report had been sidelined. Cassel continued to press for reform.[248] Every soldier tried for drunkenness or dishonesty might have his conviction reviewed by the office of the JAG. Events in Ireland in 1920 added to his responsibilities and the Empire had also become increasingly turbulent. Cassel was called upon to advise on a wide range of legal issues: could Greek civilians be tried by military courts after the Armistice?[249] Could interned Egyptian nationalists be detained outside the Martial Law Area?[250] The declaration of martial law in Ireland was an added complication for Cassel, and the first issue was a confrontation with General Macready.

General Macready complained bitterly to the War Office that Cassel was insisting on personally reviewing all convictions where the death sentence was imposed in Ireland: 'The Judge Advocate General claims he is the sole legal advisor in all cases where the death sentences are passed.' Macready argued that this would delay executions and diminish the effect of martial law.[251]

Cassel responded by pointing out that reviews by the Judge Advocate General had taken place in all courts martial or trials by military court during the Great War. 'I consider it part of my duty to His Majesty under the Letters Patent which I hold to tender my advice personally ...'[252]

This argument trumped all others and the War Office sided with the Judge Advocate General,[253] ordering General Macready to refer all cases where sentence of death had been passed to the Judge Advocate General.[254] Whether this was simply a territorial dispute between two great men is open to question but the decision gave effect to a small but significant protection for prisoners appearing before military courts. In the months that followed, the JAG acted as a brake on the policy of execution. The first case the JAG was called upon to advise on was that of Cornelius Murphy.

Cornelius Murphy faced two charges: that he was improperly in possession of a revolver and improperly in possession of seven rounds of ammunition.[255] The trial took place at Victoria Barracks on 17 January 1921. The President of the court was Lieutenant Colonel Vandeleur, who had strong connections with Ireland. His cousin, Hector Vandeleur, had owned an estate at Kilrush and as Lord Lieutenant of Clare had played a full and unrelenting part in the Land War. The family connection with the suppression of rebellion in Ireland was also long standing: one of the officers who tried Wolfe Tone in 1798 was also a Colonel Vandeleur.[256]

Murphy's answer to the first charge is recorded as: 'I do not deny having the revolver', and in relation to the second charge: 'I do not deny having the ammunition.' The court ordered that not guilty pleas be entered. This became standard procedure in capital cases.[257] The record shows that Murphy declined an adjournment to seek legal representation. There is also a note in the record which shows that the Judge Advocate explained the serious nature of the charges and that the prisoner was offered and declined legal assistance.[258]

The first witness called was Alfred Craggs, an Auxiliary stationed at Macroom Castle. He gave evidence that on 4 January he and a number of RIC men searched the farm where the accused lived at Ballydaly. As the RIC patrol approached he saw the accused and his brother, Denis

Murphy: 'As we got near to the house I saw them running away.' He shouted to them to halt. They stopped and the accused threw his coat to the ground. Found inside the coat pocket was a loaded revolver containing five live rounds. Also found, after capture, were two rounds of ammunition in the waistcoat of the prisoner. The ammunition fitted the revolver produced.

The accused was asked by the officer to account for the revolver and ammunition. He said 'I found it.' He then corrected himself and said: 'It was given me the night before.' The court then considered the question of the proclamation of martial law of 12 December 1920 and decided that the existence of the proclamation was a fact within their knowledge not requiring proof.

Murphy told the court that he had been given the revolver and ammunition by an unknown man the night before his arrest. He had been asked to hold them until the following night and he had reluctantly agreed. He had not told his brother or father about the gun and the ammunition. He stated that he had given the description of the man to the RIC.

Murphy was convicted on both charges. When asked if he had anything to say by way of mitigation, he told the court that his local RIC man, Sergeant Mulcahy, would speak for him. He was at pains to exculpate his brother and father.[259]

Cornelius Murphy was sentenced to death by shooting. The officers conducting the trial made a recommendation for clemency. They regarded Murphy as a man of 'limited education'.

One other point is worth noting. Murphy's assertion that he had provided to the RIC the description of the man who had given him a revolver was checked the day of his trial. A confidential report was sent to Cork Military Barracks 'in cypher' by the RIC inspector at Macroom. The report, dated 19 January, rebuts Murphy's assertion and describes him as a 'political character, very extreme volunteer and believed dangerous'.

The following day, Major General Strickland dispatched the case papers to GHQ in Dublin. Strickland's note reads: 'I recommend the sentence be carried out.' The case papers were then sent to London for the JAG to review. Cassel's review for Macready[260] was restrained. On the issue of the recommendation for mercy, Cassel wrote: 'The officers who composed the court and unanimously made the recommendation had the advantage of seeing the accused and of judging by personal observation whether he was a person of normal mental capacity. I think the recommendation of the court should carry great weight.'

It is a remarkable fact that the Military Court should impose the extreme penalty and then add a strong rider for mercy, although the practice was not uncommon in the courts martial of soldiers during the First World War. The definitive study of these trials by Anthony Babington concluded that officers conducting these trials often had no legal experience and were simply 'out of their depth'.[261] It should also be pointed out that during the Great War many soldiers were sentenced to death but only about 10 per cent were actually executed. And so the officers who made the recommendation may have had an expectation that the accused would be spared. If this was so, it was not a view shared by General Macready.

Cassel also noted that there was no evidence before the court that the proclamation had been posted in the area and that the accused had intimated that he was unaware of the proclamation. It should be pointed out that a great deal of energy was expended by politicians in parliamentary debate on these issues; whether a proclamation was authorised and were the procedures followed, and questions of that kind. The doctrine of martial law did not depend on the existence of a proclamation but on the events which made such a declaration necessary. There was, therefore, no requirement that the proclamation be published or even disseminated. In Ireland and the Empire, however, the government had historically placed great weight on proclamation in the old-fashioned sense of the word. This was the trigger for extraordinary powers. These proclamations were nailed up in market towns, villages or on trees or fence posts in remote areas. The logic was that once this had been done, then one and all were on notice as to their conduct. The issue raised in Murphy's case, therefore, was one of fairness: whether he knew about the proclamation. In fact there was a note on file from the commandant of Buttevant Barracks confirming that the proclamation had been posted in Rathmore. Finally, Cassel reminded General Macready of the legal test under martial law: is the execution 'essential for the purpose of restoring order and suppressing rebellion'?

The letter amounted to a veiled recommendation to avoid execution but sentence of death was confirmed by General Macready. On 30 January Murphy was handed over to the assistant provost marshal, Major Foley, and informed that he would be shot the following morning. Sentence was duly carried out. Murphy was attended by a priest. He was a single man. He was thirty-one years old.

There is no doubt that Murphy was an active Volunteer. He had been interned in 1916 but escaped and went on the run. In 1919 he assisted in the capture and trial of a gang of armed robbers,[262] while the following year he took part in attacks on RIC barracks at Rathmore and Millstreet.[263]

6.1 Sir Felix Cassel, KC, Judge Advocate General. Courtesy of Timothy Cassel QC.

Whether the court reached a factually correct conclusion may satisfy curiosity, but the more profound questions that arise relate to the legality of the trial by military court. The charge sheet is dated 15 January 1921 and is endorsed 'to be tried by Military Court'. The order emanated from Colonel Commandant Willis, who had endorsed a proforma to the effect that: 'It is not practicable that such offences should be tried by ordinary court martial. I hereby convene a military court.'

A review of surviving case papers in military court trials shows that this formula was invariably advanced as a justification for trial by military court. It raises an obvious question: if it was possible to convene three officers and a judge advocate to staff a military court, why was it not possible to convene a FGCM of the kind authorised by statute? There is no sensible answer to this question except that the army wanted trial by military court. The proclamation turned possession of arms into a martial law offence punishable by death. And the army created the military courts to deal with these offences and impose sentences of death.[264] In order to bring about a trial by military court the high command felt constrained to engage in a pretext which involved asserting that the usual trial processes were 'impractical' and therefore trial by military court was necessary and defensible after the event.

The first challenge to the legality of martial law was raised a few days after Murphy's execution. Doubts were expressed from a most unlikely quarter, the distinguished jurist Sir John Simon KC,[265] formerly Attorney General in Asquith's government. Sir John was remembered as a tall, reserved man of intellect and diverse abilities. His interest in Ireland probably dated from 1916 when he chaired the Royal Commission into the death of Sheehy-Skeffington. The following year he married Kathleen Harvey, a formidable Irish woman who became a notable campaigner on civil rights in the United States.[266] Sir John became the most articulate and trenchant opponent of the Lloyd George government.[267] So it came to pass that in 1921 it was Sir John who first questioned the proposition that the army could bypass the law and invent their own court with powers to inflict the death sentence for offences not so punishable under law. It was a question of considerable constitutional importance which would occupy the courts for many months. The policy of executions under martial law made a legal challenge inevitable, and within a few days the Republican movement initiated a response.

CHAPTER SEVEN

John Allen, Tipperary Town

John Allen was captured on 19 January near Tipperary. He was found to be in possession of a revolver, ammunition and a booklet entitled *Night Fighting*. On 2 February, the day after the execution of Cornelius Murphy, a summary of evidence was taken at the military detention barracks in Cork. The record shows John Allen was present. He had an entitlement to cross-examine but did not do so. Charges were laid the following day and the trial was scheduled for 7 February.

Two days later the army intercepted a letter from a prisoner at the military detention barracks.[268] The relevant extract reads: 'There is a chap here named John Allen from Tipp who is to be tried on Monday morning on a charge of having a revolver and dum-dum bullets. He is a co. Captain and also an FC man … he has been wanted for a long time. This coupled with the charge makes his chances of escaping the full penalty very small … but we think that in view of Sir John Simon's recent speech that expert legal advice may save the man from death …'

The trial started two days later. Despite the interception of the letter and the shortness of time, Allen was represented by solicitor Denis Boudren and barrister John Bourke, the son of the Recorder of Cork. Bourke was described by contemporaries as a tall, good-looking young man[269] of slow and heavy speech which gave his words some gravitas,[270] perhaps a little more than they deserved. Bourke went on to enjoy a successful career and he later became the Recorder of Shrewsbury,[271] but in 1921 he had only been in practice five years and since he was available to take this case at short notice we can probably infer that he was only modestly successful.

The trial was prosecuted by Captain F.E. Young, who prosecuted most of the Military Court trials. It took place in the library of Victoria Barracks. Elsewhere life had a deceptive normality: the home internationals were played; England beat Ireland. In Cork, the shops traded, schools were open, rural councils deliberated, the Board of Guardians convened, the Recorder of Cork sat in open court. But interwoven with the trappings of normality there were reports of ambushes, reprisals and shootings by masked men.

7.1 Lord Chief Justice Molony. Reproduced by permission of the Council of King's Inns.

The President of the court was Lieutenant Colonel Ernest Victor Longworth of the Royal Irish Rifles. Longworth was a barrister by training. He had been serving in Dublin in 1916 and was heavily involved in the courts martial process from that date forward. He was appointed King's Counsel in 1921.[272]

There were three charges brought against Allen. First, being improperly in possession of a revolver. Second, possession of sixteen rounds of revolver ammunition. Third, being improperly in possession of a book entitled *Night Fighting*.

Lieutenant Belcher of the Green Howards gave evidence that he was aboard a Crossley tender filled with troops en route from Tipperary to Galbally. About three miles from Tipperary they came upon Allen on the roadway: 'I jumped out and ordered the man who I now know to be the accused to put his hands up. The corporal who was driving the car came with me and I saw him take a revolver from the accused.'[273]

A number of soldiers were quickly out of the tender. Corporal Mason stated: 'I saw a man trying to scramble up the bank. The car was stopped and the officer held up the man whom I identify as being the accused. He did not put up his hands at once and seemed to fumble with his coat as if to draw a revolver.' Private Hudson of the Green Howards conducted the search and found the revolver attached to the accused's Sam Browne belt and secured also by a lanyard. A quantity of revolver ammunition was also found in a pouch in his jacket, including some 'flat-nosed bullets'. Also in his jacket were some papers, including the handbook.

Private Hudson told the court that 'the accused stated that he carried the revolver to protect his life and that he had been hounded out of Tipperary by the police'. Counsel John Bourke put in written submissions dated 7 February, the day of the trial. The submissions are handwritten, with some crossings out and obviously scribbled in a hurry. Bourke submitted that no sentence could be imposed on the prisoner other than one authorised by common law or statute. He further argued that the army had no power to create by proclamation a tribunal which could impose such penalties, the accused not being a person under

7.2 Henry Hanna KC, Counsel for the Crown in Clifford and Sullivan and other cases. Reproduced by permission of the Council of King's Inns.

military law. In support of his submissions he cited *Magna Carta*, *The Petition of Right*, *Halsbury's Laws of England* and a *History of the Criminal Law*.[274]

None of the witnesses were cross-examined. Allen gave no evidence and called no witnesses. He was found guilty on all three charges. It became the practice of the military courts to ask for a police report on the prisoner after conviction. The RIC report stated that Allen was a captain in B Company, Tipperary Volunteers and had been convicted of assault on police in November 1919 for which he had been sentenced to one month in prison. Little else was known about him save that he was a bootmaker from Tipperary. A petition for clemency attracted a small number of signatures. The petition attempted to mitigate his offence by pointing out that Allen's home where he lived with his father had been damaged in a military raid a few months before and his shoemaking business burned out during an unofficial reprisal. His father and his landlord had sought and recovered damages at Nenagh

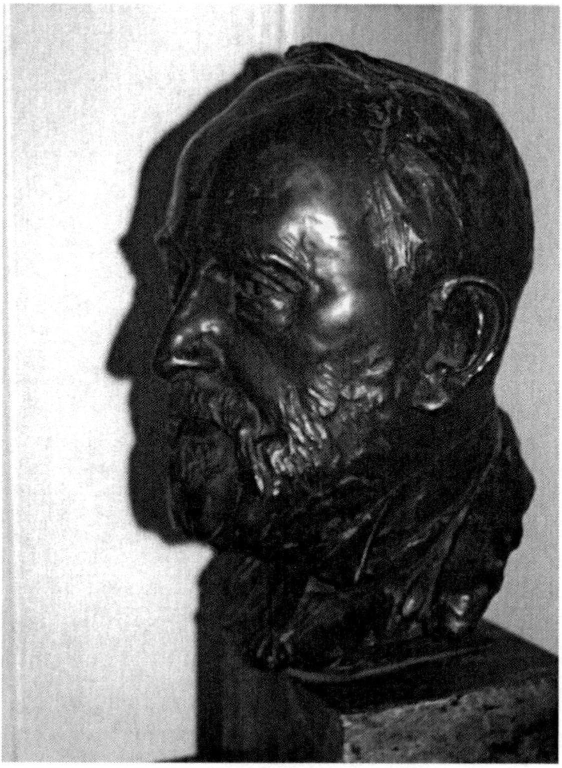

7.3 Tim Healy KC, counsel for John Allen. Healy was later Governor General of the Irish Free State. Reproduced by permission of the Council of King's Inns.

Quarter Sessions the month before.[275] These facts may explain Allen's remark when arrested, that 'he had been hounded out of Tipperary by the police'. There was probably rather more to it than that.

In any event, on 9 February Allen's solicitors made an application to the High Court for certiorari (overturning conviction), prohibition (preventing execution) and habeas corpus (securing his release). The application was heard in the High Court in front of Chief Justice Molony[276] and three other judges. Allen was represented by Tim Healy, King's Counsel. Small, bearded, portly and abrasive,[277] Healy had made his reputation defending impecunious prisoners during the Land War in the late nineteenth century.[278] With him was Patrick Lynch, King's Counsel, later Attorney General.

The Crown was represented by the attorney general, Sir Denis Henry, who would later be the first Chief Justice in the new Northern Ireland state. The Attorney General was expected to lead in cases such as this but Henry Hanna KC, who appeared with him, was probably the heavyweight advocate for the Crown. Hanna was the son of a Belfast linen merchant, a Unionist. Hanna's connections with the establishment were strong. At the outbreak of the Great War the President of the Irish Rugby Football Union formed D Company of the 7th Royal Dublin Fusiliers, an eclectic group of bankers, solicitors and stockbrokers, but Hanna had been too old to serve. And so D Company, mainly Irish, mostly Dubliners, went to Suvla Bay, where, under a baking sun, far from home, under-equipped and badly generalled, they fought with distinction and suffered a great slaughter. Hanna later wrote *The Pals at Suvla Bay*, a poignant memorial to the men of D Company.

There can be little doubt that Hanna regarded John Allen and men like him as traitors, but despite his strong Unionist leanings he also appeared for a number of nationalist prisoners in this period, subscribing to what was then still a minority view: that barristers must take every case that came to them without regard to the nature of the charge or the affiliations of the prisoner. Hanna was the emerging face of the modern Bar.

Allen's case was supported by an affidavit from his solicitor setting out the detail of Allen's arrest and trial, stating that his client had been tried by 'Field General Court Martial' and sentenced to death. The Crown responded with an affidavit from General Macready,[279] who simply observed that the destruction of barracks and the ambush campaign amounted to a state of rebellion characterised by 'actual warfare of a guerrilla kind'. His affidavit recited the casualty list in the Martial Law Area since 1 July 1920. In that time six army officers had been killed, sixteen wounded and five were missing. Twenty-four other ranks had been killed, eighty-one wounded and one missing. Sixty-two police officers had been killed and thirty wounded. He produced Proclamation No. 1 as an exhibit, which he stated had been made under 'the prerogative of the Crown'.

There is a key passage in Macready's affidavit which goes to the heart of the legality of what had taken place:

> In view, therefore, of the said state of armed insurrection prevalent in the parts of Ireland … and by virtue of my executive authority, and not otherwise, proceedings have been taken in the case of John Allen, and the charges made against him were duly and properly tried … by a Military Court.[280]

This is a crucial passage because it makes clear that this court was not convened under the ROIA, it was a new beast, a military court, created by Macready's order.

Macready's affidavit concludes with this passage: 'I considered and consider it absolutely essential in order to put an end to the terrible murders now so frequent, and for the suppression of the rebellion, that the unlawful carrying or possession of such weapons should be punishable by death.'[281]

The Crown asserted that the declaration of martial law by the Lord Lieutenant and Governor General was made by virtue of the royal prerogative and could not be challenged in the courts. This was questioned by Mr Justice Gibson:

> 'Does he have the authority?'
> 'He *is* the authority,' was the reply from the Attorney General.

So that, in a nutshell, was the argument put forward by the Crown. The argument submitted by Allen's counsel can be summarised as follows. First, if there was in fact a rebellion then the military did have the power to kill during conflict or in hot pursuit but that was the extent of the power recognised by law. Allen was, it was argued, being tried by a tribunal not known to law and sentenced to a punishment not authorised by law.

Counsel pointed out that, only a few months before, Parliament enacted the Restoration of Order in Ireland Act, which gave wide powers to meet the emergency, and it set up a statutory courts martial scheme. It was not necessary or lawful for the military to invent a new court. 'Where,' asked Healy, 'does General Macready get power to set up such a court?' He pointed out that Parliament had just passed the Firearms

Act – which increased the penalty for possession of firearms – in the full knowledge of conditions in Ireland. By avoiding the courts martial scheme set up by Parliament, the army had converted a serious offence into a capital offence.

While lawyers argued in the High Court, the trial and sentence was reviewed by the JAG in London, who simply observed that the charges were properly laid and there was evidence to justify the findings of the court, but that sentence should not be carried out until the judgment of the court was delivered.[282] The case papers then went to General Macready. It is evident from the file that the intercepted prison letter was seen by Macready, and this must have weighed heavily against the prisoner. Sentence of death was confirmed.

Allen was held for execution at the military detention barracks. He was joined by others when ten men were captured after a failed ambush at Dripsey. It is necessary to look at the Dripsey case before concluding this review of Allen's case.

CHAPTER EIGHT

Dripsey

JEREMIAH CALLAGHAN, DANIEL O'CALLAGHAN, JOHN LYONS, TIM McCARTHY, PATRICK O'MAHONY, THOMAS O'BRIEN, DENIS SHEEHAN AND EUGENE LANGTRY

The Sixth Division record shows[283] that the 6th Battalion of the First Cork Brigade of the IRA had laid ambush about a thousand yards west of Dripsey bridge on the Cork–Macroom road on the morning of 28 January. They were lying in wait for an Auxiliary convoy.[284] The main body of men were dug into rifle pits on a bank which overlooked the road on a gentle curve.

Events that day were influenced by two people. One was Father Ned Shinnick, who had preached against the 'Ambush War' from the pulpit. Another was a middle-aged widow, Mrs Mary Lindsay, who owned land at Leemount, near Coachford.

On learning of the ambush preparations, Mary Lindsay spoke with Father Shinnick and agreed to prevent the ambush taking place. She was driven to the RIC barracks by her butler, where she told the District Inspector: 'I came at once so that some poor fellows' lives might be saved.'[285] Father Shinnick passed information to a local Volunteer that their ambush position had been discovered.

The ambush party knew Father Shinnick's views on the 'Ambush War' and decided that his warning was simply a ruse to avert the attack and the reprisals that would follow.[286] The army, on the other hand, acted decisively. The information came to Lieutenant Colonel Evans of the Manchester Regiment. Evans emerges as an intriguing man – he was an able and determined officer, although it was known locally that he had reservations about the war.[287] Despite the conflict, he kept a horse at Ballincollig Barracks and hunted when he could, and as a result he was able to correctly guess the exact site of the ambush. This allowed him to deploy his troops before the rebel party were alerted to the presence of the army. By late afternoon Colonel Evans, five junior officers and nearly seventy men left Ballincollig Barracks in a convoy of lorries.

It appears that the rebel party were in the process of retiring when the Manchester Regiment arrived behind them, to the east. According to a contemporary press report the rebels conducted a running retreat. Most retreated to the west, and, as other army units closed in, they veered to the north-west and then to the north-east. It became a desperate chase on wet ground, biting cold and fading light.[288] The main party of rebels slipped away during a series of running skirmishes which culminated in an engagement just south of Peake. Householders in the nearby village watched 'the soldiers advancing up the hill firing as they came and taking advantage of every possible cover while the puffs of smoke from the civilian party firing at the military could be seen a few fields away in Peake ... the firing was intense.'[289]

It was a significant victory for the Manchester Regiment, which suffered no casualties. They took ten prisoners, five of whom were wounded. Strewn along the line of the retreat were a trail of abandoned weapons: ten shotguns, three rifles, four revolvers, six Mills bombs and ammunition.[290]

The Manchester Regiment scrupulously recorded the captured and their wounds. James Barratt of Firmount suffered a serious wound in the thigh. Denis Murphy had suffered a bullet wound to the left lung and leg. Others had suffered less serious bullet wounds: Tim McCarthy (right arm), Patrick O'Mahony (right wrist) and Thomas O'Brien (groin).[291] They were taken to the taproom of Sisk's pub where first aid and food was provided.[292]

The Trial

The trial by military court began less than two weeks later on 8 February at Victoria Barracks, Cork. Denis Murphy and James Barrett were too badly wounded to be tried with the others.[293] The accused who stood trial were Jeremiah Callaghan, Daniel O'Callaghan, John Lyons, Tim McCarthy, Patrick O'Mahony, Thomas O'Brien, Denis Sheehan and Eugene Langtry.[294] They were charged as follows:

> Count 1: Near Dripsey in the County of Cork, on 28 January 1921 did levy war against His Majesty by attacking with other persons unknown a detachment of His Majesty's Forces.
>
> Count 2: Did levy war against His Majesty by being concerned with others unknown in preparing an ambush.

The trial is significant, because until the case of Allen, most captured rebels denied the jurisdiction of the court and declined representation. An account of this trial written from the standpoint of the prisoners suggests that this practice had now been abandoned. Prior to the trial each of them had an hour with their legal representative.[295] The accused were represented by counsel or solicitor who all indicated that they were ready for trial.[296] The case was prosecuted by Major Gover, the most experienced trial advocate in the 6th Division legal branch; he had prosecuted the late lord mayor the summer before. Major Gover outlined the case and finished with the words: 'If proved, the charges are such as to merit the extreme penalty.'

The Prosecution Case

Lieutenant Colonel Evans told the court that he left Ballincollig Barracks at about 3.30 with seventy men. Arriving near Dripsey, he dropped five parties of men in a crescent shape around the area where he thought the ambushers were concealed. The parties of soldiers moved towards the presumed ambush position. Very soon they came upon the ambushers, many of whom were lying in rifle pits close to the road. Moving in extended formation and firing as they went, the soldiers quickly outflanked the ambushers, who began to run. Very quickly they captured a number of wounded. These men included O'Brien, McCarthy, Murphy, Barrett and O'Mahony. Also captured was Daniel O'Callaghan, who had barely run any distance.

The case against Langtry and Sheehan began to crumble very quickly.

> Q: 'Did you make any inquiries about these two boys, Sheehan or Langtry?
> Colonel Evans: 'I heard that they are supposed to be loyal men, and not members of any organisation. That's what I heard.'
> Q: 'From what quarters did you hear that?'
> Prosecutor: 'Now I object, though I gave you every latitude, but this is going too far.'
> Q: 'From the parties you heard it, could you rely on it?'
> Prosecutor: 'I must protest against this.'

The objection was to hearsay, though it might have been regarded as character evidence. The court did not trouble itself with these niceties and the objection was summarily overruled. Lieutenant Colonel Evans continued: 'They can be relied on.'

Langtry and Sheehan had been captured late in the afternoon. Soldiers under Lieutenant Orgill had been chasing the ambushers across the fields. Two of these men had run through the yard at Murphy's farm. The soldiers had followed and picked up Langtry and Sheehan in the farm house. According to one soldier they were out of breath. But, somewhat oddly, they were both wearing cardigans. Both appeared shocked and repeatedly protested their innocence.

The officer who captured Langtry and Sheehan was Lieutenant Orgill. He was asked a very leading question to which there was an unexpected reply:

> Prosecuting counsel: 'Will you swear to the court that the men you saw running into the farmyard were the men you arrested in the farmhouse?'
>
> Lieutenant Orgill: 'No, I will not.'

Later, Lieutenant Orgill added: 'They kept protesting their innocence.' Private Fitzgerald described Langtry and Sheehan as 'dumbstruck'.

Private Lloyd gave evidence that he was chasing a group of men. One went to ground. He identified Jeremiah Callaghan as the man: 'He was wearing a haversack and belt, and inside the haversack was a whistle and rations.' Lieutenant Vining told the court:

> 'One of them was carrying a rifle. That man jumped over a bank and I saw he had a rifle in his hand. I fired at him and hit him. He dropped the rifle and ran towards a hedge.'
> 'What did you do?'
> 'There was indiscriminate firing going on at this time, but I went after that man and arrested him.'
>
> 'Did you take that man's name?'
>
> 'He gave his name as Pat Mahony, sir.'

Lance Corporal Wright was one of a number of soldiers who gave evidence against Lyons. Corporal Wright told the court he and a party of soldiers had been chasing three men. Two had managed to scramble over a bank and through a hedge. The third had been unable to get over. This man threw a revolver over the hedge to the men on the other

8.1 General Macready. Reproduced courtesy of the Trustees of the Imperial War Museum.

side who fired on the soldiers and made off. The third man who had failed to scale the hedge was captured. He identified this man as Lyons. A search for the revolver was made but nothing was found.

A number of soldiers gave evidence that Dan O'Callaghan had been found hiding in the corner of a field by a stone wall. A shotgun had been found two yards away. One soldier, Private Donnelly, gave evidence about the capture of Dan O'Callaghan, who he said was carrying a gun as he ran. He was cross-examined and agreed that when the summary of evidence had been taken he had not mentioned that O'Callaghan had been carrying a gun.

Company Sergeant Major Cookson gave evidence that Thomas O'Brien had been one of a number of men firing at his party. O'Brien and the others had run. He had seen O'Brien captured and he searched him: 'I put my hand into his pocket and pulled out a revolver.' Private Barber gave evidence of the capture of McCarthy: 'He appeared to be wounded in his left arm, and I rolled him over and there was a revolver underneath him.'

The Defence Case

Eugene Langtry

Langtry told the court he had worked for Mrs Bowen Colthurst at Dripsey Castle for sixteen years. He had been forced to leave by threats from unnamed men. He was not a Volunteer or Sinn Féiner and he lived in a farmhouse locally with his parents. On the day in question he had been working the land. There had been an uneasy feeling abroad that day and his sister had suggested he make himself scarce. He had gone to Murphy's farm which was only a few fields distant. He had been at Murphy's farm with Sheehan when they were arrested in the aftermath of the ambush. He had not been in possession of a gun.

In cross-examination he accepted that he had guessed an ambush was in preparation because of an unusual number of civilians he had seen that day. He did not think to go to the police.

> Gardiner Wallis: 'There is no RIC barracks at Dripsey and Ballincollig is ten miles away.'
> The President of the court: 'He is an active young man; there is no reason why he should not walk ten miles.'

Perhaps the real issue related to the consequences of informing, but that remained unsaid.

Denis Sheehan

Sheehan gave evidence and confirmed the account given by Langtry. He lived with his uncle Con Murphy and had every reason to be at the farmhouse that afternoon. He had been working in the fields until about 4.30 pm. He had seen and noticed nothing unusual because the farm was over a mile from the nearest road. He then returned to the farmhouse where he met Langtry, who was a good friend. They heard shooting. At some point two men had run through the farmyard. Everyone went inside in a bit of a panic. The army arrived shortly after and he and Langtry were arrested. He insisted that he was not a member of any illegal organisation. Con Murphy, the farmer, gave evidence confirming the account given by Sheehan and Langtry.

Daniel O'Callaghan

Daniel O'Callaghan gave a muddled account. He accepted in cross-examination that he was a Volunteer and was present at the ambush site on the orders of a man he did not name. He was ordered to get into a rifle pit at the ambush site where he remained for most of the day. He said he was terrified and unarmed. When the firing started he had run west towards Coachford.

He said he was a reluctant Volunteer. He had been a member of the Volunteers for seven or eight months but had not attended many meetings. He was asked in cross-examination to name other members of his company. His counsel objected that this would expose him to retribution. The court ruled that the question could be pursued. Since O'Callaghan maintained that he was a Volunteer but did not know any of the ambushers, one would have to conclude it was a fair question. It was a question, however, which put O'Callaghan in an impossible position and he declined to answer.

Jeremiah Callaghan

Jeremiah Callaghan's mother, Julia, told the court that she had been recently widowed. She had nine children under the age of twenty. She told the court her son Jeremiah was eighteen years old. He lived with her at Coolmeagh, some miles from the ambush site. He was a stonemason, like his late father. He also repaired boots and on the day in question he had gone to Coachford by bike to buy leather to fix his boots. He had been wearing his Sunday best clothes.

Jeremiah Callaghan gave evidence that during his journey to Coachford he had been held up by three men and required 'to keep a look out' and told to blow a whistle if he saw soldiers. He said he had no connection with Sinn Féin or the Volunteers. He called character evidence from a local landowner, Major Woodley, who had known his family for a long time. Major Richard Woodley owned land at Leades near Aghinagh where his family had lived for generations. He was fond of shooting and hunted with the Muskerry Hunt. He had served in the Royal Army Medical Corps in the Boer War and in the Great War, where he had been awarded the Distinguished Service Order and was twice mentioned in despatches. His service credentials were impeccable and it is likely that he would have been known by repute to most senior army officers. Major Woodley told the court: 'I knew his grandfather and his father and I know the accused Jeremiah Callaghan as they have all been working for my family.'

John Lyons

John Lyons told the court he had been on his way to Shandy Hall to look for work. He had been crossing the fields when he saw men running and soldiers chasing. He ran at first but then surrendered. He denied being a Volunteer or a Sinn Féiner. He denied evidence given by two soldiers that he had thrown a revolver over a bank. He admitted he had been wearing khaki breeches and 'puttees' but thought nothing of it. In cross-examination he was asked:

> Q: 'Why did you run on this occasion?'
> A: 'I thought it would be safer to run, Sir.'
> Q: 'Safer from what, Lyons?'
> A: 'When the fire was opened, Sir.'
> Q: 'If you are innocent of anything that occurred that day, why did you run?'
> A: 'I thought the soldiers were angry …'

Thomas O'Brien

O'Brien did not give evidence but put in a written statement which declared that he lived with his parents at Dripsey. He had served in the British Army during the war and later worked at Dripsey Woollen Mills. He had always been opposed to Sinn Féin. On the 28th he was going from home to his aunt's when he heard firing and saw civilians running away, dropping overcoats and arms as they ran. He was caught up in the chase and was shot in the leg. A soldier came up and arrested him and when doing so picked up a revolver on the ground nearby. He denied having this revolver or being involved in the ambush.

Timothy McCarthy

Timothy McCarthy made an unsworn statement. He was an out-of-work labourer and was looking for work on the day in question. He heard firing and then saw the military coming along the road. He ran into a field and took shelter behind a hedge. A party of soldiers came into view and fired at him, wounding him in the hand. In the field where he was captured there were several guns, coats and other items of equipment lying about which did not belong to him.

Patrick O'Mahony

Patrick O'Mahony made an unsworn statement. He declared that he was the son of a local widow. He worked the family farm near Dripsey. He stated he was innocent and had never been a Volunteer. He had been visiting a neighbour at Godfrey's Cross when he heard firing and came across a party of civilians who were firing shots and running and firing back into the distance. He lay down in a field to avoid being hit by the shots. After a little while, believing it was safe to continue on his way he got up and ran when a party of military appeared and fired at him. He was wounded and taken prisoner.

Verdicts

After hearing closing arguments the court retired for twenty minutes[297] before returning the following verdicts: Jeremiah Callaghan, Eugene Langtry and Denis Sheehan were found not guilty. O'Brien, O'Mahony, McCarthy, John Lyons and Daniel O'Callaghan were found guilty. The duration of the deliberations of the court – a mere twenty minutes – calls for special mention. The court heard from dozens of witnesses and the transcript runs to over 145 pages. Even by the standards of the day, twenty minutes is remarkable – not even time to read through the transcript.

The file contains numerous character references, including on behalf of O'Callaghan, a reference from Georgina Bowen Colthurst: 'Dan O'Callaghan would not be willingly instrumental in taking life.'

All the men were sentenced to 'death by shooting'. The court made a recommendation for mercy in relation to Dan O'Callaghan, as it was not satisfied he was armed.[298] General Strickland also recommended that the sentence on Daniel O'Callaghan should be commuted: 'There is some reason to doubt whether he voluntarily took part in the ambush.'[299]

A few days after the trial, Frank Busteed, the organiser of the ambush, identified Mrs Mary Lindsay as the person who had given the army information. Mrs Lindsay and her butler, James Clarke, were kidnapped and held hostage to secure the lives of the men on trial. Mrs Lindsay was in late middle age, a jolly, 'vivacious, sincere, warm hearted' woman,[300] one of a dwindling number of the loyalist ascendancy. She was also an acquaintance of General Strickland and aspired to his friendship.

The case papers for the convicted men then went to Cassel, the JAG in London. On 15 February Cassel wrote to General Macready informing him that the charges had been properly laid and there was evidence to support the convictions. The recommendation for mercy in respect of Dan O'Callaghan, he said, was a matter for General Macready. The JAG added a note of caution that the sentence should not be carried out until judgment had been given by the King's Bench Division in the case of John Allen.[301]

On 17 February, General Macready despatched a telegram to the Judge Advocate General informing him he had confirmed sentences of death in respect of O'Brien, Mahony, McCarthy, Lyons and Dan O'Callaghan and 'propose to carry out sentences forthwith unless you give your opinion that I cannot legally do so'.[302] The same day Cassel sent a terse telegram back: 'Sentence in those cases pending the decision in Allen's case could not be properly carried out.'[303]

The following day Macready sent a formal complaint to the War Office insisting the JAG was exceeding his powers and that martial law in Ireland was being reduced to a 'farce'. The JAG rejoined by observing that the legality of martial law was being tested in Allen's case and that: 'No lawyer deserving of the name could have given any other advice.'[304]

The row between General Macready and the Judge Advocate General spread like ripples through Whitehall, with urgent memos flying back and forth. The Chief Secretary for Ireland, the Attorney General and other Cabinet ministers became embroiled and sided against Macready. There is an echo here of other disputes between the army and the civil authorities. In Ireland, the royal prerogative of mercy lay with the Lord Lieutenant and Governor General. This was a power that General Macready sought to reserve for himself as head of the army. In another case, an ROIA prosecution of Joseph Murphy, General Macready had taken this power to himself.[305] It was but one example of the developing friction between Macready and the civil authorities.

The Judgment in the Case of John Allen

Three days later judgment was delivered in the case of R v Allen.[306] The unanimous finding of the court was delivered by Lord Chief Justice Molony, who declared: 'The sacred duty of this Court is to protect the lives and liberties of all His Majesty's subjects, and to see that no one suffers loss of life or liberty save under the laws of the country.'[307] There was a qualification in times of war and rebellion, he observed. Although it was for the court to decide whether there was a state of war, the judges were satisfied that General Macready's affidavit established that as a fact. Second, following Marais,[308] a case arising out of the Boer War, while such a state of war existed the courts had no jurisdiction to intervene. This removed the last obstacle to the execution of Allen and the five men convicted of being involved in the Dripsey ambush.

The executions were announced to take place the following Monday. An attempt by the deputy Lord Mayor of Cork and a number of senior clergy to seek clemency from the Lord Lieutenant and General Macready were politely rebuffed. Meetings of public bodies were adjourned as a mark of respect and that Sunday many churches offered prayers for the souls of the condemned men. It was hardly the reaction the military hoped to evoke.

John Allen and the five men captured at the Dripsey ambush were brought up for execution on the morning of 28 February. A large, silent crowd gathered outside the barracks. John Allen and Daniel O'Callaghan were shot at 8.45 am. The others were shot in pairs shortly after.[309]

Sturgis, writing from Dublin Castle, noted the executions in Cork in his diary:

> Six rebels were executed in Victoria barracks this morning ... Now that the Allen Case is over I hope that Strickland will carry out his executions with greater despatch – the long delay gives time for all sorts of petitions and propaganda.[310]

The justification for the policy of executions rested on deterrence, and no doubt some were deterred but overall the violence seems to have been stepped up. In Cork city at about 7.15 on the evening of the executions there were a number of attacks on soldiers 'walking out'. Six soldiers were killed and eleven wounded.[311] Bizarrely, although this was an area of martial law, none of the soldiers were armed. The practice of allowing soldiers to stroll around the city centre had continued with no thought of the possibility of reprisals. Four more soldiers of the 2nd Staffordshire Regiment were wounded on curfew patrol the same night.[312]

Mrs Lindsay and her butler were held for many weeks until late one night they were both shot dead over an open grave. Clarke, the butler, had by this time suffered a complete mental collapse. Mrs Lindsay, gaunt and exhausted, remained scathing of her kidnappers to the very end.[313] The following day her house at Leemount was burned to the ground.

The propagandists on both sides seized on the executions at the detention barracks. The army distributed leaflets calling on Volunteers to wear uniforms and carry arms openly if they wanted belligerent status. The Republican movement distributed leaflets inciting soldiers to desert and return home. Demonstrations were held accusing the army of shooting prisoners of war. Attempts were also made to enlist the support of backbenchers at Westminster, some of whom were moved by concern but others relished a chance to embarrass the coalition government. Questions were raised as to how many men were being held,[314] whether those hearing trials had sufficient training,[315] whether there was a route of appeal,[316] and whether the military courts were necessary.

Privately some Cabinet ministers also shared these misgivings. Hamar Greenwood wrote a note to General Macready urging him, in capital cases, to use courts martial under the ROIA instead of military courts.[317] Macready replied with a resounding 'no'. Courts martial under the ROIA were slower, more cumbersome and open to review by the Appellate Courts.[318] Military courts were free of these difficulties, he argued.

This proposition was soon to be tested because other men were joining the list of those to be tried by the Military Court. Among them were five men captured in a failed ambush at Mourne Abbey on 15 February and eight who surrendered after a siege at Clonmult on 20 February.

8.2 Mrs Mary Lindsay of Leemount. Courtesy of the Trustees of the Imperial War Museum.

CHAPTER NINE

Mourne Abbey

THOMAS MULCAHY, CORNELIUS MULCAHY, PATRICK RONAYNE AND MICHAEL CREEDON

This trial arose out of what became known as the Mourne Abbey ambush, which took place on 15 February 1921. Drive north from Cork towards Mallow on the N20 and just before Burnfort there is a very sharp left turn which brings you over an old humpback bridge. As you cross the bridge the ground dips and bends to the right through woodland and rises to Mourne Abbey. Built by the Knights Hospitaller at the end of the twelfth century, the ruins dominate the skyline. It was here that these events took place.

On the morning of 15 February 1921 a patrol led by Major O'Brien with Lieutenants Vining and Orgill and twenty-four soldiers of the Manchester Regiment were travelling on the main road from Cork to Mallow. Major O'Brien in the leading Crossley tender saw two men dragging carts onto the road.[319] This was recognised for what it was: a favoured ambush tactic. In order to be effective the carts needed to be dragged onto the road at the very last moment but the ambushers had acted too soon. The convoy halted and troops began to deploy on both sides of the road.[320]

The ambush originated in a plan to surprise senior army officers en route from Buttevant to a conference in Cork city. The army learned of the ambush from an ex-soldier and made preparations of their own. The *Sixth Division Record of the Rebellion* sets out the army response:

> A party of police and a party of the East Lancashire Regiment were ordered to move out in lorries to the district of Ballingvuskig, and at 10 am to move in small parties across country towards Jordan's Bridge. At the same time, parties from the same Regiment from Buttevant were to move across country from the direction of Pendy Cross Roads.[321]

It was a well-conceived strategy that would result in a pincer movement

9.1 Albert Wood KC and his wife Edythe. Albert Wood was counsel for a number of the prisoners. Courtesy of Chris Wood.

and the death or capture of most of the ambush party, which numbered a little over fifty. But chance took a hand when Major O'Brien and his party arrived at Jordan's Bridge before the other army units had taken up position. The attack by the Manchester Regiment caused the ambushers to retreat and scatter.

The rebels in position ahead of the Manchester Regiment began a running retreat. Those on the east side of the road ran from the bridge and were intercepted by the East Lancashire Regiment. Those on the west side ran west and south and escaped. According to the Manchester Regiment, at least five of the ambush party were killed and others wounded. Cornelius and Thomas Mulcahy, Patrick Ronayne, Michael Creedon, Bartholomew Riordan and a number of other men were captured.

Trial by Military Court

There were four accused who were brought to trial: Ronayne, Thomas Mulcahy, Cornelius Mulcahy and Michael Creedon. The prosecution dropped the case against the fifth man, Riordan, on the morning of the trial. The only other man held for trial was Michael Looney and he died of his wounds some days after capture.

The trial by military court started at Victoria Barracks on 23 March. The President of the court was Lieutenant Colonel Vandeleur. Captain F.E. Young of the 6th Division Legal Department prosecuted. Major Meyler of the Border Regiment acted as judge advocate. The accused were all represented by counsel. John Bourke appeared for Con Mulcahy, Patrick Ronayne and Thomas Mulcahy. Michael Creedon was represented by Joseph McCarthy, later senior counsel and circuit judge. All the prisoners were charged with two counts: levying war against the Crown;[322] and being concerned in the preparation of an ambush.[323]

The Prosecution Case

Sergeant Pinchman of the Manchester Regiment gave evidence that he had been part of a motorised patrol. He told the court: '100 yards from the ruins of Mourne Abbey two farm carts were pushed out onto the road. They were about 100 yards ahead of us.' The Crossley tenders pulled up and the men began to deploy.

Sergeant Pinchman walked ahead and found the bank had been 'loop holed' to provide firing positions. At the side of the bank there lay a macintosh, empty cigarette packets and drink bottles. In the distance he saw men running. Sergeant Pinchman fired at one of the men and he fell wounded.

Lieutenant Vining told the court that he had taken a number of men to the east: 'I saw about 12 men about 600 yards away, going East, running and some carrying rifles or shotguns. I opened fire and saw some drop. Some of these were carried away and others lay on the ground. I crossed the abbey stream ... I saw three dead civilians and beside each of them was a shotgun loaded with 12 bore.'

Sergeant Quin of the Manchester Regiment gave evidence that his men fired on a number of running men. 'I saw three fall,' he said. Sergeant Quin chased one man 'but lost sight of him for a time while I was going down a dip.' The chase continued until the man 'got behind a hedge, when I was 10 or fifteen yards away he jumped up and fired at me with a shot gun but missed me. He then dropped his gun.' Sergeant Quin climbed through the hedge and arrested the man. 'I identify Patrick Ronayne, accused, as that man.'

Lance Corporal Avison gave evidence that he had been close behind Sergeant Quin. He saw Ronayne fire at his sergeant from behind a hedge at 5 yards' range. He missed, and was disarmed and captured. Private Lucas supported this account.

Private Greenhalgh of the East Lancashire Regiment was approaching from the east with a party of men. He gave this account of Ronayne's arrest: 'I saw the accused Ronayne running towards me. Immediately he saw me he put up his hands. He was breathing heavily and sweating. I asked him where he was going and he told me he was running away from the firing because he was frightened.' Private Greenhalgh added that shortly after this an officer of the Manchester Regiment, a sergeant and a lance corporal arrived on the scene. Private Greenhalgh identified these as the witnesses who had just given evidence.

These accounts cannot be reconciled, and the question of whether or not Ronayne had fired on the army might have been enough to make the difference between receiving a death sentence or not.

In the case of Thomas Mulcahy, Sergeant Larkin of the East Lancashire Regiment told the court he had been leading a party of soldiers in a sweep across country when he came on Mulcahy, who was wounded. He was searched and a shotgun cartridge was found on him. Some distance from the scene of this arrest his brother Cornelius Mulcahy was found lying under a hedge 'with a coat over his head'. This prisoner denied being involved in the ambush and said he had been returning from the fair at Donoughmore.

The case against Michael Creedon rested on evidence from Sergeant

Bourke (RIC), who told the court he was part of a group of men closing in on Mourne Abbey from the east when they had been fired upon from a corner of a field. Two men were seen running. They were fired on. Ned Creedon was killed and Michael Creedon sustained a serious head wound. He was left at the scene. No weapons were found on them or near them.

The Defence Case

Patrick Ronayne

Ronayne told the court that his family ran a 50-acre farm at Greenhills near the scene of the ambush. He had been ploughing the field that week. He had been using borrowed 'traces'. On the morning of the ambush he had gone to the creamery to buy 'traces and bolts' for the harrow. Ronayne took a shortcut across the fields. He heard shooting and ran, and found himself in a farmyard. This was about a mile and a half from his home. Here he was captured by a group of soldiers and was told that he was arrested for firing on the troops. Ronayne denied having a gun or being involved in the ambush and maintained he was not a Sinn Féiner or a member of the Volunteers.

In cross-examination he refuted the suggestion that any ammunition had been found upon him. He accepted he knew each of the accused but had not seen them that day. He also knew Patrick Dorgan who had been killed that day and Michael Looney who had been wounded and captured.

Ronayne's sister Norah gave evidence that on the morning of the 15th he had fed the cattle and left for the creamery at about 10.30 am. He was not carrying arms and she had never known him to be involved in Sinn Féin or the Volunteers.

Ronayne called as a witness a farm labourer, Michael Ronayne, who had seen him on the way to the creamery. The witness was more or less discredited when he told the court that he had been on the road that morning but heard no shooting.

One final witness, Timothy Connell from Monee, gave evidence that he had loaned Ronayne a set of 'traces'. The evening before the ambush he had gone to Ronayne's farm to collect the 'traces'. This provided the reason for Ronayne's walk to the creamery that morning.

Cornelius Mulcahy

Cornelius Mulcahy told the court that he lived close by and this at least was indisputable. Mulcahy said that the fair at Mallow had been 'abolished' by the army. For this reason he had got up that day at 2 am to drive cattle to market at Donoughmore. He was returning home when he became caught in the round-up. He maintained he was not a Sinn Féiner and he called his sister Bridget to substantiate his account. She told the court that they had always sent the cattle to Mallow until the fair was banned there and that was why the cattle had to be taken to Donoughmore, which was much further. Two local farmers, John Hassett and Daniel Coleman, also went to the fair at Donoughmore and gave alibi evidence. In an effort to test or crack the alibi, the court heard a great deal of inconclusive evidence about the speed at which a heifer could be driven and the price that might be paid. It does not seem that the officers were equipped to resolve these issues.

Thomas Mulcahy

Thomas Mulcahy told the court that he lived close to the scene of the ambush with this brother and family. He had gone that day to the creamery to buy boots, and when he heard the firing, he ran. As he ran he met another man who was also running from the firing. He was shot in the hand, shoulder and foot. He denied being a Volunteer or a Sinn Féiner. As to the shotgun cartridge found on him, he told the court he had found it a few minutes before his arrest.

The evidence showed that when Thomas Mulcahy was captured he was briefly questioned by Lieutenant Vining of the Manchester Regiment. During the prosecution case the Judge Advocate ruled that the alleged confession could not be admitted in evidence because it had not been shown to be 'voluntary' in accordance with ordinary principles of law, nor had the accused been cautioned.[324]

What happened during the cross-examination of the accused was remarkable on any view. The Judge Advocate, having excluded the confession evidence, allowed the prisoner to be cross-examined about the alleged confession. When he denied making the confession the Judge Advocate allowed the prosecutor to call Lieutenant Vining to prove the confession. It was an elementary error of law. The application should never have been made by Captain Young nor should it have been granted by the Judge Advocate. Vining then gave evidence that Thomas Mulcahy had admitted taking part in the ambush. He then showed the officer the spot where he had thrown a single-barrelled shotgun.

Michael Creedon

Michael Creedon gave evidence that he had been at home with his brother when they heard the firing. They went to look and heard shooting and running figures. They were returning back to the house when he and his brother were shot down. His brother died instantly: 'There was no stir out of him.' Michael Creedon sustained wounds to the neck, shoulder and face. He was searched by RIC men, his name was taken and he was left on the ground. He managed to get home, where his wounds were treated. Creedon was arrested at home some days later. His evidence was supported by his father, mother, sister and two neighbours. It is clear that he and his brother were on their own land when shot.

Verdicts

Verdicts were returned the following day. Michael Creedon and Cornelius Mulcahy were acquitted. Patrick Ronayne and Thomas Mulcahy were both convicted of levying war and preparing an ambush.[325] At this point Barry Sullivan instructed Albert Wood KC to make an application for a writ of habeas corpus. A conditional writ, pending full argument, was granted on 2 April.[326]

The army sent the case papers for review by the Judge Advocate General in London.[327] The Judge Advocate General, Felix Cassel, turned the papers around almost straight away. In the case of Ronayne he noted discrepancies in the evidence but concluded there was sufficient evidence to convict.

In the case of Mulcahy, Cassel observed that the Judge Advocate, having excluded the confession, had been 'wrong' to allow Mulcahy to be cross-examined about it and 'wrong' to permit the prosecution to recall a witness to prove the confession. Cassel noted that the confession may have influenced, to a great extent, the decision of the court. However, he observed: 'The rules of evidence are not necessarily applied with the same degree of strictness before a Military Court under Martial Law.'[328] There are obvious difficulties in trying to import a criminal code into a guerrilla war but the questioning of a wounded prisoner by an armed officer is hardly satisfactory.

A second area of concern was that Creedon and Mulcahy had not been present during the taking of the summary of evidence. The presence of the prisoners had been dispensed with by General Strickland, retrospectively. Defence counsel submitted, rightly, that there was no power under military law to make such retrospective orders, but this complaint fell on stony ground.

Cassel advised that, despite the evidential shortcomings, there was sufficient evidence to justify conviction and the sentences could be confirmed. And so the papers went back to General Macready for confirmation of sentence. But before General Macready turned to consider confirmation, the fate of these two men became bound up with the survivors of the Clonmult engagement, who were also challenging the legality of their trial before a military court and we need to review that case before concluding the analysis of legal proceedings in the Mourne Abbey case.

CHAPTER TEN

Clonmult

PATRICK SULLIVAN, MAURICE MOORE, WILLIAM GARDE,
JOHN HARTY, EDMUND TERRY, ROBERT WALSH
AND DIARMUID O'LEARY.[329]

On 20 February a siege took place at a cottage near Clonmult, County Cork. Twelve men were shot dead.[330] Eight men were captured, most of them wounded. The captured were William Garde, John Harty, Edmund Terry, Maurice Moore, Robert Walsh, Patrick Sullivan, Diarmuid O'Leary and Patrick Higgins.[331] All the men bar Higgins, who was seriously wounded,[332] were tried by military court just over two weeks later.

Proceedings started with the taking of the summary of evidence on 1 March. O'Leary was not mentioned in the summary. Under courts martial proceedings under the Restoration of Order in Ireland Act, he could not have been put on trial. All the men, however, were referred for trial by military court.

The trial took place a week later in the gymnasium at Victoria Barracks, Cork. Lieutenant Colonel Vandeleur presided, Major Gover prosecuted and Captain F.E. Young acted as judge advocate. Each of the accused was charged with levying war against the King. The men were heavily guarded, as one might expect, although the press and public were admitted.

Joseph McCarthy appeared for O'Leary, Moore and Sullivan.[333] McCarthy acted in many of these trials and later had a distinguished career on the bench. Michael Comyn KC acted for Terry, Harty, Garde and Walsh.[334] Comyn was emerging as a successful silk in criminal practice at that time. He had made his reputation on the Munster Circuit, where he proved a forceful and able advocate. Comyn was of average stature, with a long, angular face. He wore the heavy moustache which was popular in those days.

The case against the men was very strong. The prosecution simply proved each man was present at the house. This was done by calling an

10.1 John O'Byrne, counsel for Adam Jones. O'Byrne was later Attorney General and a Judge of the Supreme Court. Courtesy of Dr Eamonn Hall and the Office of the Attorney General.

10.2 Patrick Lynch KC, counsel for J.J. Egan and other prisoners. Courtesy of Dr Eamonn Hall and the Office of the Attorney General.

RAMC officer, Captain Young, who proved that Terry, Harty, Garde, O'Leary and Higgins has been admitted to the Central Military Hospital at Victoria Barracks on the evening of 20 February. All had wounds but only Higgins was seriously wounded. An army sergeant and a RIC man were also admitted with wounds. The other prisoners were identified by witnesses who had taken part in the siege.

Evidence was given by Lieutenant Dove of the Hampshire Regiment. He told the court:

> I was with a search party in the neighbourhood of Clonmult. It was decided to search a certain farmhouse. There were 3 officers and twelve other ranks in the party which was split into two. I approached the farmhouse with one of these two from the west. When about 300 yards from the house I heard shots. The house was not then in sight. We at once ran in the direction of the farm and to a bank about 100 yards from it when I saw four soldiers of the second party lining a bank 15–20 yards from the house. I saw the bodies of two dead civilians and then four men ran out of the front door. The second party of military had been firing at the windows of the house as we came up. There was also firing from the house. The four men who ran out of the house went to a barn. Two at least were armed with service rifles. The other two had either carbines or shotguns. We opened fire on these four. Two fell and the other two got into the barn … Desultory firing went on from both sides for about three quarters of an hour.[335]

Repeated efforts were made to get the men to give up the fight. Lieutenant Koe told the court that after one invitation to surrender the response was 'a volley' and some singing from inside the house. Reinforcements then arrived and further efforts were made to end the siege before nightfall. Lieutenant Koe described how Lieutenant Hammond 'climbed on the fencing of the cottage with a tin of petrol and succeeded in setting fire to the roof'. Lieutenant Dove continued:

> The roof of the house was fired by one of our party and we threw bombs into the house. After about a quarter of an hour 6 or 7 men came out with their hands up. We advanced into the yard to meet them and shots were fired at us from the windows of the house. A melee followed. After that about ten civilians came out of the house and joined in the melee. Later I found that we had eight prisoners.

This passage of evidence was hotly disputed. It was the prisoners' case that many of the men had been shot after surrender. This was put to

Lieutenant Dove, who replied: 'None of my men fired on civilians whose hands were up.' Lieutenant Dove readily accepted, however, that a number of men had been shot in a melee trying to escape.

The defence advanced in cross-examination was limited. First, that the amount of guns seized at the scene exceeded the number of civilians present. This was accepted by Lieutenant Dove, although Lieutenant Hook gave evidence of a large haul of weapons: 'twelve rifles and carbines, six shotguns and a dozen revolvers'. Second, that the firing from the house could have been carried out by five or six men. This was accepted. The third strand of the defence was that the men in the house were told they would not be shot if they surrendered and that they relied on that promise. This was a prelude to the real agenda being advanced by Comyn: that their surrender was conditional, obtained by a promise which avoided further bloodshed and that they should not now be executed. A number of witnesses denied hearing this said but Lieutenant Hammond went this far: 'Those inside were told that every care would be taken of them.'

The defence case was a difficult one. A particular evidential difficulty faced by the accused Sullivan was that a document had been seized in a search of his home that showed he had been a secretary to an arbitration court. It appears that he had to accept this evidence and offer some explanation. In order to understand the evidence that follows it may help to know that after the trial it emerged that Moore and Sullivan had been longstanding friends.

Sullivan told the court that he had been a secretary of the arbitration court but was suspected of passing information to the police and so had gone on the run from the IRA. He was later captured by the IRA and taken to the house at Clonmult, blindfolded and handcuffed. Moore admitted that he was in the Volunteers and that he had been asked to go to the house to identify Sullivan. Moore was asked by his counsel:

> 'Do you belong to any illegal organisation?'
> 'I do.'
> 'What organisation?'
> 'All of them (laughter).'
> 'What are they?'
> 'Sinn Féin, Volunteers and Fianna.'

The evidence of Moore supported that of Sullivan and vice versa. Although it placed them both at the heart of events it also provided each with a reason to be at the cottage and did not cause difficulties for the other accused.

10.3 Michael Comyn KC on his elevation to King's Counsel, in 1914. Courtesy of Michelle Comyn.

Each of the other prisoners gave evidence of an innocent explanation for being at the cottage, which provided an answer to the charges laid. None of the prisoners admitted to shooting from the cottage. The explanations advanced by each were, taken alone, tenable. Taken together, the accounts stretched credibility.

Diarmuid 'Sonny' O'Leary made something of an impression on King's Counsel defending; he had given his name as Jeremiah O'Leary when captured. He might have given a better pseudonym but for a head wound sustained in the siege. The false name certainly misled his family who, failing to find his name on the list of survivors, bought a burial plot and mourned him.[336] O'Leary's head injury required his head to be shaved and the result showed 'a furrow' along the top of his scalp. 'The bullet was never made that will kill Sonny O'Leary,'[337] observed Michael Comyn.

O'Leary told the court that he had come to the cottage to deliver a parcel of clothes to one of the others, Hegarty. The shooting broke out and he lay on a bed, whereupon a dog jumped on him. He raised himself up to avoid being bitten and sustained a bullet wound to the head. O'Leary was cross-examined and elaborated. 'It was a big black dog that jumped up. I never saw it before and I don't know what happened it since.' No other witness saw the dog. O'Leary was nineteen years old, naive and hopelessly out of his depth, one suspects.

The court retired for twenty minutes before returning guilty verdicts in respect of all of the men. Moore, Sullivan and O'Leary were sentenced to death, the others to twenty-five years' imprisonment.

Some complaint was later made that the court was hostile to counsel and the accused. It was in this case that Comyn is said to have uttered a famous rebuke to the officers trying the case: 'Shoot them if you must but try them first.'[338] The transcript, which is quite bland, does not support this contention. The *Cork Examiner*, working under the constraints of the censor, hints at a very different picture. Here is an extract:[339]

> 'Mr Comyn: Was the table at the left side of the door?'
> The Judge Advocate said the question is altogether illegal.
> The President, Mr Comyn, has persisted in asking illegal questions after being warned … Mr Comyn had taken no notice of his observations and he warned him now if he asked any more illegal questions he would ask him to leave the court.'

The objection appears to be that the question Comyn asked of his client was leading, one of a number of leading questions. We would need to know rather more before forming a conclusion about this exchange, although it should be said the Judge Advocate does not emerge with distinction from this trial. His ruling on an elementary point of law was wrong, and in fact was disregarded by the court.[340]

Review and Confirmation

These events were followed eagerly in the press. And the tension was increased by the kidnap of Major Compton-Smith, the commanding officer at Ballyvonaire. A note was sent to General Strickland telling him that Compton-Smith was being held to secure the lives of the men being held under sentence of death.

The convictions were reviewed by the Judge Advocate General, Felix Cassel. The papers suggest a painstaking review of the evidence. Cassel concluded the charges were properly laid and that the evidence was sufficient for the court to convict. Cassel also examined the distinction drawn by the court between the cases of those sentenced to penal servitude for life and O'Leary, Moore and Sullivan, who were sentenced to death.

His view was that in respect of Harty, Walsh, Garde and Terry there was no conclusive evidence of their involvement in insurrection apart from this occasion. One suspects that the age of the men was also a factor. Walsh was the oldest, at twenty, and Terry the youngest, seventeen. Cassel does not state this explicitly but his spidery writing has carefully noted and underlined the ages.[341]

As to those sentenced to death. Cassel concluded that O'Leary was not definitely proved to have been a member of a revolutionary association but he admitted taking a parcel to the house for one of the men who had been killed in the siege. He must, at least, therefore have been known to be an active sympathiser. However, Cassel reasoned the case for death was not as clear cut as that of Moore and Sullivan. The case papers went back to General Macready.

A Writ of Habeas Corpus

A conditional writ of habeas corpus was sought and obtained by Comyn. At the end of the hearing Comyn voiced his concern to the court: 'The prisoners had received notice they were to be shot on Saturday.'

Chief Justice Molony: 'Counsel might take it that nobody in this country would be executed in the face of a conditional order.'[342]

Molony had been Lord Chief Justice for three years and his words have the ring of a judge who expects unquestioning deference. As events would later demonstrate, Comyn's concern was not entirely misplaced. At least one prisoner in this conflict was denied access to the court, and in the Civil War that followed, another prisoner was executed[343] while his application for a writ of habeas corpus was still awaiting determination.

Returning, however, to the application for writs of habeas corpus, full argument of the case started on 20 April in front of Chief Justice Molony and four other judges.[344] The men were represented by Michael Comyn KC and Sgt McSweeny KC. The Crown was represented by Sergeant Hanna KC who had appeared for the Crown in the case of Allen.[345]

10.4 Sir John Simon, a principled and articulate critic of the Lloyd George government. He was counsel for Clifford and Sullivan. Courtesy of the Palace of Westminster Collection.

In the case of the Clonmult men, General Macready swore an affidavit setting out the mounting casualties. There was, as the General put it, 'a state of open rebellion', and therefore the courts had no power to intervene.

This time the affidavits of General Macready and General Strickland were contradicted by other evidence. A number of citizens in Cork had sworn affidavits pointing out that the normal business of the city continued; the courts sat; the churches and schools were open; businesses traded and sporting competitions took place as usual. Therefore, it was argued, martial law could not prevail.

Comyn also developed another argument. Levying war was treason under statute. And although the statutes created offences of treason, they also afforded protections and defences, such as having a copy of the indictment in advance of the trial, knowing the identities of the Crown witnesses and jurors and, since the defendants had been charged with treason, the law required evidence from two witnesses of an overt act of treason.[346] Harty, for instance, was identified by a single witness.

The Crown argued that the court should follow the decision in the case of John Allen. Counsel for the government also pressed a new argument: that the power of the King to declare martial law was delegated in the Lord Lieutenant on whose instructions the military acted and therefore the court could not dispute the assertion of the military that a state of war existed. This argument received a distinctly cool reception from the court. Judge Dodds responded: 'I for one protest.' He was joined in this by Chief Justice Molony and the argument was not pressed.

A few days later on 25 April Chief Justice Molony delivered the unanimous decision of the court refusing the writs of habeas corpus. Referring to his judgment in the case of John Allen,[347] Chief Justice Molony held that the only question which arose for decision was whether a state of war still existed. It was, he said, for the court to decide this issue, not General Macready, but the evidence of the sustained guerrilla campaign was sufficient evidence of a state of rebellion.

The very next case in the list was an application for writs of habeas corpus in the cases of Ronayne and Mulcahy[348] who had been captured after the Mourne Abbey ambush. They were both represented by King's Counsel; Michael Comyn was also instructed in this case. He was joined by Albert Wood KC,[349] a slight, moustachioed man from Norfolk who was remembered by those who met him for his urbane dress, and voice. He was known to his colleagues as 'The Thunderer'.

Michael Comyn and Albert Wood developed a new argument: that martial law had been declared under the prerogative of the King but this power had been surrendered to Parliament by the passing of the Restoration of Order in Ireland Act and could not be used without further legislation.[350] It can be fairly said that whether the argument was good or bad, Molony C.J. evaded a response on the surrender of the prerogative and followed the decisions handed down in the Clonmult case and that of John Allen. The applications on behalf of Ronayne and Mulcahy were dismissed.

It is worth digressing at this point to look at the uneasy co-existence of the courts and the military in the Martial Law Area. The following case in the list was Higgins v Colonel Comandant Willis, an action for damages for the destruction of a grocery shop in Washington Street, Cork, as an official reprisal against the householder for failing to inform the military of preparations for an ambush. There were very many cases where the occupants hotly disputed the suggestion that they were complicit in an ambush. To take a single example: at Nenagh Quarter Sessions a claim was brought by James Gleeson of Corbally for the burning of his house and, according to the pleadings, the death of his dog. The action was stayed when a military officer entered court and informed the judge that the burning had been an official reprisal.[351] As the year wore on General Macready and Major General Strickland were plagued by official complaints[352] and legal actions. Strickland gave his commanders orders not to accept writs for damages. General Macready, no doubt weary of swearing affidavits, issued Proclamation No. 3 suspending the jurisdiction of the civil courts in the Martial Law Area in respect of all actions against the military save with the consent of the Military Governor.[353] Consent was only given in respect of alleged unofficial reprisals and an army permit was needed to bring such an action.[354]

Some litigants tried to get around the difficulty by bringing cases outside the Martial Law Area. Higgins v Willis[355] was one such case. This action was stayed by Chief Justice Molony: 'durante bello'.[356] The stance of the court, as it developed, was to hear and scrutinise writs for habeas corpus but to stay all other actions. This then was the accommodation reached between the army and the courts.

Macready, having resisted this fresh and unexpected challenge to martial law, turned to review the papers relating to the Clonmult men. Much influenced, apparently, by the opinion of the JAG, he confirmed sentence of death in respect of Moore and Sullivan and commuted sentence on O'Leary. Sentence of death was confirmed in respect of Ronayne and Mulcahy, the men captured at Mourne Abbey.

10.5 The house at Clonmult. Courtesy of the Trustees of the Imperial War Museum.

On 27 April Barry Sullivan, solicitor for the Mourne Abbey men, made a last-ditch attempt to avoid execution: he issued fresh legal proceedings to stay the executions of his clients, Ronayne and Mulcahy. Senior civil servant Mark Sturgis wrote:

> Macready has had a writ delivered in the case of the two Mourne Abbey men ... I think the Cabinet should be consulted before the men are executed – but the matter is one for the GOC alone.[357]

General Macready consulted the Chief Secretary at Dublin Castle but pressed on with the executions and so Patrick Ronayne and Thomas Mulcahy were shot the next morning. Maurice Moore and Patrick Sullivan were executed by firing squad some minutes later. Outside the barracks wall the families of the prisoners had gathered and the scene was as harrowing as can be imagined.[358] The following day O'Leary was informed his sentence was commuted to penal servitude for life.[359] The sentences of penal servitude for life were confirmed in respect of Garde, Harty, Terry and Walsh.

There were a number of immediate repercussions to this trial. The first was that Major Compton-Smith, who had been held hostage, was shot dead the next day.[360]

Another sequel arose out of the evidence of Lieutenant Hammond. The officers who gave evidence at the trial had taken some care to conceal the fact that the raid had taken place as a result of a tip off. But when Lieutenant Hammond was asked what his duties were in the course of the action he told the court he was 'extra regimentally employed'. This was rightly taken to mean that he was involved in intelligence and the public correctly inferred that there had been an informant. A frantic search for the informant began. A local man, David Walsh, formerly a British soldier, was seized. He was stood over an open grave and told he would be killed if he did not confess but he would be spared if he admitted informing. Unsurprisingly he confessed. He was then shot dead.[361] No doubt he, too, would have wished for the protection of due process.

There were other dynamics driving events. At the end of the previous December, General Macready and his generals had attended Cabinet at Westminster. The advice of the Generals was that the brunt of the rebellion could be broken within four months and that elections could then take place for the Southern Ireland Parliament.[362] The months had passed and the elections set for May were only three weeks away and yet the rebellion had grown in strength.

General Macready's report to Cabinet for the last week of April shows a most remarkable four-page analysis of the Martial Law Area tracking the movements of numerous mobile columns of armed men.[363] The military position from the standpoint of General Macready was unpromising. It was in these circumstances that at the end of April 1921 General Macready wrote to Hamar Greenwood at Dublin Castle. Macready's letter threatened to issue a proclamation suspending the powers of the civil courts to grant writs of habeas corpus. 'Executions,' he argued, 'should take place within two or three days of the fight.'[364] And this is exactly what happened next.

CHAPTER ELEVEN

Patrick Casey, Ballybricken, County Limerick

The prisoner was captured on 1 May. He was tried and executed the next day. Casey's trial was later referred to by General Macready as a 'drumhead' trial, a term that has its origins in old military law where necessity required a trial in the field and execution, immediately, if need be. Even in 1921, the term was historic and had no legal status.

The engagement which resulted in the capture of Patrick Casey took place on 1 May 1921 close to Ahaphuca Bridge some miles from Kildorrery. It involved a party of soldiers from the Queen's Regiment and the Green Howards, about twenty-nine strong. They were supported by seven RIC men. Travelling in convoy they intercepted a column led by Liam Forde. The column was caught on unfavourable ground and fought a gradual retreat. Soldiers led by Lieutenant Armley of the Green Howards outflanked the rebel position and Casey and others found themselves cut off. In the course of the next few minutes two Volunteers, Patrick Starr and James Horan, were killed. Another, Timothy Hennessey, was badly wounded and captured. Casey was also captured just after 5 pm.[365]

Casey was taken to Cork. The following day Major General Strickland authorised trial by military court on two charges. First, being improperly in possession of a rifle and revolver. Second, being improperly in possession of fifty rounds of rifle ammunition. Casey was tried that day.[366] An officer, Captain Morrison, was appointed to act as prisoner's friend. An application for an adjournment made on behalf of the prisoner was opposed by the prosecutor, Captain F.E. Young. The application to adjourn was refused as 'the court did not consider this necessary'. Not guilty pleas were entered to both charges.

Two witnesses were called for the prosecution, Lieutenant Armley of the Green Howards and Corporal Jenkins of the 1st Queen's Regiment. Lieutenant Armley described leading a party of men on a flanking movement until they were within 30 yards of a group of men firing at the valley below and to their left.

> Then near the corner of a field I saw five men. One was firing at a house on my left where I had left an NCO and 3 men as fire had been coming from there. I took Corporal Jenkins with me. He was with me as I approached the civilians. We shot the civilian who was firing. We then climbed over the bank and went into the field. On the opposite side of the field there is a farm yard. There I saw another civilian who fired at us. We shot him. Both these men were firing with rifles at us. While we were lying on the bank looking around I saw a man put his hands up. He was near where the second man was shot. We told him to advance.

This man appears to have been Hennessey. According to corporal Jenkins, this man was wounded in the arm and thigh. Returning to the evidence of Lieutenant Armley:

> 'We raised ourselves slightly. As we did so I saw the accused now before the court behind a gorse bush about 30-40 yards away fire at us a shot with a rifle.'

According to Corporal Jenkins the shot had passed between himself and the officer. Corporal Jenkins continued: 'The officer then fired at him. He threw down his weapon and put his hands up.' The accused was searched. He had a haversack and a revolver attached to a belt inscribed with the word 'Volunteers'. There were four rounds left in the revolver and two empty chambers. The revolver had been recently fired. A little while later a rifle was found where the accused had been lying. The bolt was open and the clip empty. The rifle showed evidence that it had been fired recently. The accused had a quantity of ammunition on him which was shared out between the officer and his corporal and used to fire at others in the distance.

Casey told the court he was a single man. He lived with his elderly parents and sisters near Ballybricken. He had worked at Cleeve's creamery as a labourer. He told the Military Court that he had been involved in the election,[367] where he had played a part in keeping order. He had not been involved in the Volunteers since. His home had been raided a number of times and he had gone on the run to Dublin and returned to the area three weeks previously. He had been roped into the ambush against his will. He had been given the rifle and revolver. He had fired two shots. He did not fire more because he had not handled a rifle before. He denied firing at Lieutenant Armley and Corporal Jenkins. He had seen them coming but did not think to run away.

Both charges were found proved and Casey was sentenced to death by shooting. Sentence was confirmed by Major General Strickland the same afternoon. Casey was moved immediately from Victoria Barracks to Cork male detention barracks where he was executed by firing squad later that day.[368] The assistant provost marshall recorded that the execution took place at 18.31 and that Casey was attended by a priest to the last. An officer of the Royal Army Medical Corps recorded that death had been practically instantaneous. The paperwork evidencing these facts was, unlike earlier executions, filled out on typed proformas and one has the sense the army was gearing up for the process of execution.

There is no doubt that Casey was a willing and active Volunteer. The evidence he did not dispute tells a story: the haversack, a Volunteer belt buckle, a recently fired rifle and revolver. Also, perhaps more significantly, Casey was one of four Volunteers who had been cut off from the main party. Casey offered his surrender after two of the others had been killed and the third mortally wounded. His rifle had been emptied. Other evidence emerged later which made it plain that Casey was an experienced Volunteer who took a full part in the action which led to his capture.[369] This satisfies natural curiosity but it does not deal with the wider issues of legality and due process.

The proforma convening a military court is signed by General Strickland. The form records that 'it is not practicable that such offences should be tried by ordinary general court martial', although the reasons why are not stated. Nor does it state why it was impracticable to convene a FGCM under the ROIA, as laid down by Parliament.

General Macready later wrote that orders were given to try these cases by 'drumhead' courts,[370] meaning immediate trial and execution. If orders had been given to proceed by drumhead trials then this would have been recorded in General Routine Orders but there are no such orders.[371] The army being the bureaucracy it was, such an order would also be recorded in the trial papers: it is not.

Further, we have seen in earlier chapters that the Judge Advocate General insisted on personally reviewing all capital cases and was not afraid to dispute the matter with General Macready.[372] It is also clear that the Judge Advocate General had won the argument in January and General Macready had been instructed by the War Office to submit all capital cases for review by the Judge Advocate General. But in respect of this case there was no repetition of the dispute with the JAG and it is a strong inference that some communications took place which have not been recorded or perhaps not preserved.

It was later asserted in the *Record of the Rebellion* that orders for drumhead trials were given in March 1921,[373] many weeks before the trial of Casey. But this is just an assertion, as the previous chapter demonstrates no orders or arrangements were in place. It is also contradicted by the correspondence which shows a telegram from General Macready to the War Office written a few weeks after the execution of Casey seeking sanction to expedite trial and execution by drumhead court: 'Cases in point now occurring and procedure to be adopted must be settled.'[374] Finally, the *Circular Memoranda* governing trials by military court, issued in May 1921, contains no provision for drumhead trials. The earliest order for drumhead trials was issued after the Truce in August 1921.[375]

The circumstances of the execution of Casey were raised at Westminster by Major McKenzie Wood, a Liberal MP who had himself been wounded while serving on the Western Front with the Gordon Highlanders. Major Wood had extensive first-hand experience of the grim reality of courts martial in the field:[376] 'Are we to understand that the Judge Advocate General had no opportunity of looking into the case, and seeing that the due formalities of the law were complied with?' This produced no answer from the Attorney General. Another backbencher asked: 'Seeing that not merely the trial, but the execution, was within 26 hours of the occurrence was there any reasonable opportunity for those who were assigned to defend the accused to master and state the case?' Sir Denis Henry replied: 'I am sure that if any application were made, it would be duly considered by the court.'[377] With such words are the protections of due process swept away.

What was the wider significance of this trial? It is a logical conclusion that having fought off various legal challenges, the army was becoming bolder in the application of martial law and were dispensing with the protections laid down in their own regulations. The speed of this trial prevented the prisoner being represented or seeking the protection of a writ of habeas corpus and it is an irresistible inference that this was the object of what was done.

For a few weeks the army hovered on the brink of a major extension of drumhead trials. Quite why the army held off is a more difficult question. It may have been a combination of factors: adverse publicity at home and abroad; dissension at Westminster; the prospect of peace talks which were gaining ground; and a few weeks later the legal challenge raised in Clifford and Sullivan.

CHAPTER TWELVE

Daniel O'Brien, Liscarroll, County Cork

The capture of Daniel O'Brien took place on 10 May 1921 at O'Donnell's farmhouse, Aughrim, near Liscarroll County Cork. The *Sixth Division Record of the Rebellion* recounts the raid in this way: 'The East Lancashire regiment, acting on information, set out to arrest five rebels near Liscarroll. They failed to surround the house, and most of the rebels escaped. Two, however, were captured with arms.'[378]

It appears that the information was recent, specific and accurate. The army knew exactly where they were billeted and how many men were in their party. Daniel O'Brien was captured. His brother escaped and a third man, John O'Regan, was very seriously wounded and taken straight to hospital. He was unfit to be tried and was saved by the Truce. O'Brien was taken in handcuffs to a nearby lorry and then to Buttevant Barracks. The next day he was taken to Cork military detention barracks where preparations for trial were made. The charge sheet is signed by Major General Strickland and records that the accused is 'To be Tried by Military Court'.[379]

The *Sixth Division Record of the Rebellion* also shows that this was 'a drumhead trial'. This means that the process was expedited and such protections as were afforded to other prisoners were dispensed with. It was the second drumhead trial in the Martial Law Area, the first being that of Patrick Casey two weeks previously, and the pattern of events suggests the entire process was being streamlined and speeded up.

The charge sheet recorded two charges: that O'Brien was improperly in possession of a revolver, and that he was improperly in possession of twelve rounds of revolver ammunition. The trial took place at Victoria Barracks on 14 May.

The record shows that O'Brien declined to be represented by counsel or an officer acting as a prisoner's friend. He did not make any request for an adjournment and made no attempt to contest the case. When asked for his plea, he replied: 'I was caught as a soldier and you can try me.'[380] Not guilty pleas were entered. He was prosecuted by Captain Staveley-Dale, RFA. The Judge Advocate was Lieutenant Colonel Meyler. The President of the court was Lieutenant Colonel Vandeleur.

The trial record shows that a party of men from the 2nd Battalion East Lancashire Regiment had been detailed to raid the O'Donnell farmhouse near Aughrim. Arriving on foot, they surrounded the house. An officer approached the front door. Lance Corporal Hudson described what happened:

> I saw an officer go up to the door and knock. He got no reply at first and then the door was opened and banged in his face. Immediately after I heard a revolver shot fired at the back of the house and I saw 2 civilians run out of the back of the house and run crouching down the back away from me. Accused was one of them and he was 30 yards away when first I saw him. The corporal called three times for them to halt, but they did not do so, so I fired at them with the Lewis gun and both dropped.

Before the raid Sergeant Sandham had taken some men to a wood overlooking the rear of the O'Donnell farm. Sergeant Sandham told the court what he saw:

> I saw a man run through a gate at the corner of the hedge of the next field. I then saw the accused with another man about 30 yards from me, on the other side of the hedge in the next field. As I looked over the hedge several shots came over my head from the direction of where I had seen the first man go. I had noticed the first man had something like a sporting rifle in his hand. The shots appeared to be rifle and revolver shots.

Shots were fired by the army and then the men 'dropped down'. The soldiers advanced and found O'Regan seriously wounded. O'Brien lay close by. Sergeant Sandham continued:

> I searched the accused. In the right-hand trouser pocket of accused I found the ammunition (twelve rounds of .45 revolver ammunition) …

> About a yard from the accused I found the Webley revolver … covered with a stone and a little dirt but not entirely covered. It had a dark green lanyard on it. I examined the revolver and found it loaded in all six chambers.

When the Webley revolver was found, O'Brien simply said: 'You did not find that on me.' A nickel-plated revolver was found at the feet of O'Regan. It contained five unfired rounds and one fired. There was no evidence as to whether the gun had been fired recently.

According to Sergeant Sandham, O'Regan asked for first aid. This he provided. 'I thank you,' said the wounded man. An officer arrived and continued to provide first aid and a soldier brought blankets from the farmhouse.

None of the witnesses were cross-examined. The record shows that O'Brien called no witnesses. Here is an extract from his brief statement: 'I expect the treatment of a captured soldier. I would not shoot a soldier if I captured him myself, & you can do as you like with me.'

The officers conducting the trial then found the charges proved. The record shows that O'Brien declined to say anything in mitigation. He was sentenced to death by shooting. The following day Major General Strickland confirmed the sentence and O'Brien was informed that sentence would be carried out the next morning.

Sentence was carried out at 8 am on 16 May. The record shows that O'Brien was attended by a priest and that death was instantaneous. Little is known about the prisoner. The summer before, O'Brien had been convicted by district court martial for possession of seven automatic bullets. General Strickland had declined to confirm the conviction because of shortcomings in the evidence and O'Brien was released.[381] Cabinet records show that in the spring of 1921 the family home near Liscarroll was destroyed in an official reprisal.[382] At the time of his death he was a single man, a farmer's son aged thirty. A photo of him survives and shows a slim, rather intense young man with a heavy moustache.

The capture of O'Brien is also fully documented in records held by the Bureau of Military History. The man who escaped was Patrick O'Brien, brother of Daniel. He had met the others at the O'Donnell farmhouse on the night before the raid. The house was judged safe enough for a night-time meeting but not safe to stay the night because the area was well served by roads. But it was some time after midnight when they finished talking and, being tired, they stayed the night, against their better judgment.

They were woken the next day by the farmer with the news that three lorries of soldiers had just passed. They dressed quickly and were on the point of leaving when there was a knock on the door. The knock was answered by John O'Donnell, the farmer, who, finding an army officer outside, promptly slammed and bolted the door. The three men ran out the back door. What follows is taken from the BMH statement of Patrick O'Brien:

> We made for a gateway leading to a small enclosed haggard adjoining the yard, when we were immediately confronted by about ten soldiers who were lined up outside the ditch. I fired one shot with a Colt automatic and turned to make for another gateway leading to the yard. We succeeded in getting through, and after proceeding for forty yards along by a fence O'Regan was leading at this time having been first to turn on my firing at the military. My brother was about five yards behind O'Regan and I was about ten yards in rear of my brother. I saw O'Regan stumbling, but the ground was very rough at that particular place. It never struck me that he may be wounded, although shots were coming from about three different points at the time. The Brother, Dan, stopped to assist O'Regan and they both shouted at me to keep going as they were alright.[383]

There is something of an irony here. It is highly likely that Daniel O'Brien was executed because the troops had been fired on, although he himself was not charged with firing on the troops, nor did he do so. A close review of the facts reveals that the shots were fired by Patrick O'Brien, who escaped, and O'Regan, who was too badly wounded to be tried before the Truce. The gun attributed to Daniel O'Brien was not fired and he may well have escaped had he not stopped to help O'Regan.

CHAPTER THIRTEEN

Clifford and Sullivan

PATRICK CLIFFORD, BALLYARTHUR, MITCHELSTOWN AND MICHAEL SULLIVAN OF JAMES STREET, MITCHELSTOWN.

It is necessary to go back in time by three weeks to pick up the threads of this case. These men were captured on 23 April in possession of handguns. The two men were taken back to Fermoy Barracks where a note was found on Clifford directing him to parade his section at 9 pm at Ballygiblin. At this point both men were all but forgotten as the army organised a sweep to trap others making for the rendezvous.[384]

Two days later a direction was made by General Strickland that it was 'not practicable'[385] to convene a general court martial and therefore the men would be tried by military court. Both men were charged with being improperly in possession of a handgun and being improperly in possession of ammunition. They were tried on 3 May, Sullivan first and then Clifford, the evidence in both cases being much the same. Captain F.E. Young prosecuted; Lieutenant Colonel Vandeleur presided.

Both men were represented by Joseph McCarthy,[386] and both entered guilty pleas to the charges. The Military Court, acting in accordance with the usual procedure in capital cases, entered not guilty pleas.[387] The record shows that defence counsel protested against the refusal of the court to accept the guilty pleas. It was an odd start to a case which became a minor landmark in constitutional history.

Lieutenant Coleman of the Machine Gun Company gave evidence that he had been leading a patrol comprising two armoured cars and a Crossley tender in the area of Ballyporeen, near Mitchelstown. The time was between 8.30 and 9 pm. They had challenged some men, who ran off into the fields. Then they came upon Clifford and Sullivan, who were on bicycles. They were ordered to stop and dismount, and were found to be armed.

Evidence was given by Private Finch that Sullivan had a pistol in a holster. Sullivan had told the officer when asked that he was on his way to find lodgings. Sullivan was asked how long he had the pistol and he replied: 'Since 1916.' A revolver was found on Clifford. It had five full chambers and one empty. In answers to questions, Clifford told the officer he had found the revolver at the roadside. Clifford was searched again at the police station and a note was found on him directing him to 'parade your section tonight at Ballygiblin Chapel without fail'.

Neither Clifford nor Sullivan gave evidence. They both relied on a Church of Ireland vicar, the Reverend O'Connor DSO, who gave evidence that the area had been quiet and that no policemen or soldiers had been killed in the area. Both he and the local parish priest had denounced the ambushes. They also called a Constable Ashe of the RIC and a local building merchant, Patrick O'Neill, to give character evidence. At the conclusion of the evidence, objection was made to the jurisdiction of the court on the ground that no proclamation had been produced. This objection was overruled by the court.

Both men were convicted on each count. It appears that the sentence was pronounced the next day and both men were ordered 'to suffer death by being shot'. Clifford arranged for a sergeant of the Cameron Highlanders to send a telegram to his solicitor, Mr James Skinner of Mitchelstown,[388] who immediately made contact with Michael Comyn KC: 'Do anything but do something,'[389] was the request. It was difficult to do anything, having regard to the case of John Allen which gave legal sanction to the military courts. As Comyn began to formulate new arguments, the army was moving to confirm the sentences.

On 8 May Major General Strickland forwarded the case papers for confirmation. His note of recommendation indicated that Sullivan had been on the run since his hunger strike and escape from Wormwood Scrubs the year before. Intelligence reports indicated that he was an officer in the Volunteers and that when the men had been captured they had both been en route to a meeting to organise an ambush. General Strickland recommended confirmation of the sentences of death by shooting. It is a reasonable inference that this intelligence, which was only partially correct,[390] resulted in the decision to try these men by military court. The self same intelligence was then used, following conviction, to recommend execution.

This analysis tends to suggest that the process by which capital sentences were recommended for confirmation might be based on matters not proved before the Military Court and about which the accused had no opportunity to comment or contradict. This was certainly in keeping with the procedure in the courts martial of servicemen at that time[391] and also in trials before criminal courts. It is perhaps an example of procedures which were unremarkable by the standards of the day but which would not withstand scrutiny in the modern age.

On 10 May an application was lodged at the High Court for a writ of prohibition[392] against General Macready and General Strickland preventing them from taking any further steps to confirm sentence. The argument centred on the writ of prohibition as a remedy against an illegal court. Mr Justice Powell refused their application. He took the view that he was bound to follow the decision in John Allen, the Clonmult case and that of Ronayne and Mulcahy.

Michael Comyn KC then went to the Court of Appeal which heard the case on 12 May. The argument before the Court of Appeal turned on whether the case involved was civil – in which case the court had jurisdiction – or 'a criminal cause or matter', in which case the court had no jurisdiction.[393] The Master of the Rolls, recognising the gravity of the case, observed that if the court had jurisdiction, 'it would gladly exercise it'. However, the court ruled that the issue raised was a criminal cause or matter and therefore the court had no jurisdiction. Comyn seized his opportunity and appealed to the Lords against the refusal of the Court of Appeal to consider the case.

As to the decision to go to the Lords, this was an expensive course of action. In Ireland barristers negotiated their own fees and Michael Comyn KC had a natural diffidence on such issues. Occasionally in these capital cases he simply waived his fee,[394] but in this case there were other heavy expenses. It was thought sensible to secure the services of Sir John Simon, who had first articulated the legal argument against the military courts. There is no doubt that Sir John was one of the heavyweight barristers of his day and his interest in Ireland had already been stirred but perhaps not to the extent of taking cases without fee. Sir John's fees were said to be £300 'on the brief' and 'refreshers' of £300 a day. It was a small fortune, money beyond the dreams of most men. The money was collected by public subscription in the Mitchelstown area[395] and carried by night across country to be deposited in the solicitor's safe.[396]

While these preparations were in hand, the executions were suspended until the Lords ruled. When the case first came before the Lords on 16 June it was thought that the Lords would rule immediately on the preliminary matter: was the case a criminal cause or matter and was it, therefore, susceptible to appeal? Henry Hanna argued for some hours to persuade the Lords to find for the Crown on the preliminary point but Sir John Simon successfully urged the House to give more time for research into the constitutional issues.[397] An adjournment was granted and the stay on executions remained in force until the judgment of the Lords, and this is a subject to which we shall return.[398]

CHAPTER FOURTEEN

Thomas Keane, Limerick

The stay on executions came too late for one prisoner, Thomas Keane, who was tried in mid-May before the case of Clifford and Sullivan had gone to the Lords. Keane faced two charges: first, that 'at Singland, in the county of Limerick in Ireland, on the 1st day of May 1921, did levy war against His Majesty the King by joining with others in attacking members of His Majesty's Royal Irish Constabulary'; and second, 'being improperly in possession of arms, viz one revolver'.

The trial began on 14 May at New Barracks, Limerick. Keane was prosecuted by Captain Colis of the North Staffordshire Regiment[399] and represented by Robert J. Kinehan, who was led by Patrick Lynch KC, who had famously lost the East Clare by-election of 1917 to Éamon de Valera. During the election Lynch was described by a Sinn Féin opponent as a strong candidate: 'He has defended one half of the murderers in Clare and is related to the other half.'[400] Others described him as 'a place hunting ex-Crown prosecutor'.[401] Neither description was remotely fair; Lynch stayed at the Bar, where he was remembered as a man of probity.[402]

Evidence was given by Sergeant James Horan of the RIC that he had been in charge of a convoy consisting of 'an armoured car and two Crossley tenders' which had left William Street Barracks in Limerick at 3.15 pm. The convoy travelled along the Tipperary Road. As they approached Singland Bridge they saw a number of men on the bridge and also under the bridge. The bridge was crowded with people but as they approached they saw two men in particular running between the railway line and some cottages. The officers ran after the men and spread out. There was then firing from behind the cottages.

The men were pursued and fired on the policemen. The sergeant appears not to have seen who fired but, coming up on the scene, Keane and the other man Clancy threw their guns under a bush. Both were captured. The guns were recovered. One was a Colt, fully loaded. The other was a Webley which contained 'five rounds and a spent cartridge'. Sergeant Horan gave evidence that Keane had told him 'he was just after getting the gun from a man on the bridge'.

What exactly transpired at the point of arrest is not clear, but Sergeant Horan's evidence was that 'the other man who surrendered was killed'. The circumstances in which the other man, Clancy, was killed were not explored in evidence.[403] A suggestion in cross-examination that the accused was 'roughly handled' was denied by the sergeant.

Sergeant William Hickie gave evidence that 'seven or eight shots' had been fired at police. Hickie identified Keane 'kneeling or crouching' and firing at the police officers. He told the Military Court that Keane was then no more than 20 yards away. He fired once. Sergeant Hickie then fired at the accused, who ran a short distance and threw his weapon into a bush. Constable Michael Nolan told the court that Keane had fired at him and that he had fired two shots in reply. The two men threw revolvers into a bush and put their hands up. There was a suggestion, denied by the officers, that the accused had been beaten with rifle butts.

Keane gave evidence. He told the court that he had been on his usual Sunday walk when he met a man he knew as Clancy on the bridge. There was a third man there. The third man put the revolver in his hand saying: 'Take this bloody thing out of my hand. I am finished with the IRA.' He took the gun, not knowing if it was loaded or not, and a few seconds later he saw the police lorries close by. He and Clancy ran. Unknown to him, Clancy had a revolver also. He, Keane, was caught and could not remember what he did with the revolver. He denied firing at the constables but accepted that they had fired at him.

Keane's counsel referred the Military Court to the standard legal textbook and submitted that evidence that the police had been fired on did of itself not prove levying war against the King as opposed to some other criminal activity.[404] His defence to the second charge was that he had been an unwilling recipient of the gun – and had not time to hand it over to the police.

In summing up, the Judge Advocate put three questions to the court:

1. Were they satisfied that the evidence of the prosecution is what actually took place?
2. If so, does that amount to levying war?
3. The accused admits having the revolver. Does the court believe his explanation of how he got it?

These were the directions given by the Judge Advocate to the court. The first two correctly set out the law but the third wrongly placed the burden of proof on the prisoner. Keane was convicted on both charges and sentenced to death by shooting.

Petition

A petition for mercy was sent to General Macready which recited the bare facts. There had been no previous executions in the Limerick area and it was argued that mercy in this case might bring dividends. The petition was signed by a formidable body including the Bishop of Limerick and Father MacNamara, a local priest who had exercised influence in favour of peace. It was also signed by three peers who were prominent in the area and James Goodbody, a successful corn merchant and notable loyalist. His name was noted by the commanding officer at Limerick, Brigadier General Cameron, as 'a strong character and a man I respect'. A second petition was sent to General Macready, under cover of a note by the military commander which observes that the signatories were men of 'known loyalty' and considerable local influence.

The papers were sent to Cassel, the Judge Advocate General, in London for review and consideration of the petition. Cassel observed that the charges were properly laid and there was evidence to justify the convictions. The question of clemency was a matter for the commander in chief. The argument about the propriety of a conviction for levying war was not addressed.[405]

A few days later, the petition for mercy was rejected. There was, oddly, no High Court challenge launched, possibly because it was thought that the petitions would succeed.

There had been no executions in the city for nearly forty years. The last was the hanging of 'Francey' Hynes for the murder of a herdsman[406] and the impending execution of Keane generated wide controversy. Thomas Keane was executed by firing squad at 8 am on 4 June at the military detention barracks at Limerick. A crowd of many hundreds gathered outside the barracks, including his mother and his pregnant wife. He was the last man to be executed as a consequence of conviction by a Military Court. There is no doubt that Keane was an active Volunteer. However, a review of local sources suggests that neither Keane nor Clancy fired on the RIC nor were their guns loaded.[407]

The War of Independence and the Civil War generated many last letters home. One reads 'Dearest mother', another 'My life is sworn away.' They are all moving and painful to read. Many of the letters are preserved and sustain the memory of what took place. British soldiers captured during the spring of 1921 were also killed by way of reprisals for the executions carried out under martial law.[408] Ernie O'Malley wrote a harrowing account of one such incident near Fethard in which three British officers had strayed from barracks. They were captured some days after Keane was executed and shot dead the following day.[409] One of the men, Lieutenant Toogood, wrote a last letter, which remains in the archive: 'My dear Colonel, I am to be shot in half an hour ...' When the regiment found the bodies a photo was taken.[410] It shows three young men in casual clothes lying in a field by a hedge. But for the provenance of the photo it is not possible to say if the men were British or Irish.

CHAPTER FIFTEEN

John Joseph Egan, Ennis

There were a number of military court trials following the execution of Thomas Keane, but the critical case would prove to be that of Egan. The trial of Egan took place on 11 June 1921 at New Barracks, Limerick. Captain Tapling prosecuted the trial and Egan, like most of the Military Court prisoners from Clare, was represented by Patrick Lynch KC.[411]

There was a single charge: 'On the 26th May 1921, near Quin, County Clare, in Ireland, was improperly in possession of ammunition, namely ninety-seven rounds of revolver ammunition and five rounds of service ammunition.'

Major Gillette DSO of the Royal Scots Regiment gave evidence that he had been leading a motorised patrol from Galbally towards Ennis. At a point about a mile outside Quin, the convoy came around a corner and he saw the accused on a bike coming towards him: 'When the accused saw them, he dismounted and threw a brown paper parcel over the wall'. The patrol stopped. The Major looked over the wall and found a parcel tied with string. It was about 8 feet from where the accused was standing. The accused denied having a parcel or throwing it over the wall. The parcel was examined and found to contain two boxes with ninety-seven rounds of .45 ammunition and a clip of .303 service ammunition.

In cross-examination Major Gillette told the court: 'We were going at about 18 miles per hour.' The accused was cycling towards them around the corner 'at a moderate pace'.

Constable Stanley Laylor was driving the Crossley. He put his speed at over thirty miles an hour and said they had seen the accused come around 'a bend in the road'. He told the court that when the accused had seen the convoy coming towards him, he ran to the side of the road and threw the parcel over the wall. He told the court that he knew the accused, who turned 'very white' when he was stopped.

Constable Laylor told the court that on the way back to barracks the accused had admitted that he had thrown the parcel over the wall. There was a short legal argument on the admissibility of this confession.

Laylor admitted that he had pushed the accused and said: 'You are caught now, old man.' He denied striking the accused. The confession was 'volunteered', the officer said, not made as a result of questioning. The confession was ruled admissible by the court.

Sergeant Major Taylor gave evidence corroborating the account given by Major Gillette and told the court that minutes after the arrest and after the convoy had only moved '100 or 150 yards' a shot had been fired in their direction.

Egan told the court that he was an engineer with the county council. He had been travelling on county council business from Ennis to Sixmilebridge. Egan's counsel called a local shopkeeper, his mother May, his sister Mary and two other local men, Thomas Mangan and Patrick Hogan, to show that he had been seen at various stages in the journey and had not been carrying a parcel. He also called his work supervisor, Michael O'Brien, to confirm that he, Egan, was undertaking his journey to Sixmilebridge to get parts for an engine.

Other evidence was called from two local men, Martin Hannon and Martin Cullinan, which showed that two men had been seen close to where the parcel had been found.[412] Written evidence of character was submitted by the clerk of the county council and Charles Keane, then the principal land agent in Clare, who had known the accused for many years.

Egan was convicted and was sentenced to death by shooting. He lived with his parents in Ennis where his father was the caretaker of the old infirmary. The family house was thoroughly searched after the arrest and the mother and father were 'frantic'.[413] It is likely that they paid for his representation and no doubt pressed his lawyers to do all they could. Egan's case became a test of the law. It may be that the execution of Keane one week earlier had spurred on Patrick Lynch or it may be that the facts of Egan's case readily lent themselves to a test case: the prisoner was of impeccable character, the evidence against him was not strong and the charge on which he was sentenced to death carried only imprisonment under civil law. Although there remained great uncertainty that the prisoner might be executed before the case was heard.

Soon after conviction, notices were posted in Ennis town centre inviting people to go to the town hall and sign a petition. It is clear that this petition was well organised and attracted support from a wide cross-section of society,[414] including a surprising number of ex-servicemen. The petition was sent to the Lord Lieutenant and Governor General, Viscount FitzAlan, the head of civil administration in Ireland.

The JAG advised General Macready that the sentence could be carried out and the army could properly ignore the petitions sent to the Lord Lieutenant.[415] While this standoff between the army and the civil government loomed, Hugh Kennedy and Patrick Lynch appeared in the Chancery Division before the Master of the Rolls in Dublin and applied for a conditional writ of habeas corpus.

The Master of the Rolls, Sir Charles O'Connor, had refused Clifford and Sullivan's appeal to the Court of Appeal on a jurisdictional point but it had become clear during legal argument that he had an open mind on the central issue: the legality of the Military Court. And it seems, therefore, that the case was brought before the Master of the Rolls for that reason.

Patrick Lynch had made his reputation in criminal cases, and although it was his efforts that brought the case to the High Court, it was probably Hugh Kennedy's intellect that lay behind the legal challenge. Kennedy was then a little-known civil practitioner.[416] A rotund man in his early forties, a photo shows an unlined face and a pince nez. Within three years he would become the first Chief Justice of the new state. Kennedy informed the Master of the Rolls he intended to take the case to the Lords, if need be, and after a succinct argument a conditional writ was issued, pending full argument.

By chance and by the efforts of counsel, the hearing in Clifford and Sullivan in the Lords was delayed and the executions remained suspended pending a decision in that case. This provided a brief respite for others. It was in these circumstances that Egan's case went for hearing in the High Court at the beginning of July 1921. Hugh Kennedy suggested to the court that the case be adjourned for two weeks pending the judgment of the House of Lords in Clifford and Sullivan. The Master of the Rolls agreed but asked for an undertaking from the army that the sentence would not be carried out until the court ruled. 'It is a matter of life or death,' observed the Master of the Rolls. Counsel for the Generals informed the court that his clients were 'unable to give any undertaking'.[417]

General Macready's difficulties were never more acute. The disputed events were taking place in the Martial Law Area but Dublin, seat of the High Court, was not under martial law. General Macready needed to win the case to maintain the credibility of martial law, but on the other hand he could not publicly acknowledge the supremacy of the civil court without endangering the whole edifice of martial law.

The whole strategy underpinning the Military Court had depended on shutting out the Civil Courts, but General Macready had not quite dared to go that far. He perhaps recognised that if all went badly he could not rely on Lloyd George. He might yet be relieved of his command, recalled under a cloud like General Dyer, or abandoned like Governor Eyre. And so Macready hesitated.

In the absence of any undertaking from General Macready the case went ahead. The primary argument can be distilled to a few lines: the Crown had released the prerogative power to wage war in Ireland to Parliament, by passing the ROIA to deal with the rebellion. And therefore only Parliament could embark on new measures. It followed that the military courts were unlawful.

Counsel for General Macready argued that the court should simply follow the decision of the court in the cases of John Allen[418] and Garde and Others.[419] He further argued that when the ROIA was passed the country had not been in a state of war and therefore the main argument for the prisoner had no merit.

At the end of the second day the Master of the Rolls reserved judgment. The question then arose as to what would become of the prisoner in the meantime. Counsel for General Macready told the court he had 'no instructions one way of the other'. The Master of the Rolls then made an order staying execution until judgment.[420]

CHAPTER SIXTEEN

Egan v Macready And All That

Judgment in Egan v Macready was reserved while the Master of the Rolls considered the law. While he did so, momentous events were taking place: the Truce came about on 11 July.[421] There were no more trials by military courts,[422] although courts martial under the Restoration of Order in Ireland Act continued throughout the summer. Those interned or otherwise imprisoned remained in custody.

At this point a writ of habeas corpus was sought for another prisoner, Patrick Higgins, one of the men captured at Clonmult. Higgins was fortunate to have the same legal team that acted for Egan, with the addition of the young John Costello, later Taoiseach; a formidable legal team opposed by Henry Hanna KC, who pressed the Master of the Rolls to defer judgment until the decision of the Lords in Clifford and Sullivan. 'I must hear the case,' replied the Master of the Rolls.[423] His view reflected centuries of law that a writ of habeas corpus was a swift measure to test the legality of detention, which should not be deferred. A conditional writ was granted and the case of Higgins became linked to that of Egan, and both men then came back before the Court on Tuesday 26 July when the Master of the Rolls ruled in favour of the prisoners.

The central argument advanced by the Crown rested on the decision of the High Court in John Allen which itself hung on the decision in Marais:[424] 'Where war actually prevails, the ordinary courts have no jurisdiction.' This decision was distinguished by the Master of the Rolls on the ground that a state of war was in existence at the time of the passage of the Restoration of Order in Ireland Act, and that the prerogative powers under which the military acted had been invested in that statute. A fresh initiative had to come through Parliament. Therefore, a person charged with a capital crime could only be tried by a court martial convened under the ROIA.[425]

The judgment of the Master of the Rolls concluded with an echo of Lord Cockburn's observations in the Jamaica case: 'There are considerations more important even than shortening the temporary duration of an insurrection. Among them are the eternal and immutable principles of justice, principles which can never be violated without lasting detriment to the true interest and well being of a civilised community.'[426]

Stripping away the ornate language, this was simply a judicial reminder to the government to stay within the law. For these reasons, ruled the Master of the Rolls, the writs of habeas corpus would issue and the Crown must produce the prisoners at court on Friday 29th. General Macready was in London when the news came through. He telegraphed Dublin GHQ with orders to disregard the writs.[427]

The confrontation between the army and the courts threatened a constitutional crisis of some gravity. The position was further complicated when the House of Lords delivered their speeches in Clifford and Sullivan on 28 July;[428] the prisoners lost the case.[429] The Lords decided, first, that the case was 'not a criminal cause or matter' and therefore the Court of Appeal had been wrong to refuse to hear the prisoners' appeal. But on the merits of the case an order of prohibition did not lie against the military.[430]

The case of Egan v Macready came back before the Master of the Rolls the following day. Henry Hanna for the Crown had taken on board the decision in Clifford and Sullivan. Hanna pressed for more time: 'An appeal lies,' Hanna argued, 'and notice of an appeal having been served, the Crown did not propose to produce the prisoners or release them pending the appeal.' [431]

> The Master of the Rolls: 'I will not listen to any such answer to the writ. The writ must be answered in the ordinary way. Has the writ been obeyed?'
> Lynch KC (for the prisoners): 'No, my Lord.'
> The Master of the Rolls: 'Then I will order a writ of attachment to issue against the three parties for whom Sergeant Hanna appears. It is a quite deliberate contempt of court.'[432]

Writs were then issued for the arrest of General Macready, General Strickland and Brigadier General Cameron. The news travelled swiftly around the globe: 'Writs out to seize the Generals'[433] was the headline in the *New York Times*. In London the news created a sensation, although in Dublin excitement was tempered by amusement at the expense of Sir John Harley Scott, the High Sheriff, charged with the duty of arresting the generals. The office of High Sheriff was in large part ceremonial, a relic of a distant era. Sir John maintained an uncomfortable silence.

16.1 The Emerging Judiciary of the Supreme Court and the High Court.

Standing (left to right): Thomas Lopdell O'Shauhnessy, William Wylie (who prosecuted most of the leaders of the 1916 Rebellion), William Johnston and James Murnaghan.

Sitting (left to right): Gerald Fitzgibbon, Timothy Sullivan, Chief Justice Kennedy, Charles O'Connor (who gave the judgment in Egan v Macready) and James Creed Meredith. Courtesy of the *Irish Times*.

General Macready's weekly report to Cabinet tersely recorded events and finished with these words: 'The situation will have to be cleared up as it affects the power of the British army all over the world.'[434] This was only a slight exaggeration. At that time martial law prevailed not just in south-west Ireland but Egypt, Mesopotamia, Constantinople and occupied Germany.[435]

The next day the government at Westminster gave way and ordered the release of Egan and Higgins. One final hearing took place in Egan v Macready when the Master of the Rolls was informed of the release of the two men. He then stayed the writs for the arrest of General Macready, Strickland and Cameron.[436] The crisis was averted.

No doubt the High Sheriff of Dublin, relieved of his obligation to arrest the generals, breathed more easily. Clifford and Sullivan and others awaiting execution by order of the Military Court remained in custody. Their position remained fraught with uncertainty.

General Macready's next weekly report to Cabinet recounted, with barely concealed fury, the release of Higgins and Egan and also a number of imprisoned members of Dáil Éireann, freed so that they might take part in the Treaty debates: 'It might have been useful had I also been informed.'[437] Back at Westminster the Commons were informed that 'the action in releasing Higgins and Egan was based solely on the existing situation, and the importance of avoiding conflict between the civil and military authorities'.[438] General Macready described his position as 'impossible and degrading' and threatened to resign,[439] but afterwards put on a brave face and issued a Special Order of the Day to all commands: 'Where martial law applies writs of habeas corpus do not run.'[440]

Something more needs to be said about the two critical legal decisions that we have examined. Clifford and Sullivan[441] became a very famous case and it remains a landmark in constitutional law but it has also generated a number of myths. It has been said that the argument about prohibition was a novel legal point but, as Comyn must have known, it was at best a speculative argument which was floated but not pursued in the case of John Allen. As a seasoned campaigner his strategy was to filibuster: even in mid-May there were signs of peace talks on the horizon[442] and a delay might buy time that would save the lives of the prisoners.

It was also later said that Clifford and Sullivan were two of forty-two men then under sentence of death by the Military Court for possession of arms.[443] That also is incorrect. An analysis of the Register suggests that when Clifford and Sullivan were tried there were no other men awaiting execution following trial by the Military Court,[444] although there were certainly a number of men awaiting trial. Another error that has crept in was that the prisoners won the case and it resulted in all executions in the Martial Law Area being stayed.[445] That is also incorrect. Clifford and Sullivan lost at the High Court, in the Court of Appeal and the Lords. The practical significance was that when the appeal went to the Lords the army stopped executions until the case was resolved.[446] Whether this was the sole reason that executions stopped is open to doubt, but in essence it was the delay in concluding the case that saved lives: the Truce then intervened and the rest is history.

As to Egan v Macready, the decision was disputed by General Macready, who implied that the Master of the Rolls had 'acquired merit' in the eyes of the new administration. That is altogether too cynical an assessment, although the Master of the Rolls had a vain streak. He would not be the first or last judge to reach out for a niche in history, but if non-legal considerations affected his thinking, it may simply be that he realised he had an opportunity to bring the executions to an end.

Constitutional lawyers still argue over the decision, notably on the ground that the power to implement martial law flowed from the common law principle of necessity rather than the exercise of the prerogative. On this issue, history provides another perspective on the case. A review of events in the autumn of 1920 demonstrates that martial law was sought by the military in order to put in place official reprisals and to achieve unity of command. Martial law was never sought by the army on the grounds that ROIA trials were ineffective, under strain or that necessity required them to be replaced.

If the government at Westminster considered that increased sentences were required, Parliament could have acted swiftly. It is an inference that the government of Lloyd George did not legislate because it did not wish to be associated with this policy. If that is so, the common law justification of necessity simply cannot be sustained.

16.2 Chief Justice Kennedy. By permission of the *Irish Times*.

Egan v Macready was never appealed because the Truce held and the government at Westminster was anxious to avoid any step that might jeopardise the position. There is, however, another wrinkle to the story of the military courts which should be told.

There is evidence that had the Truce not come into being, martial law would have been brought into effect throughout the twenty-six counties. Preparations for an extension of the powers of the army had begun some weeks earlier. In late May 1921, Lloyd George reconvened the Irish Situation Committee under the chairmanship of Neville Chamberlain. The Committee met within days and recommended that if the Southern Parliament failed to function, martial law would be extended to the twenty-six counties.[447] The decisive factors were the advantages of unity of command, censorship of the press and a desire to discontinue official reprisals but find an effective substitute. General Macready argued that martial law could be imposed flexibly, deploying a light touch where appropriate. In terms of reinforcements this meant another 16–18 battalions and two or three cavalry regiments. Plans were made to use the navy to blockade ports and act in support of sweeps by the army. The Cabinet considered and approved the recommendations.[448]

The review of the measures that worked and those that did not gave rise to other changes of strategy. Official reprisals were abandoned. In the course of the previous six months the army had destroyed 191 homes and 20 other properties in the Martial Law Area as part of official reprisals.[449] The policy had proved counterproductive because the rebels responded in kind and began to burn the homes of loyalists, and so many of the finest Georgian residences were burned to the ground in the spring and early summer of 1921. As Hamar Greenwood put it: 'The loyalists own everything that is worth burning, while the Sinn Féiners who are the sons of farmers, shopkeepers, publicans, own nothing.'[450] And so official reprisals were abandoned and a more potent response was sought and identified.

Another key meeting of the Irish Situation Committee took place on 15 June when Macready's draft proclamation for martial law was considered.[451] Macready's personal view was that force would fail and the record shows his reluctance to engage in coercion but if it had to be tried then it must be 'all out or get out'. He questioned whether the Cabinet would support the measure: 'There might be as many as one hundred men shot in a week?'[452] This figure was a reference to executions, not casualties.[453]

Anyone found with guns or bombs would be tried by military court and 'executed on the spot'. Other proposals included: identity cards, requisition of goods without payment, the closure of fairs, markets, race meetings, ports and a complete prohibition on any person bringing legal action against the Crown without the permission of the Military Governor. These proposals were accepted subject to refinement by the Irish Situation Committee.[454] It was agreed that unless the new MPs swore allegiance to the Crown, martial law would be declared in the twenty-six counties. The date for declaration of martial law was fixed for 14 July.

While this was taking place, General Macready's staff continued to refine a series of draft proclamations which extended the scope of martial law to the twenty-six counties. These new proclamations repeated those already in force in the Martial Law Area and added new provisions: death was prescribed as a punishment for membership of Dáil Éireann, the Irish Republican Army and the Volunteers.

Under the new proclamations the jurisdiction of the law courts to grant writs of habeas corpus, mandamus and prohibition were suspended. The jurisdiction of all courts to make orders in respect of any claim for damages against the army was to be forbidden without the express sanction of the Military Governor General.[455]

Proclamation No. 8 extended the list of persons who would suffer death following trial by military court. The detail is worth relating:

> 'Any person or persons
> 1. Who may see or come into contact with any party of rebels;
> 2. Whose house may be visited by rebels; or
> 3. Whose relatives may join the rebels; or
> 4. Who may know of ambushes and 'possible' attacks on His Majesty's Forces, and who neglects to give full information immediately to the military or police authorities; and
>
> Any person or persons who, in any way, may consort with rebels or assist the rebels by giving them information or by providing them with money, food, horses, vehicles, clothing, arms, forage, goods or stores render themselves liable to suffer death.'[456]

As the proclamation put it: 'Neutrality is quite inconsistent with loyalty.'[457]

During the summer the Truce held, sometimes by a fine margin. As steps towards peace gathered momentum, the protagonists on both sides made plans for a renewal of hostilities.

In early August 1921 General Macready issued orders for convening military courts.[458] These were to apply to persons captured in action with arms, bombs or explosives or where there was clear evidence that they had possessed such items immediately before capture. These rules, summarised below, were to apply to all combatants whether in uniform or not.

Application was to be made at once to the nearest officer of field rank to convene a drumhead court which would be held at the nearest convenient place. The trial was to take place with the utmost expedition and everything but the most urgent military operations would give way to that need. No adjournments would be allowed and no considerations were to prevent the commencement and conclusion of the trial. The sentence would be confirmed by the nearest officer of field rank available. Nothing was to be permitted to cause delay in confirmation. There is a note appended to these instructions which states that the instructions only apply to cases where the evidence appears to be clear beyond possibility of doubt.

Other aspects of military planning developed as the year wore on. Macready asked that provision be made to house 20,000 more internees.[459] More detailed plans were submitted to Cabinet in September when Macready wrote stating that in the event of the Truce failing he proposed to take 'immediate and drastic action'.[460]

Macready emerges as an increasingly marginal figure as the peace talks gather momentum. There is evidence that some of his letters to the Cabinet went unanswered and unacknowledged.[461] This might have changed swiftly. The Treaty talks hung in the balance in the summer and autumn of 1921. There were serious infractions of the Truce on both sides but there was also determination to hold the ceasefire. However, there were concessions which neither side would give, and it seems likely that if the Truce failed, the politicians would call on the Generals.

In this volatile atmosphere, the prisoners Clifford and Sullivan were again beginning proceedings for writs of habeas corpus. There was an additional argument to be advanced: the country had been at peace for some four months. Could martial law still prevail?

In fact the position of prisoners under sentence of death was even more parlous than they thought. The day before the House of Lords delivered speeches in Clifford and Sullivan, the Law Lords had conferred. There was a broad consensus that the appeal must fail, although if the prisoners wished to renew the argument, their only remedy could be by a writ of habeas corpus. The Law Lords agreed to confine themselves strictly to what was necessary to deliver their decision and to say nothing that might prejudice an application for habeas corpus or the Truce. It was a very delicate issue. Only Lord Sumner refused to go along with this view and hinted in the course of his speech that an action for habeas corpus would fail.[462] In the Lords debates on the Amritsar Massacre the previous year, Lord Sumner had spoken in defence of General Dyer. This was the backdrop in which the decision was made to seek writs of habeas corpus for Clifford and Sullivan.

The Cabinet at Westminster had allowed the release of the prisoners Egan and Higgins in order to keep the peace process on track, but the Cabinet had resolved in early August that any future writs of habeas corpus would be ignored.[463] It seems that General Macready feared the determination of the Cabinet might weaken. A letter from GHQ Dublin to the JAG reads: 'The Habeas Corpus season has now opened and the Master of the Rolls is performing on the 15th instant.'[464] There was concern at Dublin headquarters. There is a handwritten note in the margin referring to General Macready: 'The Chief will not release or produce.'[465]

General Macready wrote to the War Office in London asking for instructions.[466] Macready intimated that he intended to refuse to produce the men unless ordered by his superiors. He was developing a new argument: that although peace prevailed, the sentences were passed in time of war and could therefore still be carried out. He pointed out the consequences if the impending action by Clifford and Sullivan was successful: there were 16 men under sentence of death, 133 men serving prison sentences passed by military courts. A further 790 prisoners were interned under martial law. All of these might soon be freed.[467] Another constitutional crisis loomed. A solution was found by the law officers: if the prisoners continued to seek writs of habeas corpus, then an order for internment under the Defence of the Realm Regulations would be made. This was a provision created by statute and would be a complete answer to the writ.[468] This proposal was endorsed by the Cabinet.[469]

Clifford and Sullivan, then on Spike Island, did not go back to court the following week but their lawyers did and an order was made 'by consent' adjourning the action until either side sought to re-list the case. An undertaking was given by the Crown that no executions would take place while the Truce held or until the final determination of the constitutional question by the courts, whichever was the longer.[470] It is likely that Clifford and Sullivan's lawyers took the view that if the Truce broke down they would still have one final card to play and that the army acquiesced because it allowed martial law, which had become the status quo, to continue. But the Truce held and the Treaty was signed and the radical plans for martial law were shelved.

PART III

CHAPTER SEVENTEEN

Thomas Malone, Tyrrell's Pass, County Westmeath

Malone was captured on Christmas Day 1920 near Parnell Bridge in Cork. He was taken to Union Quay Barracks and later transferred to the military detention barracks and held for trial. He was the first Republican prisoner tried by military court.

The trial took place at Victoria Barracks on 3 January 1921. Malone was charged with having in his possession twenty-one rounds of .303 ammunition and sixteen rounds of sporting rifle ammunition. He was unrepresented. The brief record shows that he declined, in the most courteous terms, to acknowledge the jurisdiction of the court, although this did not stop him from taking a full part in the proceedings.[471]

A Black and Tan told the court that he was returning to Union Quay on Christmas Day with despatches when he saw the accused and another man who 'looked suspicious'. They stopped them and searched the first man and found nothing. As they were about to search the accused, he ran off towards Anglesea Street. He was followed and caught but struggled and resisted arrest. The officer knocked him down and held him but the accused tried to take his revolver off him. The accused was put against a wall and again tried to seize the officer's gun. Failing to gain control of the gun, the accused ran off again but was captured and searched and the ammunition was found. The accused gave a false name and produced a motor permit in support.

Malone cross-examined this witness and put to him that he had tried to seize the gun because the officer was intent on killing him. This was denied by the officer. This line of cross-examination was taken up by the court. In response to questions by the President of the court, the officer said that fourteen shots had been fired at the prisoner during his attempt to escape. It seems that all these shots missed. A second officer gave supporting evidence of the circumstances of the capture.

It is not clear from the brief record of this trial if Malone gave evidence or simply made an unsworn statement. It is suggested that the rules governing the Military Court were still evolving, and at the time of this trial prisoners were not entitled to give evidence in their own defence. The record simply notes that the prisoner 'did not deny having the ammunition on him.' At this point the prosecuting officer intervened: 'It was only right to say that the accused had said at the time of his arrest that the ammunition had been handed to him.'[472] Malone added that he had given a false name because if he gave his real name he 'thought he would be shot'.

It is necessary to digress to point out that Malone had been 'on the run', a fact which he disclosed to the court to explain why he tried to escape.[473] Malone explained to the court that he had produced a motor permit in the name of another man to save himself, and the owner of the motor permit knew nothing whatever about the matter. He told the court that he had later given his correct name to the District Inspector.

Many years later Malone made a statement to the BMH. Much of what Malone later said is supported by the record of trial. He describes running from the officers but, it being Christmas Day, the streets were empty and there was nowhere to hide. He was caught. 'The first fellow that came up fired straight into my face with his revolver … I instinctively ducked and grappled with him. The two of us struggled for possession of the gun. I was a little bit stronger than he was and I pulled it around until it was pointed at him. I pressed his own finger on the trigger.' It transpired that the gun was now empty. Another RIC man came up and hit Malone rendering him unconscious.

Here is another extract from Malone's account of his trial.[474]

> I questioned one fellow – the Tan who had tried to shoot me – and I brought out that he was trying to kill me. I said, 'Did you fire so many shots at me at point blank range?' He admitted he did. I said, 'When you came up to me and I had my hands up, did you fire into my face?' 'I did,' he said, 'and I am sorry I did not … get you too!' I said to him, 'Did you try to shoot me?' To which he answered, 'Yes.' 'When I closed with you, did you not struggle with me for the revolver?' He admitted he did. I explained to the court the circumstances of this struggle and said that in this case, where it was clearly a question of my life or his, I felt entitled to defend my own life …

According to Malone's account, the officer was sufficiently provoked by this cross-examination to reach for his side arm and was placed under arrest by the President of the court. The record shows five years' imprisonment was imposed.[475] Malone was sent to Spike Island, from where he escaped in the spring.

According to Malone's account to the Bureau of Military History, he was charged with attempted murder and possession of ammunition. He also suggests that he was sentenced to death and the sentence was commuted. In these respects, his recollection may not be reliable. The Register shows he was charged with possession of ammunition only and that he was not sentenced to death.[476] The Register has proved reliable in all other respects and is likely to be correct. This analysis is supported by the fact that the charge related to 25 December 1920. Proclamation No. 1 confined the death penalty to acts done after 27 December.[477] Finally, had Malone been sentenced to death, one would expect to find a record in the minute book of the Judge Advocate General. As far as can be established, there is no such record.

Whether the rest of Malone's account is factually correct cannot now be determined. The report in the *Constitution* is brief but there is evidence that in some of these trials discreditable conduct by the police was not reported or was referred to obliquely.

CHAPTER EIGHTEEN

Gabbett and Fenton, Mount Rivers, Newport, County Tipperary

These trials concern William H. Gabbett and his maid, Mamie Fenton, of Mount Rivers, Newport, County Tipperary. The record describes Gabbett as a landowner. Other government records show he was of the Church of Ireland faith, formerly a captain in the Royal Yeomanry. At the time of his trial he was fifty-three.[478]

Gabbett was charged with improper possession of arms, ammunition, and military equipment.[479] He was tried at New Barracks, Limerick on 16 February 1921. The record shows that he was represented by Arthur Blood-Smyth, solicitor. The evidence showed that a search of the accused's farm at Mount Rivers took place on 31 January. An army officer gave evidence that Gabbett gave all assistance during the search. Found at the farm were a rook rifle, several rounds of rifle, revolver and gunshot ammunition and a quantity of unspecified equipment.

The brief report of this case indicates Gabbett gave no evidence. He called as a witness Sir Charles Barrington, Vice-Lord Lieutenant of County Limerick. Sir Charles gave evidence that Gabbett was 'loyal'. He had served in the army. He was 'the last man who would keep a gun for an unlawful purpose', a lapse he ascribed to carelessness.

Gabbett was acquitted of possession of the rifle. In respect of the other matters he was convicted and sentenced to £75 fine with six months without hard labour in the alternative.[480]

There is no doubt that the Military Court gleaned a great deal from the background of the witness called by the accused. The accused's choice of legal representation could also be revealing. Gabbett was represented by Blood-Smyth, whose name has a certain resonance. Cornelius Murphy chose not to be represented, a fact which told a tale. John Allen's solicitor, Denis Boudren, quickly became known for representing IRA men and it is probable that this told against them. Cases such as Gabbett excited the view that the Military Court was partial. That much is plainly correct. Men like John Allen were perceived as part of the armed threat to the Union. Gabbett was not.

One final matter. Two weeks before this trial, the Military Court tried Mamie Fenton, also of Mount Rivers, on charges of possessing a revolver and ammunition. No record of this trial survives. We can glean something from the census, which shows that Mary Fenton was a Catholic, one of William Gabbett's domestic servants. She would have been thirty when she was tried. She was sentenced to two years' imprisonment, which was later commuted to a £20 fine.[481] It might be surmised that the raid on Mount Rivers was directed against her and that during the search evidence came to light which implicated William Gabbett.

CHAPTER NINETEEN

Rahanisky House

MICHAEL BAYLOR (AKA FITZGERALD), SEÁN MACSWINEY, TIMOTHY MURPHY, CORNELIUS CONROY, LAWRENCE DRISCOLL, JEREMIAH DENNEHY, MICHAEL BOWLES, JOHN TWOMEY, JOHN O'KEEFE, JAMES THOMPSON, CORNELIUS TWOMEY, JAMES CAREY, MICHAEL RENEHAN,[482] MRS McKAY.[483]

According to the *Sixth Division Record of the Rebellion*, information was received that a party of rebels were billeted at Rahanisky House, near Cork. The unnamed female informant expressed a particular interest in the timing of a raid. It was thought that she might be selling information to both sides and so she was told the raid would take place at 10 am the following morning while plans were laid for an early arrival.

Rahanisky House was a detached residence set back behind hedges and fencing in the Whitecross area, a respectable suburb of Cork that was largely untroubled by the conflict until 8 February 1921, when a raiding party of the Hampshire Regiment arrived just before dawn. Before a cordon could be thrown around the grounds, a man was seen. He was challenged and shot at. He disappeared, although some of his fingers were found close by.[484] Fourteen prisoners were taken and a quantity of handguns and ammunition was seized.

A summary of evidence was taken in the presence of the prisoners on 15 February,[485] and the trial commenced in the library at Victoria Barracks on 22 February. The gallery was crowded with press and families. All the prisoners were represented by solicitor or counsel.[486] The Judge Advocate was Captain F.E. Young. The trial was prosecuted by Major Gover. The President was Lieutenant Colonel Vandeleur. The prisoners were all charged with conspiracy to levy war.

Lieutenant Roe of the Hampshire Regiment told the court that they arrived at about 6.30 am. They came upon a man in the driveway. Lieutenant Roe ordered the man to put his hands up. The man fumbled in his macintosh, before turning and running. The officer fired at him and the man was not seen again. The officer led his men around the side of the house and came on a man climbing out of a window. He was told to go back into the house and he did so.

Orders were then shouted for everyone in the house to come out. After some minutes three men emerged and put their hands up. One of these men gave his name as Fitzgerald. He was searched and found to have a loaded automatic on him. After a few minutes seven more men emerged. All the men were stood at the front of the house. One was known to the officers; Conroy had been a clerk to the garrison adjutant at Victoria Barracks. Lieutenant Roe searched the house and in an upstairs bedroom he found Bridie McKay, a 44 year old woman who had made a fortune dealing in scrap metal, and Carey and Renehan, her domestic staff. They were arrested. On the bed under a blanket the officer found five loaded revolvers. Most were loaded with flat-nose bullets.

Lieutenant Roe was cross-examined and his identification of Fitzgerald as having a gun was challenged by defence counsel. Lieutenant Roe replied: 'A man charged with possessing arms may pay the death penalty and it was necessary to be very particular about identification.' In answers to questions, Lieutenant Roe told the court Mrs McKay appeared to have just got up. Carey and Renehan were servants in her employ. Mrs McKay told the officer that they knew nothing of the revolvers in the bedroom and were at a loss to know how they had come to be there.

MacSwiney, it emerged, was the brother of the late Lord Mayor. This exchange in cross-examination of Lieutenant Roe gives the flavour of events: 'Did you say to the prisoner we finished your brother and you won't be long after him?' 'I said his brother had died in prison through his own fault and that he would probably be shot for consorting with rebels.'

Lieutenant Dove of the Hampshire Regiment gave evidence of movement in a shed outside the house. Orders were given for the person inside to come out but no one emerged. A bomb was thrown into the shed.

Mrs McKay gave evidence that she was the wife of Joseph McKay, who ran a business manufacturing ploughs. She had a house in the city and Rahanisky House on the outskirts of Cork. She told the court that Renehan and Carey were employed by her and 'lived in'. They were respectable men. She had been living there at the time of the raid. She told the court that Conroy was an acquaintance and had a standing invitation to 'come in for a cup of tea' or 'stop for the night' if the curfew prevented him from travelling home. The night before the raid Conroy and another man came to the house. Conroy told her they had been to a dance and were in danger of breaching the curfew. She had fed them and let them stay over. Later that night a number of other men had arrived and also stayed over. She had seen no guns and had no reason to believe the men were armed. They played the piano and she served tea. Later that night after she retired she had heard the men 'reciting the rosary'. She was awoken by the raid. She went to the door and on finding the military there she called out to the men in the house. A number of men came downstairs. She said she had never seen the revolvers seized from her room and when she left her bed there were no revolvers in the bed.

She was cross-examined about her friendship with Conroy and the arrangement for him to stay over.

> 'Conroy is a friend of yours?
> 'I suppose you could say an acquaintance.'
> 'Would you call him a friend?'
> 'Well I have never found a friend yet in my life.'

The relationship between Conroy and Mrs McKay remains ambiguous.

Sergeant Sullivan, Sergeant John Dowling and Constable James West all gave compelling evidence of Mrs McKay's character. They had all known her many years. They described her variously as a lady of 'excellent character', 'loyal' and 'respectable'.

James Carey gave evidence that he had been employed by Mrs McKay for six years. On the night in question he had heard voices downstairs but he 'did not see any men enter the house'. He was awoken by the sound of shouts the next morning. He heard Mrs McKay calling him and as he came down there was some confusion with people going and coming. No electric lights were on. It was the first time he had seen the men in question. He denied being a member of any illegal organisation. Renehan gave evidence that he went to bed at about 9.15. He had no knowledge of men coming to the house. He said he had never been a member of any illegal organisation.

One curious feature of the case bears examination. According to the prosecution evidence, only one man, Fitzgerald, was found carrying a weapon, a Colt .45 automatic. Fitzgerald denied that he had the automatic. His case was that MacSwiney had the gun and MacSwiney accepted this.

MacSwiney gave evidence that he had been in possession of a .45 that night. He was the brother of the late Lord Mayor and a member of the Volunteers. He said he had never taken part in an attack on Crown forces. He told the court he did not carry arms 'habitually'. That night he had a

Colt automatic .45. He had had it some time and carried it for self-defence – he had information that his life was under threat from a group of RIC men, 'what we call the murder gang'. It should be added that self-protection was not a defence to carrying a weapon under martial law. MacSwiney, who was represented, would have known that. This factor, and his claim to possess a gun which the prosecution did not allege was his, exposed him to the death sentence, a stance which conveys an echo of his late brother's protest.

MacSwiney declined to answer any questions about the battalion he belonged to or the membership of that battalion. As to the Colt, MacSwiney said the gun seized and produced to the court was not his but he had a similar one that night. His gun, he told the court, had a safety catch that was in a poor state of repair.

MacSwiney's defence was a difficult one to advance. He admitted he was a Volunteer. He admitted carrying a gun that night and he chose not to answer questions about other Volunteers. His admission that he had a gun but not the gun produced to the court was an improbable scenario. In his case there was an unlikely twist after the close of the prosecution case. Prosecuting counsel, Major Gover, announced to the court that it had come to light that the gun seized and produced to the court had been taken to the armourer at Victoria Barracks the night after the raid. The safety catch had been repaired and returned to Lieutenant Hook of the Hampshire Regiment. This disclosure by the prosecution bolstered the account given by MacSwiney and by implication the case for Fitzgerald.

Cornelius Conroy was twenty-six. He told the court that he joined the Royal Navy in 1912. He saw service in the British Cameroons, east Africa and Russia where he served as a medic. He had been invalided out in 1920. None of this was in dispute, although the nature of his disability is unclear: he was described by a contemporary as a 'big and athletic' man.[487] He became a clerk at Victoria Barracks. He had left that employment and was proposing to go to America. He produced a passport and a ticket to sail to America on 20 February. His difficulty was that, on his account, most of the other men were at the house at his invitation and none save MacSwiney admitted possession of a gun.

All the other men gave evidence and they all advanced innocent reasons for being at the house: 'a bit of sport,' said one, or the danger of being caught in the street after curfew. The picture that emerged showed Conroy playing 'ragtime' piano and the others singing until late into the night.

None of the men produced an explanation which the court accepted. None admitted to knowing about any of the guns found around the house. Fitzgerald's position was further complicated when it emerged he had given a false name on arrest and kept up the pretence until cross-examination when prosecuting counsel produced a watch from the prisoner's property held at the detention barracks. Fitzgerald admitted the watch was his. He was asked to turn it over and his real name, Baylor, was scratched on the case. He was forced to admit he had lied about his name and address and continued the deception until caught out in cross-examination. It followed also that the position of the co-accused who admitted knowing him also suffered because they had supported the subterfuge.

One other factor which may have affected the trial: Conroy's job as the clerk to the garrison adjutant at Victoria Barracks was crucial and sensitive. In fact, some weeks earlier soldiers raiding a house in Cork had found a mass of blank official entry passes to the barracks together with confidential papers relating to sentry postings.[488] The finger of suspicion pointed at Conroy, who was arrested and his home searched but nothing was found. Conroy was sacked. He was arrested some weeks later in the Rahanisky House raid, a fact reported with some glee in the *Hampshire War Diary*.[489] It is almost inconceivable that the officers presiding over the court at Victoria Barracks did not know this fact. It was the elephant in the room.

Verdict and Sentence

James Carey, Mrs McKay and Michael Renehan were all acquitted. All the others were convicted of conspiracy to levy war.

Michael Baylor, Seán MacSwiney, Timothy Murphy, Cornelius Conroy, Cornelius Twomey, John Twomey, Jeremiah Dennehy and James Thompson were each sentenced to fifteen years' penal servitude. John O'Keefe, Michael Bowles and Lawrence Driscoll were sentenced to ten years' penal servitude.[490]

There is a sequel to this trial which throws some light on these events. The pivotal figure in the case was Conroy. It was Conroy who was a friend of Mrs McKay and Conroy who seems to have invited the others to join him. Conroy next appears at Spike Island as a leader and organiser of long-term prisoners.[491] He later tunnelled his way out of Kilkenny prison. That would seem to settle that issue. MacSwiney escaped from Spike Island in the spring and was elected to the second Dáil in May. Evidence later emerged that Baylor, (alias Fitzgerald) had taken part in the Dillon's Cross ambush.[492]

This trial generates two issues of note. First, what is now known as disclosure: the process by which the prosecution releases unused material that may assist the defence. That process is now highly regulated and strictly enforced in most civilised countries. In 1921 the process was far more rudimentary and a great deal turned on the conscience of prosecution counsel. In this case the decision by Major Gover to disclose repairs to the safety catch of the automatic pistol was crucial to the defence of Fitzgerald and MacSwiney.

The second matter which calls for comment is that this was one of the first multi-defendant trials during martial law. One of the main purposes of the Military Court was to provide for death sentences where this was not available under civil law, particularly in firearms cases.[493] The *Sixth Division Record of the Rebellion* recorded this trial as a missed opportunity: 'The failure to execute these desperados ... had the worst possible effect, it encouraged the rebels to think that the full penalties prescribed in the proclamations would not be carried out.'[494] The Rahanisky House trial was one of a number of cases in which officers serving on the Military Court declined to pass death sentences. It is an inference that some officers serving on military courts were not prepared to support the full rigour of martial law.

It later emerged that Bridie McKay had been the informant. She went into hiding in England for some time and later returned to live out her days in Cork where she was shunned by her neighbours.[495]

CHAPTER TWENTY

John McBride, Knockmoylan, County Kilkenny

This trial concerned John McBride, then aged twenty-two. McBride lived in the house overlooking the Knockmoylan crossing of the main railway line from Dublin to Waterford. He was a 'milesman' with the Great Southern and Western Railway, whose job was to 'pass' trains and operate the crossing. His father, Robert, had also been a 'milesman' at the same crossing.

The trial arose out of an attack on the RIC barracks at Mullinavat, County Kilkenny. Mullinavat was then a village with an RIC barracks and a railway station serving the Great Southern and Western Railway. In the early hours of 17 January there was an attack on the barracks. It was one of thirteen garrisoned barracks attacked that week.[496] The attack followed a pattern: roads were blocked off to prevent reinforcements getting through. The attackers then laid siege to the barracks in the small hours. At Mullinavat the attackers attempted to lay mines against the barracks wall but lost the element of surprise when a constable peered out the window at a crucial moment. The barracks was defended vigorously with rifle fire and grenades. Verey lights were fired into the sky and the attack was broken off. Reinforcements were brought up from Waterford in the south and Kilkenny to the north. The passage of reinforcements was impeded by roadblocks which had been laid on all main roads in the hours leading up to the attack.[497] One of the blocked roads was at the level crossing at Knockmoylan.

The prisoner was charged contrary to Regulation 50 of the Restoration of Order in Ireland Regulations, that on 17 January 1921, he knew of a possible attack on His Majesty's forces but failed to give full information. In the alternative, he was charged that on the same day he came into contact with a party of rebels but neglected to give information to the authorities. He was tried at Waterford on 2 March 1921.[498] He was represented by a solicitor.[499]

The case opened for the Crown was that a party of police and military going to the assistance of the besieged barracks found the gate at the level crossing at Knockmoylan blocked with stones to about half the height of the gate. One of the stones weighed 4–5 cwt. The prisoner lived in a house on the other side of the crossing and it was therefore a reasonable assumption that the prisoner had known of the barricade. There was an inference, alleged the prosecutor, that the barricade was part of the attack on the barracks.

A witness was called to prove that martial law proclamations had been posted nearby at Lukeswell. The witness also gave evidence of the attack on Mullinavat RIC barracks. In cross-examination, the witness conceded the barracks were four and a half miles from the level crossing.

An RIC officer gave evidence that the relief party arrived at the level crossing and found it blocked by stones. The accused was standing on the railway line. He said he was leaving the barrier there until 'the ganger' came up. When he did so, he would report it to him. The officer then arrested the accused. Cross-examined, the officer said that he had seen no rebels in the area. He accepted the accused would not have been able to move some of the stones but the stones could hardly have been put there without the knowledge of the accused. A second officer gave evidence that the accused had helped to remove the stones. It took three men to move the largest stone. And there were very many large stones in the vicinity.

The accused's supervisor – 'the ganger' – gave evidence. He told the court that the prisoner had responsibility for the level crossing. He told the court that if something untoward happened it was the duty of the 'milesman' to wait to be relieved by a 'competent person' before going to report it to the supervisor, who would then pass the matter on to the inspector. As far as the witness knew, the accused was not a Sinn Féiner. Character evidence was called for the accused. His mother Brigid gave evidence that he was not involved in politics. Nor was he involved in any political organisation.

John McBride gave an unsworn statement to the court as follows: he had locked the gates at 10 pm the night before. He got up at 7.30 am and he saw the 7.40 train pass. He then looked out of the house and saw the barricade. He was unable to move the barricade and helped police move it. He did not belong to any political organisation. McBride was acquitted.

This was a slightly unusual trial. The first charge was contrary to the Restoration of Order in Ireland Act, and would ordinarily have been tried by statutory court martial under the Restoration of Order in Ireland Act. By the spring of 1921 the military courts asserted jurisdiction over all martial law offences and all contraventions of the ROIA.[500] The second charge alleged a contravention of the proclamation issued on 3 January when Kilkenny became part of the Martial Law Area.

The basis of the charges was also unusual because the accused had not done any positive act. The prosecution rested on the common law principle that every citizen had a duty to actively suppress disorder and insurrection.[501] This logic was also used to justify official reprisals against property belonging to civilians who had failed to inform the military of planned ambushes.[502] Both the army and the IRA laid claim to the active loyalty of all citizens. Those who informed risked death and those who did not risked reprisal. The prosecution may be seen in that context.

CHAPTER TWENTY-ONE

Michael Kelleher and James Keogh, Youghal, County Cork

On Saturday 5 March, 1921, these men were tried by military court at Victoria Barracks.[503] The prisoners were both charged on two counts: that of being improperly in possession of arms and of being improperly in possession of ammunition. They pleaded not guilty to both charges, and were defended by Joseph McCarthy.[504]

The evidence showed that on 17 February a motorised patrol was passing near Youghal, and at around 8.30 in the morning the patrol had come up from a by-road onto the road between Youghal and Killeagh. An officer had seen three men standing in a field around 300 yards away. The men were challenged and began to run. A shot was fired at the men. The first man had run across the fields and escaped but the other two (later identified as the accused) had made for a wall near the corner of a field. Another officer told the court that the men were found 'in a crouching position three or four yards from a gate in the wall'. They were searched but nothing was found in their possession.

An officer went back up to the wall where the two men had been standing and called for a spade. From this spot he dug up a 'short Webley revolver', which was loaded with three ordinary and three dum-dum bullets. Apart from the mud covering the revolver, it appeared to be in good working condition. Later inquiries were to reveal that this revolver had been stolen from the army the previous summer. A second revolver was found close by in a sluice in the wall. The revolver was in good working order and fully loaded.

The record of this trial was not preserved at the National Archive. The only other record was compiled by the court reporter, who left court before the end of the trial to avoid being caught out after curfew. It is known from other sources that Kelleher and Keogh were found guilty on both charges and were sentenced to five years' penal servitude.[505]

CHAPTER TWENTY-TWO

Denis Murphy, Godfrey's Cross, County Cork

Denis Murphy was wounded during the engagement at Dripsey recounted in Chapter 8. He had suffered a bullet wound to the lung and was unfit to be tried with the others.[506] He was tried on 9 March 1921 at Victoria Barracks on a charge of levying war against the King and a second charge of preparing an ambush. Like many such trials, it took place in the gymnasium, and 'a large number of ladies attended'.[507] Murphy was represented by solicitor and counsel.[508] He was prosecuted by Major Gover, who had conduct of the case against the others captured at Dripsey.

The prosecution evidence was much the same as that called in the trial of the other Dripsey men: Lieutenant Colonel Evans gave evidence of the background to the raid; the disposition of his forces which advanced on the ambushers, who were quickly routed: 'All the civilians appeared to be armed and numbered about 40.' After capturing a number of men, Lieutenant Colonel Evans recounted going back to the bank by the road where he found 'a trench and some rifle pits near the road'. He recounted that 'a lot of shotguns, rifles and revolvers were collected'.

A private soldier gave evidence that as the army advanced on the ambush site he saw about forty civilians spring up out of the trench in front of him. There was an exchange of fire and the ambushers ran. The private fired on one man, who fell over a hedge. He came up and captured the man, whom he identified as the accused. The soldier gave evidence that Murphy was covered in blood. He 'had a shotgun over his shoulder. He also had a haversack, ammunition and bandolier.'

Murphy told the court that he was aged twenty-two, a farm labourer from Meenachoney near Godfrey's Cross. He had been out on horseback running an errand for his mother when he came across the ambush party. They had taken his horse and held him at the scene. One of the ambushers had put his equipment on the ground and gone off on the horse. Murphy had been required to carry the man's equipment. A little while later the soldiers were seen and he had run with the others until he came to a fence: 'As he was going through the gap a bullet hit him in the leg and he fell.' He also sustained a wound to the shoulder. He denied being a member of any illegal organisation.

Murphy called his employer, his father and his step-mother as witnesses. The trial lasted for no more than two hours. Murphy was convicted on both charges. His defence, in essence, was duress, which was certainly available as a matter of law. It follows from his conviction that the court was satisfied that he took a full and willing part in preparations for the ambush and the ambush itself. Murphy was sentenced to death by shooting. No recommendation for mercy was made. His sentence was later commuted to penal servitude for life.

The case papers have not survived and the reason for commuting sentence is not clear. It was surprising, having regard to the death sentences imposed on all the others convicted of participating in the Dripsey ambush. Murphy later suggested that his father had gone to see Major Woodley, who owned land at Leades near Aghinagh.[509] This seems the most likely explanation. In the Dripsey trial, Major Woodley had given evidence for Jeremiah Callaghan, who had been acquitted against the run of evidence. Major Woodley had a distinguished record in the Boer War and in the Great War. It is likely that his word carried great weight with the army.

Murphy survived the war. He did not dispute the verdicts passed in his case.[510]

CHAPTER TWENTY-THREE

Patrick Coakley, Lissanisky, Near Upton, County Cork

The old Cork, Bandon and South Coast Railway ran west from Cork near the Owenboy river until it reached Upton station, a single-storey redbrick with slated roof and barge board eaves. On 15 February 1921 the 9.30 am Cork to Bandon train was crowded with soldiers and civilians. The train was ambushed as it pulled into Upton station.

The background to this ambush may be briefly stated. In early 1921 the trenching of roads and destruction of bridges in south-west Ireland made the moving of troops slow and hazardous because the lorries were vulnerable to grenade attack and ambush and they were also noisy and incapable of surprising rebel units.[511] Following the defeat of the rail strike in December 1920, the army began to use the railways to transport men, sometimes in small groups, but they were also vulnerable to attack. On 11 February a train travelling from Cork to Killarney was ambushed near Millstreet. The fourteen soldiers of the Royal Fusiliers were crowded together in a single carriage and after a short and fierce fight they sustained a number of casualties and surrendered.[512]

The ambush at Upton railway station took place four days later; the ambush party numbered fourteen.[513] They had imprisoned the station staff before the ambush and placed themselves alongside the railway line, around unused rail trucks, the goods store, where sacks of corn and meal were used as sandbags and in Cronin's pub overlooking the tracks.

The plan was to attack a group of twenty soldiers believed to be travelling from Cork to Bandon. It had been noted that the soldiers tended to travel in a single carriage. The disposition of the ambushing party was laid with this in mind. Three unexpected events occurred. First, as a result of the Millstreet ambush the army issued an order requiring officers to ensure that when travelling by train, their men were dispersed along the length of the train and to post lookouts.[514] A second, important factor arose quite by chance. A large party of soldiers unexpectedly joined the train at Kinsale Junction and they too dispersed along the length of the train. The train usually waited at Kinsale Junction before setting off for Upton, a mile and a half down the track. It was intended that two scouts would check the number and disposition of troops and cycle on to Upton to make a report to the ambush party. That morning, for the first time in living memory, the train pulled out after only a few minutes before the scouts could set off.

The train pulled into Upton at 10.25 am. Firing began immediately and continued until 10.40. Trapped amid the shooting were a large number of civilians, travelling salesmen, railway staff and families out on a day trip. Caught up in the fighting, these civilians endured a terrifying ordeal which many did not survive. The soldiers emerging from both ends of the train began to outflank the attackers. According to a contemporary account the ambushers began a running retreat.

The shooting resulted in an appalling death toll among passengers. One woman and nine male civilians were killed and others wounded.[515] Two Volunteers were killed at the scene and three were wounded, of whom two died of their wounds.[516] Five soldiers were wounded.[517] According to army records, two men were captured after the ambush.[518] One was Patrick Coakley, who was the only man tried for involvement in the Upton railway ambush.[519] Coakley was tried at Victoria Barracks on 21 and 22 March 1921 by a military court convened in the library. The accused was charged with levying war. He was represented by Joseph McCarthy, led by Michael Comyn, King's Counsel.[520]

The evidence showed that the accused had been arrested in the round-up after the ambush. An officer gave evidence that he searched Cronin's pub near the station. He found the accused there with a priest and a number of women. A discarded rifle was found concealed in a cupboard. It was unloaded but had recently been fired. Coakley was questioned and he gave his name as John Buckley. The officer told the court that Coakley was searched but nothing was found except a list of names which had the appearance of an 'Arms Levy list'. He had no ticket but said that he had been sent into the pub by the ambushers and told to stay there. He was asked about the gun and said that 'one of the attackers had put it there'. Coakley was 'excited' and protested he was innocent.

A sergeant of the Essex Regiment gave supporting evidence. He told the court that he 'counted twenty attackers'. He added that the people in the pub had been 'very kind and friendly'. They had supplied brandy to the wounded. He added that the accused, when questioned, was 'not unduly excited'. Evidence was called from a local man, who proved

Coakley's identity and thereby confirmed that he had given a false name on arrest. The witness added that the Coakley family were farmers and 'most respectable'.

Michael Comyn KC made a lengthy opening address which commenced with some old-fashioned flattery of a brazen quality. He described the officers trying the case as 'calm, serene and enlightened minds'.

Coakley gave evidence that he lived at Lissanisky about a mile from Upton station with his parents and brother and sisters. He was the eldest. They ran a farm. On the morning of his arrest he had gone to Upton station to catch the train to Bandon. He had been going to see a dentist and to do other errands. When he arrived at the station he saw a number of armed men. They compelled him to go into a pub by the station where he joined other passengers. Shortly afterwards they heard shooting, which lasted for some time. Then he heard a whistle and a man ran in and threw a gun under the stairs and then ran off. Shortly afterwards, a military officer entered the public house. Coakley was asked his name and he gave a false name. He was arrested.

23.1 Royal Fusiliers near Killarney. Courtesy of the Royal Fusiliers Museum.

He admitted he had been a member of the Volunteers until the previous September. He had resigned because he was against physical force and against the Ambush War. He said he had spoken out against the Ambush War. He admitted being a 'Sinn Féiner' and to being on the run for some months. He had feared arrest by the military and RIC. Here is an extract of the cross-examination:

> 'Did you know the man who met you at the station with a revolver in his hand?'
> 'No.'
> 'Why did you give a wrong name?'
> 'I happen to be a member of the Bandon Rural Council. I wanted to wait until I would be properly under arrest and more safe.'
> 'When did you give your right name?'
> 'When going to Cork.'

He was pressed about membership of the Volunteers.

> 'You said you were in the Irish Volunteers?'
> 'Yes, up to September last.'
> 'You left as a protest against ambushes?'
> 'Yes …'

The accused was asked for details of others.

> 'Do you know which company took part in this ambush?'
> 'No.'
> 'What company were you in?'
> 'I am afraid I can't tell you that.'
> 'Do you know what company you were in?'
> 'I admit I know the company I was in, but I would be afraid to answer it.'

Although pressed by the President of the court, he declined to name the commander of that company on the ground that it would leave him open to reprisal.

Coakley was also cross-examined about a list found on him, which the prosecution contended was a 'levy' on local people of the sort that had been declared illegal by proclamation a few days previously.[521] This Coakley denied. He asserted it was a subscription list for a dog club.

A young woman gave evidence for the defence. She said that she too had been held prisoner in the pub beside the railway station with others.

She gave evidence that the accused had been there throughout the ambush. At some point a man had run in and dropped a gun under the stairs and ran off. She denied being acquainted with the prisoner.

The parish priest, the Reverend Patrick Desmond,[522] gave evidence. He said he had campaigned against the Ambush War from the pulpit and had read out the bishop's letter excommunicating those who took part in the war.[523] He explained the 'levy' document as a list of members of a dog club. He gave character evidence for the accused.

Coakley was acquitted and released.[524] Subsequently evidence came to light which suggests that Coakley took a part in the ambush.[525]

23.2 Soldiers inspect bullet holes following a train ambush. Courtesy of the Royal Fusiliers Museum.

CHAPTER TWENTY-FOUR

Laurence Medlar, Paulstown, County Kilkenny

We are concerned with Gowran in County Kilkenny, well known now for golf, hurling, racing and for St Mary's, a medieval church, and the siege in 1650 when all but one of the captured garrison's officers were executed.

In 1921 Gowran was a quiet town with a railway station and a substantial RIC barracks adjoining the courthouse. Despite the war, the area was generally quiet until an attack on the barracks in the early hours of 13 February. Laurence Medlar lived a few miles north at Paulstown, where his family ran a blacksmith's forge. Medlar was the only man charged in connection with the attack on the barracks.

The prisoner was tried on 2 April on two charges. First, possessing thirty-nine sticks of gelignite. Second, levying war on His Majesty by taking part in an attack on the RIC barracks at Gowran. Medlar was represented by a solicitor, Mr Colbert. The case for the Crown was opened at some length, prosecuting counsel drawing attention to the charge of levying war and observing that if the accused was convicted 'he was liable to suffer the extreme penalty.'

An RIC officer gave evidence that he had been at Gowran barracks on the evening of 13 February.[526] At about 10.45 a volley of shots had been fired at the barracks from the rear. Bombs exploded in the yard. Verey lights were sent up. The attack was intense for about three-quarters of an hour before it was broken off. It appears there were no casualties. The following morning an inspection of the barracks showed damage to the roof. Thirty-seven windows had been broken. The police went directly to the Medlar family home, a thatched cottage opposite a smithy's forge off the main street in Paulstown. It was about three miles distance from the barracks.

The second officer told the court that Medlar was in bed when police arrived. He dressed and then was searched. He said he had been with a girl the previous evening but would not give her name. He was asked where his bicycle was and said it had been borrowed by a friend but did not know the name of the man who borrowed it. The outhouse was searched and a bike was found which the accused admitted was his. There were 'wet marks on the rims'. In the loft a sack was found. Inside was a bag containing thirty-nine sticks of gelignite. The bag and the gelignite were damp but the loft itself was quite dry. The accused said he knew nothing about it.[527] A book was found in which there was a slip of paper: 'Have men for demolition, start operations at 9 pm sharp.' Another piece of paper was found containing a list of arms held by local companies.

At the taking of the summary of evidence on 1 March the accused made the following statement: 'On the 12th February I was outside our house when two men came up and presented revolvers at me. One of them had a bag and small parcel, and asked me to keep it. I refused and they blindfolded me and took me to the back of the house. One of the men went away and when he came back said that men would call on the following Monday night, and if I told anyone about it I would take the consequences. I told nobody.'

The accused did not add to what he had said during the taking of the summary of evidence.

Michael Medlar gave evidence. He was a 55-year-old blacksmith, the father of the accused. He told the court that his son lived at home and, as far as he knew, was at home in bed on the night in question. The solicitor, Colbert, who had an uphill task in his closing address, related that the father of the accused had been to the parish priest to ask for a character reference for his son – 'a character', as it was then called. The priest wrote back: 'You asked me for a character. I am not giving it. But instead of a character I will give you a note that he should be committed to a lunatic asylum.'

The meaning of this note is clear enough and it was not that contended for by the defence solicitor. There was, in any event, no other evidence of mental incapacity. No prosecution witness mentioned this, nor did the father of the accused. It is clear that this was a desperate and inept red herring thrown in by the solicitor defending and this was acknowledged by the prisoner after the trial.

The Judge Advocate gave directions in summing up which are worth looking at. He stated that the case against the accused on levying war was circumstantial, involving a chain of evidence: the proximity of the barracks to the home of the accused; the fact the accused had a bike; the attempt by the accused to conceal the bike; the condition of the bike only hours after the attack; the wet gelignite found in a dry loft. Then there were the slips of paper which told their own story.

The Judge Advocate commented unfavourably on the accused's failure to mention his defence when arrested and his silence at trial: 'The court would have been considerably helped in coming to a conclusion if they had the evidence of the accused.' This amounted to inviting the court to draw an adverse inference against the accused from his failure to give evidence. Had the prisoner been tried in a criminal court or before a ROIA court martial the law would have prevented him from giving any evidence. He also commented on the failure of the accused to call his brother, with whom he had shared a bed on the night in question. As the law then stood, the Judge Advocate was entitled to make this comment in strong terms.

In his summing up the Judge Advocate commended the ability of the solicitor. Although, as he pointed out, Mr Colbert's persistent questions as to why the police had gone to Medlar's address brought an unwelcome answer: the accused was reputed to be the commandant of a local battalion of Volunteers. This piece of intelligence, which was plainly hearsay, was elevated by the Judge Advocate into evidence supporting the Crown case. Even where hearsay is inadvertently introduced, it does not become probative of any fact. It was a significant error.

The accused was convicted of the charge of possessing gelignite. He was acquitted of levying war. He was sentenced to fifteen years' imprisonment.[528] The prisoner was extremely fortunate to escape conviction on the charge of levying war. He was released in 1922. He did not dispute the verdict.

CHAPTER TWENTY-FIVE

O'Brien's Castle, County Clare

WILLIAM MACNAMARA, PATRICK COOTE,[529] JOHN HASSETT, JOHN KEARNEY.

These men were captured in February 1921 at O'Brien's Castle[530] near Carrahane, some way north of Ennis on the road to Gort. The captured men were taken to Ennis where a rumour of a rescue attempt prompted the army to move the men to the military barracks at Limerick. The trial took place at New Barracks, Limerick on 25 March 1921.[531]

The men were charged on two counts, that of levying war against the Crown and improper possession of arms, while Kearney was charged with harbouring rebels. They were represented by a local solicitor, Jack Lynch, who instructed Patrick Lynch, King's Counsel. The name of the prosecuting officer is not known.

The trial began with a now familiar challenge to jurisdiction, which was overruled by the court. The proclamation was proved in evidence and then witnesses were called.

An army officer gave evidence that at about 11 am on 12 February, a party of army and Auxiliaries had raided Kearney's home, O'Brien's Castle near Carrahane. The military disembarked from their vehicles about 100 yards from the house and from there the soldiers made their way up on foot. A big man had appeared at the front doorway, and then quickly disappeared back inside. This man was later identified as Hassett. The witness stated that he had gone in and seen Kearney who, when questioned, had indicated to the back of the house. At the back of the house he saw three men running down the lane. These men he identified as Hassett, MacNamara and Coote.

The witnesses described Hassett as a big, tall man wearing puttees. MacNamara was stout, medium height, carrying a rifle and sporting leggings, while Coote was a slightly built youth, who wore a shirt and tie. A chase began as the three men tried to outdistance their pursuers. The chasing soldiers shouted for them to 'halt' but the men kept running and their pursuers began firing as they ran. The fugitives were seen trying to discard a variety of incriminating objects while in flight. Hassett was seen to throw away a revolver holster and MacNamara to throw his rifle into a nearby ditch, while Coote was seen to throw a small bag into a bush. The chase was strung out to well over a mile. Occasionally the pursuing party lost sight of the men because of the undulating countryside and the thick furze bushes. For a time they were spotted only sporadically, sometimes running through hedgerows and at others even crawling through the thick undergrowth. Eventually all three men were captured and taken back to Kearney's. Hassett admitted to the officer that he had stayed the previous night at Kearney's. Kearney was asked about this and denied it. He was then confronted by Hassett and admitted it. Kearney was then arrested.

This was a case where the Crown witnesses were subjected to detailed cross-examination as to what they had seen and from what vantage point. Later in the case Patrick Lynch KC was to produce a detailed model of the house and the surrounding area which contradicted some of the identification evidence given. The court then adjourned and visited the scene and resumed the following day.

A short Lee Enfield rifle said to be carried by MacNamara was recovered, along with a revolver and holster. The bag discarded by Coote was retrieved and was found to contain a quantity of ammunition. Three obsolete and rather rusty Martini-Henry rifles, two carbines and a sporting rifle were also found in or around the farm. A wooden box containing 'egg bombs' was also found. In the course of the search two haystacks were set on fire, which generated a series of explosions in one of the haystacks.

It was suggested by defence counsel that Kearney, Hassett and Coote had been knocked about after capture and that Kearney's home had been looted and damaged by fire. These allegations were denied. Later, a police witness who dodged counsel's question on these issues was rebuked by the Judge Advocate: 'That is not an answer to the question.' It should be said that this intervention was typical of the Judge Advocate in this trial.

MacNamara told the court that he was a grocer and a farmer. He said that on the night before his arrest he had been staying at his mother's home in Ennis. He set off the next morning in order to buy peat for her. His route had taken him near Kearney's house, where he heard firing. Frightened, he took refuge in a nearby bog where he had hidden in the long grass. He was soon spotted by the military and arrested. He told the court that he had served some time in prison in

1917 for 'marching a body of men'. This, as it turned out, was a reference to the East Clare election where his counsel, Patrick Lynch KC, had fought and lost to de Valera.

> Patrick Lynch: 'Was that before the Volunteers?'
> MacNamara: 'It was during the East Clare election.' [laughter]
> Patrick Lynch: 'Really, that is hard on me. I am sorry for that. [more laughter]
> Judge Advocate: 'I think the only way you can clear yourself is to ask him how he voted.' [laughter]

The East Clare constituency had been held for a quarter of a century by Willie Redmond, who had volunteered to serve in the Great War. Many had followed his lead, hoping that Home Rule would be the reward for loyalty. Major Redmond was killed leading the men of the 6th Battalion of the Royal Irish Regiment towards Messines Ridge in June 1917. He was fifty-six years old and a little out of condition, but he was still one of the first out of the trenches and was wounded twice before taking even a few strides. He died within a few hours, one of many who perished that day. Redmond's tragic death, the heavy casualties in France and the threat of conscription in Ireland provide the context for the East Clare by-election.

As to the candidates, their credentials summed up the divide in Irish life: 'Patrick Lynch KC was a former Crown Prosecutor, he came from one of Clare's leading families. Éamon de Valera came from Lewes prison having been prosecuted by the Crown.'[532] There was a little more to it than that, but the result was that Lynch lost the election by a decisive margin, Sinn Féin gathered momentum and the War of Independence followed.

MacNamara might have been unwise to acknowledge his connection with the East Clare by-election but he did so and told the court that he had left the Volunteers after he came out of prison in 1917. He had never gone 'on the run'. Character evidence was called for MacNamara from a Lieutenant Colonel of the Royal Army Medical Corps. Another witness gave evidence that MacNamara worked at his farm and sometimes stayed with his mother at Ennis. Yet another witness stated she had seen MacNamara at his mother's house that night. This evidence was adduced to demonstrate that he was not 'on the run' and that his presence near the house when the raid took place was coincidental.

Coote gave evidence. He lived in Ennis with his parents. On the morning of 12 February he was walking to Derryvet and had taken a shortcut which took him past Kearney's house. He heard shooting, and out of fear and panic, began to run. While in flight his course joined up with that of Hassett and MacNamara. The former was a stranger to Coote but he knew MacNamara by sight. He denied being a member of Sinn Féin and he asserted that he would not join them if asked, nor would he join the British army. It appears that he accepted giving a false name when captured.

Coote's father also gave evidence, affirming that his son did live with his parents in Ennis. He told the court the prisoner worked as a tailor but business had not been brisk. On the day in question he had been going to visit his mother's family at Derryvet. He was used to visiting them in the holidays. Another witness stated that he had seen Coote walking on the morning of his capture. He was not carrying anything. Coote had asked him the way to Derryvet. This piece of evidence seems to have raised a few eyebrows on the bench: if Coote was visiting his mother's family he would hardly need to ask the way. Character evidence was also called for Coote from a police officer who had known him since he was a small boy.

Kearney relied on four police officers who told the court he was a respectable and industrious farmer who had no known connections with the rebellion. One police officer gave evidence that Kearney had voluntarily surrendered a fowling piece after the proclamation was published.

Kearney's sister who lived with him gave evidence that Kearney was fifty-six and took no part in politics and had recently declined to subscribe to the Volunteers. He had a bad heart. She told the court that Hassett had stayed over the night before but no one else. He had come to do some ploughing and to break a young horse to the plough. Later she had seen her brother struck with a gun. The prisoner Kearney gave evidence corroborating this account.

Kearney's case was supported by Hassett, who said he had given up politics some years before. He had never been 'on the run'. He was at Kearney's that morning when a woman ran in very excited. He heard her say the word 'military'. He went out the back door and saw Kearney falling. He thought he had been shot and he began to run. Other witnesses corroborated the claim that Hassett was an able ploughman who had worked at Kearney's and elsewhere. He had at one time been involved in the Volunteers but had dropped out after the proclamation was issued.

Coote was acquitted of all charges. He was promptly taken before the Summary Court at Kilmallock and tried for giving a false name.[533] Kearney was convicted of harbouring rebels only. MacNamara and Hassett were acquitted of the arms charges but were convicted of conspiracy to levy war. Evidence of prior convictions showed that both men had served time in prison. MacNamara had been sentenced to two years' imprisonment with hard labour in 1917 for drilling and training men contrary to the Defence of the Realm Act. He was released after a lengthy period on hunger strike in 1918. Hassett had a conviction for riot and had also served a short sentence of imprisonment.

MacNamara was sentenced to fifteen years' imprisonment, Hassett to ten years and Kearney to one year. The convicted men were sent to Limerick prison. MacNamara was sent on to Cork male prison, then to Spike and Kilkenny, from where he and others escaped through a tunnel in November 1921.

Many years later MacNamara made a statement to the Bureau of Military History which showed that he was an active Volunteer and so was Coote, who he referred to as a 'scout'. His statement makes no mention of Hassett and Kearney having any involvement.[534]

CHAPTER TWENTY-SIX

John Duane, Ballina Cross, County Cork

The accused was tried at Victoria Barracks on 8 May 1921.[535] He faced two charges: improper possession of an automatic pistol and improper possession of two rounds of ammunition. The accused was represented by counsel, Joseph McCarthy.[536]

The case had been put back for consideration of the accused's mental condition and whether he was fit to plead. A doctor gave evidence for the defence, a specialist. He described the accused as 'a fool and a simpleton. The prisoner was always an imbecile and might one day be dangerous.' When he saw the prisoner at the detention barracks he asked him why he was there. To which the accused replied: 'I don't know.' When pressed, the prisoner said: 'They found an automatic pistol in my pocket.' The accused said he had not fired the gun and would never injure anyone. These statements were delivered in 'a very simple manner'. The accused appeared unsure how many brothers and sisters he had.

An army doctor gave evidence that he had examined the accused and found him fit to stand trial. He answered the doctor's questions intelligently. A lance corporal gave evidence that when the accused was arrested the gun was seized from him. He was questioned by an officer. At the end of the questioning he replied: 'May I go home now sir?' The mother of the accused told the court that he was twenty-nine or thirty. He had not spoken until he was seven. He had attended school but could not be taught anything. He did not attend fairs or work on the farm. He spent his time with her in the kitchen. There was a history of mental illness in the family, she told the court. The report reads: 'The witness then wept', and told the court she had 'never seen a pistol with her son'.

The court then adjourned to report to the convening officer. John Duane was found to be unfit to plead.[537]

CHAPTER TWENTY-SEVEN

Timothy Dennehy, Clash, Kilbrin, County Cork; Cornelius Cunningham, Drominagh, County Cork

This trial arose out of an ambush on a train near Millstreet on the night of 11 February 1921. After the ambush the army captured some documents in a raid which showed the railway line had been watched by a Volunteer for some nights. The *Sixth Division Record of the Rebellion* recounts that: 'On the 11th February this man, having satisfied himself that the military party was one of suitable size for attack, boarded the train with them, and having been joined by a man at Rathcoole station, he held up the engine driver and forced him to stop the train when they had reached the position selected for the attack.'[538]

The army party comprised of one officer and fourteen other ranks from the 1st Battalion of the Royal Fusiliers who were returning by train from Buttevant where many of them had been giving evidence in a court martial. They were en route to their headquarters at Rathmore. These men found themselves trapped in the train, overlooked by an embankment on both sides.

According to an account given to the BMH the attackers had four Lee Enfields, two single-shot rifles and a quantity of revolvers. They intended to offset the lack of firepower by relying on surprise and the favourable ground. As the train came to a halt the attackers lit torches made from dry sacking soaked with kerosene which were thrown down to the train.[539] Firing began and a call for surrender was refused. It appears that the entire military party, barring the officer, were sitting together in a single carriage. So lit up by burning torches and the gas lamps inside the carriages, and confined to a single carriage, the Royal Fusiliers stood little chance of fighting off the attackers hidden above the embankment.

The engagement lasted fifteen minutes. Sergeant Frederick Boxold was killed[540] and another soldier, John Holyome,[541] later died. The officer escaped wounded. Five other soldiers were wounded. The rebel party collected up the arms and ammunition and made a fruitless search for the officer, who had run off into the darkness. First aid was administered to the wounded, who were put back on the train with the other captured soldiers. The train was then sent on its journey.[542]

The army, having departed from the scene, was unable to recover any physical evidence. In these circumstances the only real possibility of prosecution rested on 'information received' and identification evidence, and so it proved.

Cunningham was arrested near Drominagh some weeks later. He was found in a house near his family home. He was partly covered in soot and it may be inferred he had been hiding in a chimney. Dennehy was arrested when the intelligence officer of the Gloucesters received an anonymous letter naming him as an active Volunteer who owned a shotgun. Lieutenant Grazebrook was sanguine about the tip-off. As he put it, these letters might be 'a trap for the army' or just written out of 'spite'.[543]

Dennehy worked for Mrs Elizabeth Nash, who ran a substantial farm at Clash House near Kilbrin. A search was made and nothing was found. He was taken to Buttevant Barracks where he was held in 'the cage'. Most army camps in the 6th Division area had a cage where suspects might be held for some days[544] and picked out by passing soldiers. It was in these circumstances that Dennehy and Cunningham were called out and put on a formal identification parade. Both were picked out by two soldiers.

The trial by military court took place at Victoria Barracks on 9 May.[545] Both men were charged that: 'On or about the 10th February near Millstreet, County Cork, levied war against His Majesty the King, by joining, with certain persons unknown, in an attack with arms, against a detachment of His Majesty's forces.'

Dennehy was represented by C.K. Murphy, a Cork solicitor. Joseph McCarthy, counsel, appeared for Cunningham. Joseph McCarthy stated at the outset that he was not ready for trial because he 'only got instructions on Saturday evening'. The prosecutor responded that 'the court was pressed for time and the witnesses were present from a long distance'.[546] The application for more time was refused.

The first soldier gave evidence that he had been in the second compartment with his sergeant and a number of soldiers. He had seen a light flare up and then the train stopped. A shot was fired and then 'a volley was fired into the carriage from both sides of the embankment'.[547] Four of the soldiers were wounded in the first volley. Fire was returned. The inside of the train was lit by gas lamps. He and the sergeant had fired at the lamps to put the lights out. A number of civilians came down the bank and ordered the soldiers to come out with their hands up. He identified Cunningham and Dennehy as part of this group. Cunningham had a revolver but Dennehy had not. The wounded were put back on the train and the driver was given orders to carry on.

The soldier gave evidence that he had identified both men at a parade at Buttevant Barracks. An officer had conducted the parade, which took place in the compound. He had stood in a nearby hut while the line-up was prepared. Cross-examined, the soldier said that when he left the carriage he thought he was going to be shot. Cunningham had removed his shoulder straps and numerals from his tunic. This took some time. The scene was lit by 'a flare from an oily rag' which was lying burning on the embankment. There were a number of such flares. The rebel party numbered about 200 but only 20 or so came close to him.

A corporal gave evidence about the ambush. He told the court that the soldiers were unable to keep up the resistance because the carriages were lit up: 'They were in the light but the attackers were in the darkness.' He identified Cunningham as the man who had removed numerals from the tunic of soldiers. He identified Dennehy as the man who was seizing rifles. He said he picked both men out at the identification parade at Buttevant and pointed them out to the officer and a sergeant in the presence of the accused. Cross-examined, he said it was 'pitch black' outside the carriage.

Evidence was given by a sergeant about the identification parade at Buttevant Barracks. Witnesses were brought out of a nearby hut and walked down the line of men in the compound. Both accused were identified by two soldiers.

Dennehy told the court that he lived at a farm at Clash near Kilbrin, County Cork, where he worked for the owner, Mrs Nash. He was arrested there but no charge was put to him. He was taken to Buttevant Barracks and put in the compound with the other prisoners. He was put on an identification parade with Cunningham and a number of others. He was picked out by two soldiers. The second soldier was present when the first one made his identifications.

He gave an alibi for 11 February. His employer had sent him to Kanturk on the evening in question. He did some 'messages' and met a friend. They shared a drink and walked their bikes towards home.

He met a girl he was courting at Currabella Cross. He then went home. In the morning he took the milk to the creamery. He produced in evidence the creamery book. Dennehy was cross-examined about his alibi and maintained his account. Here is an extract:

> Q: 'Is the young lady you met that night here today?'
> A: 'She is, sir.'

Having established she was likely to give evidence, further questions followed to establish the detail of the alibi.

> Q: 'What is her name?'
> A: 'Miss ----'
> Q: 'How was she dressed?'
> A: 'She had a shawl and black skirt.'
> Q: 'Had she a blouse on?'
> A: 'She had.'
> Q: 'What colour was it?'
> A: 'I don't know, sir. I didn't go as far as that.'[548]

Dennehy's employer, Mrs Nash, gave evidence. She told the court that Dennehy had worked at her farm for five and a half years. She gave alibi evidence that Dennehy had worked at the farm on the day of the ambush and gone into Kanturk to post letters in the evening. He later returned and had supper and slept at the house as he always did. He was hard working and 'a very satisfactory boy'. She learned of the ambush the next day or on the Sunday at church. When cross-examined she insisted she remembered the day because it was the day before the fair at Kanturk. Millstreet was '14 Irish miles' from her home. Mrs Nash was a 46-year-old widow with two teenage children. She ran a substantial farm and her brother was a justice of the peace. It is likely that her evidence carried some weight.

Four other friends or acquaintances of the accused supported his alibi. An unnamed prisoner gave evidence corroborating Dennehy's account of the identification parade which tended to suggest that the parade had not been supervised and that no steps had been taken to ensure that witnesses viewed the parade separately.

That ended the case of Dennehy. The transcript ends abruptly at this point with the case being adjourned indefinitely. We can piece together the reason from other records. It transpired that Cunningham's witnesses had gone missing, apparently under the impression they were not required. Lieutenant Grazebrook's diary entry reads: 'The witnesses had apparently been present once but had cleared off home.'[549]

Three officers and thirty men from the Gloucester Regiment were detailed to search for the witnesses in the area of Drominagh and Clonbanin in north Cork. This was by no means an easy or safe undertaking as the King's writ no longer ran in this isolated area. Colonel Commandant Cumming had lost his life at Clonbanin some weeks previously. The witnesses, however, were found and brought to barracks and then to Cork 'to swear black was white', as Lieutenant Grazebrook put it.[550]

The trial restarted some weeks later but the record does not survive. We need to go back to the Register to learn that both accused were acquitted. Dennehy was interned for the duration.[551]

Very little is known about these men. Dennehy was twenty-eight, he spoke English and Irish. He was one of ten children raised at an isolated farm at Coolmahane near Kilbrin. Cunningham was twenty-five, a farmer's son from Drominagh. Neither man made a statement to the Bureau of Military History. A review of BMH statements tends to suggest that neither Cunningham nor Dennehy were involved in this ambush[552] but there is insufficient information to make a conclusive judgment.

CHAPTER TWENTY-EIGHT

Michael Casey, Newmarket on Fergus, County Clare

The accused was charged with the murder of John Reilly near Newmarket on Fergus. The deceased was found shot dead close to the village. A card pinned to the body stated he had been shot as a spy.[553]

There is evidence that a mail raid on the Limerick to Ennis train took place in the spring of 1921. These raids were usually directed at stealing the mail with a view to identifying possible informants. According to one account, this mail raid resulted in the interception of a letter from the RIC to John Reilly. The letter suggested he had given information to the RIC.[554] An officer told the Military Court of Inquiry that there was 'no truth' in the suggestion that the deceased had given information to the security forces.[555] He was described by Sergeant Harrison as a 'steady, sober kind of man, in constant employment'.[556]

Reilly was known to be a loyalist and was the secretary of the Old Comrades Association at Ennis.[557] He worked as a labourer in the quarries and part time for Lord Inchiquin at Dromoland Castle in the kitchen garden. At the time of his death he was forty years old. He had fought in the Boer War and in the Great War. He left a widow and a twelve-year-old daughter.

The killing was witnessed by a local priest, Father William Kennedy, who was stopped on his journey by a number of armed men and asked to administer the last rites to a man. Father Kennedy was kept waiting until late at night when some of the men returned with their prisoner. Father Kennedy heard the confession of John Reilly, who was then blindfolded and forced to kneel in the roadway and shot to death. This is the context in which the trial took place.

Casey, a tailor by trade, was charged with the murder of Reilly. He was tried at New Barracks, Limerick on 16 May. He entered a not guilty plea. He was represented by H. O'Brien Moran, who was then an experienced and respected solicitor with a busy practice in Limerick.[558]

Mary Reilly, the widow, gave evidence that on the night in question she, her husband and their daughter had retired to bed. There was a knock at the door: 'Who is there?' A voice answered: 'Police.' The door was opened and six men came in. All were masked. Only one man, a tall man, spoke. He told her husband to put his boots and clothes on and to 'bring some holy water as it would be wanted'. The man told her that her husband would not be harmed and he would be back within the hour. They left. Mrs Reilly and her daughter stayed with a neighbour until morning. She told the court she could not identify any of the men. They all wore big coats and masks. In reply to questions by the court, she said that she could not say who the men were. She had told the police she thought the accused was one of the men but she could not now say.

An RIC man told the court that the accused had been interviewed. He had given an account of where he was on the night. No further evidence was adduced. Mr Moran made a submission that there was no case to answer and in passing expressed his regret to the widow. His opponent replied that Mr Moran 'was justified in making his application'. The accused was acquitted. A review of BMH statements suggests Casey was not involved in the killing.

This is one of four cases tried by a military court where a civilian gave evidence for the Crown. Tellingly, this witness retracted what she told the police. We cannot know for certain whether she did so because she thought she was unsure of her evidence or because she had been threatened or was simply too fearful to give evidence. It is a wretched story. At the Ennis Quarter Sessions Judge Bodkin made an order for a substantial payment to Mrs Reilly and expressed his regret at 'the brutal and horrible murder of her husband'.[559]

CHAPTER TWENTY-NINE

Edward Punch and Timothy Murphy, Limerick

The weekly report to Cabinet shows that at about 9 pm on 23 April 1921 three unarmed RIC men were walking on Carey's Road in Limerick. They were attacked with Mills bombs and revolver fire.[560] Constable Redfern was injured and Constable McCann received a serious head wound.

Punch and Murphy were brought to trial at New Barracks in Limerick on 17 May. They were charged with levying war against His Majesty. They were also charged with improper possession of revolvers on the occasion of their arrest. Both accused pleaded not guilty. They were represented by Patrick Lynch KC and R.J. Kinahan.[561]

The central issues on the charge of levying war were whether the accused had been correctly identified and whether the identification parades were contaminated.[562] On the charge of possession of firearms: the guns had been seized from the lodgings of the accused, a multi-occupancy address. On this charge the issue was whether possession of the guns could safely be imputed to the accused.

Constable Redfern told the court that he was stationed at Boherbuoy Barracks in Limerick. He and two other officers were going to a dance. They were in plain clothes and unarmed. One of their number stopped at a barber shop in Edward Street for a shave and arranged with the other two to meet in O'Donnell's pub. They stopped for a drink at O'Donnell's and went on to Noonan's where a man came in who looked at them in a 'suspicious' way and left. They left the pub and separated briefly to look for the other officer. The witness, who was now on Carey's Road, then noticed that people 'were getting off the street quickly'. He saw the other officers about 80 yards away and saw 'a bomb thrown at their feet'. He saw the constable 'fall to the ground'. While he was waiting to see how his friends were, he was fired on from behind. He was wounded 'in the left calf'. Another shot was fired but missed. He turned and saw a man with a revolver with 'a long barrel'. He was six yards away. He 'would never forget him'. He identified Murphy to the court: 'That's the man, sir.' He was the man he had seen earlier at Noonan's pub. The witness 'made a run for it' in the direction of the railway station and he was 'bombed' as he ran.

As he ran he saw a man coming out of King's laneway. This man threw a bomb at him. This man he identified as Punch. The blast caused him to stumble and he ran on pursued by a number of men. He managed to escape and make his way to hospital. He made his statement some days later. He picked out both accused at an identification parade at William Street Barracks.

Constable Redfern, when cross-examined, stated that he had not been drinking that day. He had one glass of stout at O'Donnell's and another at Noonan's. He said he was shot a few seconds after the first bomb was thrown. He did not see Murphy fire the shot which wounded him and he was stumbling when he saw Murphy fire the second shot. After his release from hospital he was taken to William Street Barracks for the identification parade. He was accompanied by a sergeant. Before the parade he was kept in a room with opaque windows. The facts of the case were not discussed nor was he shown any photo of the accused or given a description of their clothing. There were a dozen men on the parade. He was told to look over the men carefully to see if any of them were those who attacked him. If he was able to make an identification he was to place his hand on the man's shoulder but not to speak. He said he did not notice that the two men he picked out had several days' growth or that the others were clean shaven. He did not notice any blood on the clothing of the men he picked out.

The report then shows an intervention from the President directed at the witness: 'I am not satisfied with the way you are answering the questions. You are not answering civilly and I expect a civil answer to counsel.'

Cross-examination continued. The witness said he had not conferred with the other witness on the day he made his identification. In answers to questions from the President the witness said he was in hospital for seven days and he was visited there. He told one of his visitors he could identify his assailants but he did not provide any description. In answers to questions from the Judge Advocate he said that the lighting was 'bright night and not dusk'. He had seen both accused previously in the area but not together.

A second officer gave evidence that he had identified Murphy at an identification parade. He had seen him at Noonan's bar when he appeared to be observing who was in the bar. He had seen this man in the district a number of times before. He saw Murphy pursue the first witness and he saw Punch throw a bomb at him from King's Lane. He was cross-examined and accepted that he had seen both accused after their arrest and before the identification parade. It was put to him that when he saw them, he said: 'Who are these two?' He denied saying this. It was put to him that he said: 'I suppose ye're two of the fellows that bombed us in Carey's Road.' This was also denied by the officer.

The witness maintained that he had not conferred with the first witness while awaiting the identification parade. He did not realise the parade was in connection with the men who he had seen under arrest at the barracks. He did not see the prisoners exercising in the yard.

Another police witness gave evidence of the arrest of the accused during a search of the Ahabeg area near Caherconlish. Both were found sharing a bed. Both gave false names. Also found during the search were two revolvers; one was 'nickel plated' and the other was described as a 'Webley'. A senior RIC officer gave evidence that each of the accused was cautioned and questioned individually on the day of the arrest.

Patrick Lynch KC submitted that the interviews were not admissible. A number of grounds were put forward. The report on this part of the case is entirely obscure save that the court excluded the interviews. It is now apparent that this vagueness arose because the newspaper was unwilling to report allegations of misconduct by the RIC. The review later conducted by the JAG refers to serious ill-treatment of the accused as an established fact 'most regrettable and unfortunate' and it is a strong inference that this is why the interviews were excluded.[563] This concluded the prosecution case.

Murphy gave evidence that he had served in the army and had been wounded in the Great War. He gave evidence that prior to 23 April his house had been searched by police and threats had been made against him. On the night of the 23rd he had not stayed at home that night and he did not learn of the Carey's Road bombing until the next day. He was arrested on the 29th where he had slept. He did not see the police find any revolver. He did hear an officer ask who the revolvers belonged to. He and his co-accused were then 'bashed about' with the guns. A constable arrived and asked who they were. He heard the constable say: 'Were these the two —— who threw bombs in Carey's Road?' They were then taken to Bohermore where they were beaten and kicked and thrown into a dyke. At the barracks the constable had said: 'If you were never there I will put the rope around your neck.' The next day they were paraded and saw the two officers who had come to identify them looking through a window before the parade. He said the other men on parade were freshly shaven and therefore different in appearance.

Punch gave evidence that he was a 'sawyer' by trade. He denied any part in the bombing or possession of a gun. He had not slept at home for many weeks because he had heard that the police were looking for him to shoot him. They had apparently found a 'drill book' during a search of his home. He did not repeat the allegations of ill-treatment made by his co-accused. It is probable that this was because he had a prior conviction which under the rules governing criminal trials at that time would go before the court if he attacked the character of a prosecution witness. In fact the *Circular Memoranda*[564] confined the circumstances in which the prosecution could adduce evidence of bad character to where the accused asserted his own good character. Plainly, defence counsel were not aware of this provision. It has been argued elsewhere in this book that the rules governing trial by military court were not published or disseminated to defence counsel. This aspect of the trial tends to confirm that view.

The men were convicted on both charges. Punch had a prior conviction for taking part in an armed attack on an RIC patrol in 1917. He had served a sentence for that.[565] Both men were sentenced to death by shooting.[566] In fact the prisoners were very fortunate because the sentences were commuted to life imprisonment for reasons which are remarkable. The JAG advised that convictions might be confirmed although he expressed the view that identification procedures should be conducted in a way that was not open to criticism.[567] He also intimated the officers responsible for ill-treating the prisoners should be prosecuted and the executions deferred or commuted so that the prisoners could give evidence.

The case papers then went back to Macready, who commuted sentence of death on both men to imprisonment for life. The credit for commutation of sentence was attributed to the efforts of Father Bernard Vaughan, a prominent English Jesuit[568] and also claimed[569] by Captain Redmond MP, the Home Ruler, but it appears the army was rarely influenced by outside interventions and took their own course.

The prisoners were released in January 1922. They did not dispute their involvement in the Carey's Road bombing.[570]

John O'Sullivan, Abbeyfeale, County Limerick

The prisoner was tried at Victoria Barracks on 20 May 1921.[571] He was charged with (i) being improperly in possession of arms, namely an automatic pistol and revolver; (ii) improper possession of ammunition and (iii) being improperly in possession of a document entitled *Night Fighting*. He was represented by Patrick Kelly, counsel, of Ardagh, County Limerick.[572] He pleaded not guilty to the charges.

An army officer gave evidence that he was leading a military patrol passing through Knocknadike on 24 April. The witness was in the leading car which came upon a trench in the road. Five civilians were seen running away. The army gave chase and called upon the civilians to halt. They did not do so and fire was opened on the running men. The accused was seen to discard an item as he ran. The accused halted and was captured and searched and found on him was a book and a slip of paper entitled 'Numbers of Enemy Transport Cars'. A search was made and a haversack was found. It contained an automatic and ammunition. The haversack was inscribed with the name Seán Sullivan. A belt was also found inscribed '2nd West Limerick Brigade'. As it transpired, the prisoner was from west Limerick. He was asked why he ran and said he was frightened.

In cross-examination the officer stated that the other men had also been captured but they were not in possession of arms. All five men had run from a cottage. And, he added, if the accused was innocent he would not have run. The witness added that he had seen the accused throw something away as he ran.

> 'Could you see what the accused threw away?'
> 'No.'
> 'Might it have been anything at all?'
> 'Yes. It might.'[573]

A second witness, a soldier, told the court that he had chased the accused for about 400 yards and fired upon him. At some point the accused had stooped as if to discard something. After capture a search was made of the area where the accused had stooped and some items were recovered. These were the haversack and other items including a Sam Browne belt and a revolver holster. A third witness gave evidence that the pistol recovered was loaded and in good working order. The prosecution case was closed at this point.

Defence counsel applied for an adjournment until the following day because his witnesses were unable to be at court owing to transport difficulties. The President ordered that counsel press on with calling the accused. A fifteen-minute adjournment was permitted to allow counsel to consult with the accused.

After this short break the accused gave evidence as follows. He told the court that he was twenty-one years old and was an assistant manager in a creamery. On 24 April he went to mass at Tournafulla. Afterwards he stopped off at a 'hurling field' for a short time. His boot was hurting him and he stopped again at a labourer's cottage and took a tack out of his boot. He was about to leave when he heard the lorries and saw the soldiers run into a trench on the road. He ran and he saw five other men running in front of him. He stooped at one point because they were being fired on. He ran along the main road for half a mile and then turned into a lane where he saw another man running. Shortly after, he saw three soldiers. He tried to run but shots were fired upon him and he put his hands up. He denied being armed or having the holster and belt. He accepted the slip of paper and the book on night fighting was found on him. He said he had found these a few days before in a ditch and he had kept them out of curiosity. He said he was not a violent man and was not a member of any political organisation. He added that when he left the hurling pitch he had met five or six men but he was afraid to mention their names.

He was cross-examined and denied being a member of the 2nd West Limerick Brigade. He accepted that he knew it was illegal to carry arms but said he did not know it was illegal to have seditious documents. He was afraid to give the names of the other men for fear they would be arrested. The accused maintained that he ran because he was afraid the soldiers would think he dug the trench and he might be beaten.

Defence counsel addressed the court on the facts and the character of the accused: 'He bore a good character.' The application for an adjournment does not seem to have been renewed. O'Sullivan was sentenced to death by shooting on each charge.[574]

The process of confirmation began at once. The speed of the process is remarkable. The case papers went to London for consideration by the Judge Advocate General, Cassel, who advised on 25 May, only five days after the trial. In this case, however, Cassel declined to endorse the conviction. He noted that there had been an application by the accused to adjourn the trial to call witnesses and the application had been refused. The trial record did not show who the witnesses were or why they were not at court.

The case papers hint at an untold story. The father of the accused was Patrick O'Sullivan, a 57-year-old farmer. He was a father of six, of whom the prisoner was the youngest. It appears that he was present at the trial and we can infer that he had organised and paid for legal representation for his son. He had also arranged for witnesses who had failed to show at his son's trial. Patrick O'Sullivan had sat in the public gallery waiting anxiously for the witnesses, who did not come. He watched his youngest son convicted of a capital charge. With the persistence that every father bestows on a wayward son, he composed himself and wrote a letter which he managed to persuade an officer to put in the case papers. The letter stated that there were three witnesses for his son who had been unable to attend the trial because the train services had been 'dislocated'. Patrick O'Sullivan maintained that the witnesses could have given evidence on the issue of whether his son was armed or not.

There is no doubt that the train services were badly affected by the war. General Macready's reports to Cabinet show the rail service was disrupted by raids on the mail, sleepers torn up and trains diverted or attacked.[575] A rail journey from west Limerick to Cork city could be very difficult.

The Judge Advocate General's note indicated a degree of scepticism but he directed that an inquiry should be made into what was said at the trial about the reasons for the witnesses not being present, and if there had been a genuine reason for the non-attendance of witnesses, a new trial should be ordered.

It is not clear if a new trial was ordered, but Patrick O'Sullivan's letter introduced a life-saving delay. A few weeks later, executions were stayed pending the decision of the House of Lords in Clifford and Sullivan. This prisoner was released in January 1922.

CHAPTER THIRTY-ONE

Jack Shine, Athea, County Limerick

Jack John Shine was tried at New Barracks, Limerick on 28 May. He faced a single charge, namely that on 11 May he was improperly in possession of an automatic pistol and nineteen rounds of ammunition. He denied the charge. Shine was represented by counsel.[576]

Details of this trial are very sparse. Evidence was called from a parish priest who told the court that the accused was 'mentally afflicted'. He did not consider Shine responsible for his actions. Shine was convicted and sentenced to death by shooting.[577]

Conviction and sentence were reviewed by the JAG, who directed that the conviction could not be impeached but that sentence of death should not be carried out until a medical report from the prison doctor had been seen.[578] There is no record of the result of this examination but Shine was released in January 1922.[579]

CHAPTER THIRTY-TWO

O'Connell and Cregan, Limerick

Michael O'Connell and Patrick Cregan were both charged with being in possession of a revolver, eleven rounds of revolver ammunition and one round of automatic pistol ammunition at Newtown on 22 May. They were tried three days later at New Barracks, Limerick.[580] They were represented by Robert Kinahan, counsel.

The report of the trial is very brief but it is noteworthy for the way in which the court dealt with an allegation that one of the prisoners had confessed after ill-treatment.

An RIC sergeant told the court that he was leading a motorised patrol from Limerick to Ballysimon and back. While going through Newtown he saw the accused leave the road and go into a field. They were called upon to halt and they obeyed but before doing so, O'Connell 'dropped a revolver on the grass'. Following a search, ammunition was found on Cregan. It appears Cregan made a confession after capture.

It was suggested in cross-examination of the sergeant that Cregan had been questioned by a police officer while lying on the ground. The officer, it was suggested, was threatening to shoot the accused if he did not tell where the gun was. The sergeant denied the allegation: 'These allegations have created a very bad feeling against the police. I had not to restrain at any time any member of the patrol.'[581]

Cregan was called on the admissibility of the confession. He told the court that after his arrest he had been struck with the butt end of a rifle and questioned. He was beaten with a rifle while on the ground. He said that a constable had come over and put a cartridge into his rifle and said if he did not admit to where he had got the gun and ammunition he would shoot him. Cregan then made admissions. He also volunteered that the sergeant was not present when this happened.

A number of constables present at court were paraded. Cregan pointed out two who he alleged had struck him and threatened to shoot him. One of the constables identified was then called by the court. The constable gave evidence that he had seen the accused being searched and saw something seized from Cregan. He spoke to the accused while he was being searched. He asked Cregan where he got the ammunition.

> The Judge Advocate: 'Did you do anything else to him?'

In reply to this question the constable said he struck the accused with his rifle.

> The Judge Advocate: 'I rule that the statement made by the prisoner is not admissible.'[582]

This ruling reflected the common law rule that a statement made by an accused was not admissible in evidence unless it was shown to be voluntary, that is, not obtained by fear of prejudice or hope of advantage held out by a person in authority.[583]

Another police sergeant proved the finding of the ammunition on Cregan. Both accused gave evidence. They were convicted. Both were sentenced to twelve years' penal servitude.[584]

CHAPTER THIRTY-THREE

Mallow Barracks

The Mallow Barracks raid resulted in the trial of six men on a charge alleging the murder of Sergeant Gibbs of the 17th Lancers. This was a court martial under the ROIA and it is the only such court martial in this study. It is included because it took place in the Martial Law Area and by a side wind it provides some insight into the fairness of trials by the Military Court.

In the summer of 1920 a company of the 17th Lancers, 'the Death of Glories', was posted to Mallow, a market town just over twenty miles north of Cork. The Lancers had been deployed with their horses, for which there was little operational need, and this cavalry unit would later be seconded to carry out hazardous amphibious operations in the west of Ireland. But first they were to suffer a different indignity: Mallow Barracks would be the only military barracks to be captured by rebels during the war.

The outer wall fronted onto Barrack Street, close to Main Street. It was flanked on two sides by houses and on the third by a field which fell away to the Blackwater. Around the barracks square there was a magazine, a forge, a guardroom and the soldiers' quarters with a cook-house behind it. The barrack warden's house also looked out onto the square. The garden was used as 'horse standings'. The barracks were occupied by thirty-five men and an officer, Lieutenant McCreery.
The regimental record recounts what took place:

> Shortly after 9 am on the 28th September, most of the men and horses had gone to exercise, a civilian appeared at the gate, which was kept locked, and stated he had a letter which was to be delivered to the barrack warden, which was to be delivered personally. After examining the letter through the peephole, the sentry opened the gate and was immediately overpowered by a second man. Immediately about 30 Sinn Féiners, having scaled the wall on the river side, shot down Sergeant Gibbs who was inspecting some horses that had not gone out. Meanwhile two painters who

> had been engaged in painting the walls of the guardroom … produced revolvers and held up the guard.

The painters were Dick Willis and Jack Bolster, who were helped by a third man posing as the clerk of the works.[585] From a variety of sources it can be said with certainty that the man at the gate was Ernie O'Malley[586] and it is relevant to the trial to recall that O'Malley had red hair and a pale complexion.[587]

The sentry later stated: 'The main gate was then open and I saw a lot more civilians. There would be about thirty altogether inside the barracks.'[588]

First aid was administered to Sergeant Gibbs by O'Malley, while the other captured soldiers were herded into the square where three cars were pulling up. The magazine door was smashed and ransacked and equipment and guns were loaded on to the cars. Two Hotchkiss machine guns, thirty rifles, a quantity of handguns and ammunition were seized, and on one account a quantity of cavalry lances were also taken.[589]

The barracks were set alight and the raiders fled. One soldier had been left free to tend to the wounded sergeant. He released the others and the flames were quickly put out. According to the regimental record the entire raid lasted only fifteen minutes. The first the town knew of the raid was the sight of a trooper galloping his horse through Main Street to raise the alarm. Lieutenant McCreery was found and rode back to barracks, where Sergeant Gibbs had died.[590]

33.1 Barry Sullivan, solicitor for many of the prisoners tried by military court including Ronayne and Mulcahy, Moylan, and also those tried in connection with the Mallow Barracks Raid. Courtesy of Helen Sullivan.

Reinforcements were summoned from Buttevant, some seven miles distant, but help was delayed by a combination of an obstructive telephonist[591] and roadblocks. As it is put in the regiment history: 'Great care had been taken in the preparation of the coup. At least two hundred men were so employed, mainly in blocking all access to the village; trees were felled to interrupt communications and all wires cut.'

The *History of the 17th Lancers* records an enigmatic entry: 'That night Mallow knew the word fear. Though the troops who had suffered took no part. Discipline prevailing. Mallow was in flames.'[592] It appears that soldiers from Buttevant and Fermoy were involved in the reprisal, and one of the Lancers' officers who later wrote about the raid candidly observed that although 'the NCOs had been excused from any involvement', he was quite sure they had taken a full part in the looting and burning. It was a dry summer night and the town was lit up by fires, which burned all night. Cleeve's creamery, the town hall, Williams' steam mills, Hanover's hotel, and a number of shops and homes were destroyed.[593]

Events at Mallow made an immediate impact at Westminster, where the sacking of Mallow was about to become part of a wider debate on reprisals. That night Sir Henry Wilson, Chief of the Imperial General Staff, wrote in his diary:

> The report tonight that Mallow had been sacked after the murder of one of the sergeants of the 17th Lancers may well prove the 17th Lancers had sacked the town. All this was terribly dangerous. What was quite evident to me after this long talk was that neither Lloyd George nor Bonar Law had the faintest idea of what to do.[594]

Sir Henry Wilson's comments on events at Mallow were part of a longer speech to Lloyd George and Bonar Law:

> I told them what I thought of reprisals by the 'Black and Tans', and how this must lead to chaos and ruin. Lloyd George danced about and was angry but I never budged. I pointed out that these reprisals were being carried out without anyone being responsible; men were being murdered, houses burnt, villages wrecked.

Within weeks, the aftermath of the raid and the frantic search for suspects became part of a wider argument when the opposition at Westminster, under Asquith, brought a motion of censure against the government.[595] The motion failed and the spiral of killing continued.

The Court Martial

The body of Sergeant Gibbs was returned to England and carried on a horse-drawn carriage through his home town of Bedford, where the High Street was lined four deep with mourners.

Back in Cork, six men were brought to trial by court martial under the Restoration of Order in Ireland Act. Those men were Owen Harold (Bank Place, Mallow), John Murphy (Fair Street, Mallow), David Buckley (Farren), Denis Barter (Mourne Abbey), Daniel McCarthy (Mourne Abbey) and Timothy Breen (Lombardstown). We know little about them save that they were all single, all local. Harold was the oldest, aged thirty, he had a conviction for possession of a firearm. He was described by a local RIC inspector as 'a very bad lot'.[596] The others were in their early twenties. Murphy had been a railway porter at Mallow station and had been sacked for refusing to handle munitions. It is relevant to the trial to record that he was young, thin and, like O'Malley, had red hair.

The court martial was delayed when the Lancers were transferred to Cork and a grenade was thrown into one of their lorries, injuring a number of witnesses. Subsequently, Lieutenant McCreery was killed in an ambush[597] and this caused further delays until late May 1921.

The court martial took place at Victoria Barracks in Cork.[598] All of the Military Court trials were prosecuted 'in house' by the 6th Division but most of the more serious ROIA trials were prosecuted by senior counsel brought over from England. Although the case was prepared by captain F.E. Young, this court martial was prosecuted by R.E. Otter, a barrister in chambers at Garden Court at the Temple. Otter was a decorated veteran of the Western Front, who was often instructed to prosecute these trials. Otter came over with Kenneth Marshall, a barrister who had been appointed Judge Advocate for the trial. Marshall had acted as Judge Advocate over many years; back in 1914 he had tried Carl Lody, the first German spy to be shot during the Great War. Marshall and Otter travelled by 'first class smoking compartment' to the Holyhead ferry. Once at Dún Laoghaire they were picked up by a destroyer and taken down to Cork.[599]

The identity of the other officers trying this case is not known, save that H.M. Meyler, the legal officer for the 6th Division, acted as the 'legal member'.[600] The men, however, were all represented by a formidable array of legal talent: Albert Wood KC, Patrick Lynch KC and John Bourke.[601]

Counsel for the accused applied to stay the trial because of non-compliance with the rules of procedure relating to the taking of the summary of evidence. As we have seen elsewhere, the summary of evidence was recognised as a significant safeguard for the accused against prosecutorial misconduct and also in knowing the case the accused had to meet.

The following facts emerged. The summary of evidence had been taken some months before, in November. Captain F.E. Young, who had conduct of case preparation, had undertaken to supply copies for the summary of evidence to Barry Sullivan, who acted for most of the men. He failed to do so[602] and it appears the reason for this was that a decision had been made to take a more complete summary of evidence at a later date. Captain Young also agreed in writing to ensure that Sullivan would be present when any further summary of evidence was taken. In fact Captain Young reneged on his undertaking and a further summary of evidence was taken without notice being given to Sullivan and he was not present.[603] As Captain Young later admitted in cross-examination, when the taking of a fresh summary of evidence took place he destroyed part of a summary of evidence which related to the accused, Buckley, which on one view was unhelpful to the Crown. It appears that Buckley seized the document, saying words to the effect of: 'My solicitor will want to see that.' In fact, as it transpired, the revised summary for this soldier showed that he identified Murphy coming through the guardroom door; at the trial, he insisted this man was Buckley. As will be seen, evidence subsequently came to light that Buckley was not involved in the raid on Mallow Barracks.[604] It does seem, therefore, that there may have been some substance in this dispute.

Captain Young told the court that he had taken back the summary from Buckley because it had the name of a witness upon it and he simply wished to re-write the statement to put the evidence in chronological order. He said he had not notified the solicitor of the date for the taking of the summary of evidence because 'it was not the rule for solicitors to be present on such occasions'. The combination of the failure to permit the solicitor to be present and the destruction of a statement taken from a witness was unfortunate to say the least. All that can be said with certainty is that the court had Young called and accepted his explanation. It was in these circumstances that the court refused the application to stay the trial but ordered the prosecution to disclose the summary of evidence created the previous November.

The Prosecution Case

After a short adjournment for the discarded summary to be produced, the court then started to hear evidence. The sentry told the court: 'There was a knock on the gate. The witness looked through the hole and saw a man with an envelope in his hand. He said something and the witness opened the gate about six inches.'[605] The door was forced. The witness identified Murphy as the man at the gate.

When the door was forced, the sentry was 'caught around the neck by Murphy, and another man seized his rifle. Another man fired some shots.' The sentry, now overpowered, was marched out on the square: there were about thirty civilians armed with service rifles and revolvers. Civilians were taking arms, equipment and clothing out of the barracks and onto the square.

The barracks warden told the court that he was with Sergeant Gibbs. He saw 'the sentry beckon the sergeant and the sergeant take a few steps when there were shots fired'. The warden then 'took cover in the wc'.[606]

The NCO in charge of the guardroom told the court he 'heard shots ... then saw a man in Khaki stumble and fall just beside the guardroom door; two men rushed inside the guardroom and fired two shots and said "Put them up".' The NCO added that he was taken into the square, where he saw a large number of armed civilians. Some men were carrying arms and equipment out of the gate and loading a car. He remembered one man who gave orders, recalling: 'He had a watch in one hand and an automatic pistol in the other.'

The summary of evidence taken from the late Lieutenant McCreery was read to the court. The lieutenant's statement showed that 'a detachment from his regiment took horses to exercise about four miles from Mallow Barracks; as they were coming home about 10 am a private galloped up to him and made a report; they trotted back to barracks, arriving at 10.15; he saw Sergeant Gibbs lying dead and also the woodwork of the barracks was slightly burned.'[607]

In this case all the men, save Buckley, were arrested in circumstances which suggested that they were Volunteers. Murphy was caught out after curfew and McCarthy and Harold were found with arms. As to Barter, some uniforms and equipment were found at his address. All this provided some support for the Crown case but ultimately the case against each man turned on the correctness of identification evidence, which was disputed at their court martial. In the case of Barter, Harold and McCarthy, the Crown case rested on a single identifying witness.

McCarthy was identified by a soldier as a man he had seen at the barracks 'with a grey cloth cap pulled well down over his eyes'. In the case of Murphy, he was identified by the sentry as the man at the gate with a letter and by a number of other soldiers. Buckley was identified by two soldiers as being in the barracks.

A number of parades took place. The method of conducting the parade was to assemble a number of suspects and bring in soldiers one at a time to carry out identifications. Several prosecution witnesses stated that officers or NCOs had attended the parades and taken notes of the results. Despite requests from the defence, these potential witnesses were not produced, nor were their notes. This was an important shortcoming since it was well recognised even at that time that what an identification witness says when he makes an identification may be crucial: it may assign a role to the suspect or may indicate doubt or confusion. A further shortcoming was that all the accused, save Murphy, had been arrested by the soldiers who later identified them. These soldiers had been responsible for transporting the men to Mallow Barracks and later to Cork for the taking of a summary of evidence.[608]

The Defence Case

The Restoration of Order In Ireland Act did not permit the accused to give evidence in their own defence and therefore each of the men were confined to making an unsworn statement in their defence.

Denis Barter called alibi evidence from two national school teachers, Jer Cronin and Daniel Barry, who told the court they were on their way to the schoolhouse at Analeentha when they had seen Barter repairing a bridge some six miles from Mallow. This alibi evidence was supported by Robert Love, a local magistrate. Love was a former RIC man. According to his evidence, he was a vociferous opponent of Sinn Féin and was the only justice of the peace at Mallow not to resign in the face of 'a campaign of intimidation'. He said he recalled the morning of the raid because court adjourned early as a mark of respect for Sergeant Gibbs.

Owen Harold called evidence from his employer that he was working at his farm, 'stacking corn' some eight miles from Mallow, on the morning of the raid.

John Murphy called Eyre Tarrant, who ran a grocery shop at the junction of Fair Street and Main Street. He told the court that Murphy had been in his shop, reading a newspaper and helping out when news came of the raid. They went to the front of the shop and saw 'a soldier on horseback galloping through the town'.

Other supporting evidence was called: John Neal of Chapel Street and Maurice O'Brien who ran a farm near Ironmines. One final witness was Mary Ellen Walsh, who lived in Barrack Street opposite the gate. She told the court she had just come back from Mass. She was standing in the road and witnessed the man at the gate, the sentry being overpowered, other men coming up in support and the raid unfolding in front of her. She knew Murphy, she said. He was not the man at the gate, nor did she see him at the barracks.

McCarthy also relied on evidence from Robert Love JP to the effect that Love had seen McCarthy with a horse and cart at Mourne Abbey railway station on the morning of the raid. The evidence of the magistrate was supported by Mr Mannion, the station master, who told the court that McCarthy had been taking delivery of a load of coal. Paperwork relating to the transaction was produced. This evidence was supported by some neighbours of the accused.

Breen called alibi evidence that showed that on the morning of the raid he was at home early in the morning and later at work at the creamery in Lombardstown in the company of his manager, Joseph Healy, and sub-manager, John Looney. He also called his brother Jerome, who had served in the US army on the Western Front and had just returned from America. Breen also called two RIC men and an RIC sergeant, who gave strong evidence of character.

Buckley called his brother, cousin, a local farmer, Edward Lenihan, and his son to substantiate an alibi that he was at home on the farm 'cutting corn' or 'attending to some pigs' on the morning of the raid. Buckley's brother also gave evidence that he had stood on two parades and had seen two men picked out who were not on trial. Buckley's case was that he had 'a halt' (a limp); this fact was not disputed, although none of the identifying witnesses had described a man with a limp.

Summing Up

As to the summing up by the Judge Advocate, Kenneth Marshall, although the directions might not pass legal scrutiny today, applying the standards of the time it was full, fair and correctly set out the law and even mildly rebuked prosecution counsel for taking a bad point against the accused. Where the case against a prisoner rested on a single identifying witness the Judge Advocate directed the court as follows:

> It is my duty to warn you that where there is only one witness against the accused you should act with very great caution before

> accepting that evidence and convicting the accused, unless you are actually satisfied that the man had the fullest opportunity (to see the accused) and there could reasonably be no mistake in what he was telling you.[609]

The Judge Advocate finished with these words: 'If there was any doubt in relation to any of the accused it was their duty to find the accused not guilty.'

Verdict and Sentence

The court retired before returning to deliver a not guilty verdict in respect of Breen only. Denis Barter, Owen Harold, Daniel McCarthy, John Murphy and David Buckley were convicted and sentenced to death. No recommendations for mercy were made. The duration of deliberations of the court was just forty-five minutes. It was hardly sufficient to deliberate on the fate of one man on a capital charge, let alone six.

The death sentences on the men could not be carried out until the review by the Judge Advocate General in London and confirmation by General Macready. The papers would not go to the Judge Advocate General until the notes of evidence were typed up. The solicitor for some of the men, Barry Sullivan, persuaded the typists to delay the typing for as long as possible while he and Albert Wood prepared a petition for clemency and an affidavit to support a challenge to the verdict in the High Court.

Albert Wood KC drafted a petition asking that the men be spared the death penalty. The King's prerogative of mercy rested with the Lord Lieutenant and Governor General, Viscount FitzAlan of Derwent.[610] The petition argued that the evidence was uncertain and that in any event the men should be spared death because they had been in custody for seven months at the detention barracks in Cork where there had been many executions by shooting within earshot of the prisoners, who had suffered 'an agony of mind'.

The petition went off to Dublin Castle. Sullivan crossed over to London, where he met various backbenchers, notably Captain Wedgewood Benn and Commander Kenworthy. He circulated the petition and prevailed on them to intervene on behalf of his clients. While Sullivan was conducting this campaign, the JAG advised that the convictions might be confirmed in early July but the Truce intervened only days later.[611] There were no more executions, although the prisoners remained under sentence of death until Christmas of that year.[612]

Sullivan's affidavit in support of the challenge to the verdicts is important because he made two key points about the role of Colonel Meyler, who was the legal member of the court. Meyler was also the legal officer of the 6th Division and the prosecution of these men was being undertaken by his subordinates. In the circumstances, Sullivan argued, the legal member was not unbiased.

Second, Sullivan asserted that Colonel Meyler subjected the alibi witnesses to close cross-examination but did not test the evidence of prosecution witnesses in the same way. The record of the evidence is not sufficiently detailed to evaluate this point nor is it mentioned in other accounts of the trial.[613] But it may be that Sullivan hit on a significant point. In the *Record of the Rebellion*[614] there is a letter written by Bryan Kelly, a prisoner from Mallow awaiting trial at the detention barracks. Kelly's letter was intercepted and found to contain a request to his friends on the outside to help set up a false alibi for John Murphy, who was then awaiting trial. It is inconceivable that Meyler, who was the legal officer for the 6th Division, did not know about this letter. If he did, it must have affected his view of the evidence.

But what of the other officers on the court? The evidence in this trial consisted almost entirely of identification evidence of questionable reliability. A review of the evidence suggests that the parades were not well conducted, by contemporary standards. There remains a question as to why the officers conducting this trial accepted so readily the identification evidence. It should be noted that officers serving in Ireland received an intelligence briefing on the prevalence of false alibis.[615] The army cannot be criticised for briefing officers in this way, but it may have made a dispassionate evaluation of evidence more difficult.

Many years later John Murphy made a BMH witness statement.[616] He had been identified as the man at the gate with the letter. He did not dispute that he was involved in the raid but his role involved opening up the town hall for the raiders in the early hours and later carrying out wire cutting near the town centre. There is every reason to accept this as a reliable account because there is a wealth of evidence that the man at the gate was O'Malley. He, therefore, had been wrongly identified as one of the raiders in the barracks. Perhaps for no better reason than that he, like O'Malley, was a young man with red hair and a pale complexion.

Owen Harold recounted his memory of the raid in his BMH witness statement. In general terms, there is no reason to doubt his account and it is consistent with other statements.[617] He had taken part in the raid but he had never been in the barracks because he had been leading a party of Volunteers engaged in blocking roads to the south of Mallow. He had therefore been wrongly identified as one of the raiders in the barracks.[618] Of his co-defendants Barter and Buckley, Harold observed that they had not been involved in the raid. According to Harold, Buckley was not even a Volunteer.

CHAPTER THIRTY-FOUR

Seán Moylan,[619] *Newmarket, County Cork*

The prisoner was captured in the early hours of 16 May near Kiskeam, County Cork in a raid led by Lieutenant Grazebrook of the Gloucestershire Regiment.[620]

Grazebrook was a graduate of Sandhurst. He had won a Military Cross at the battle of Sanctuary Wood in 1915. Soon after he took a bullet in the lung and was invalided back to England where he served out the war as an instructor. In 1921 the 1st Battalion of the Gloucestershire Regiment was posted to Cork and Grazebrook, a small, immaculately turned out man, became a successful battalion intelligence officer. Moylan went to the national school at Drominarigle, leaving at fourteen. He had been struck down by Spanish Flu in the pandemic of 1918 and although he survived, like thousands of his generation he was dogged by ill-health. He was fortunate to have the help of a former British Army surgeon, Algie Verling, who had first-hand experience of the illness on the Western Front. He rose through the ranks of the Volunteers and, as the war intensified, he was hunted by the Gloucestershire Regiment.

On the evening of 15 May, Grazebrook led sixty men on an all-night march through hostile country, from Kanturk to Boherbue. 'The going was exceedingly heavy and the Irish banks and deep ditches exhausting.'

The cross-country night march was a difficult feat of navigation in an area where there were few landmarks and no moon. Grazebrook later recalled the march: 'We were helped by a wonderful and unique display of the Aurora Borealis. The whole sky to the south was diffused with purple rays of light.' Grazebrook's men arrived above the village of Boherbue just before dawn. They sheltered in a disused barn during the following day. Late that night they marched again across country to Riordan's farm near Kiskeam. Grazebrook had arranged for the telephone wires around Newmarket to be cut that evening to prevent a warning being transmitted. He correctly anticipated that his troops would be spotted by local people in the final stage of the operation and arranged for a large detachment of men on bikes to move up swiftly in support.

By mid-May 1921 the prisoner had been living rough for some time and was waiting hospitalisation. He appears to have avoided the initial round-up by running into a field and ducking under a furze bush, and through a combination of fatigue and illness he fell asleep and was found just after dawn. Twelve others were captured in the round-up, together with a code book, despatches and a machine gun captured from the 17th Lancers in the Mallow Barracks raid.

The following day Moylan was taken to the detention barracks in Cork. He later recalled his condition as 'ragged unshaven, bloody'.[621] He also recalled a kindly, older Scottish sergeant who provided him with a bath.[622] The army view at GHQ in Dublin was more unkind: the prisoner 'was in a disgusting condition and needed much fumigation'.[623]

The witnesses from the battalion journeyed up to Victoria Barracks to give evidence the next day. Grazebrook, as intelligence officer, remained in the background – a legacy of events at Clonmult where the presence of the intelligence officer had precipitated a hunt for the informant.[624] The trial did not go ahead that day, probably due to a backlog of other cases. Three days later the general election took place and the prisoner was elected to the second Dáil.

Moylan acquired a solicitor at this point: Barry Sullivan, a local man who had been acting for some of the men in the Mallow Barracks trial. Sullivan had qualified the year before. He was then twenty-two years old. Those who knew him describe a quiet young man, fond of cricket and passionate about his work.

Moylan described meeting his counsel, Albert Wood KC, for the first time: '... beautifully dressed and groomed, with an accent which seemed to me then to be the quintessence of Oxford'.[625] Moylan later wrote: 'Wood insisted that negotiations were going on and that a Truce was imminent. He said it was very important for many reasons that my case should be defended. It might mean eventually saving the lives of other men ...'[626]

The case of Clifford and Sullivan had just gone to the Lords and the only way forward was to adopt the arguments being advanced in that case. On 26 May at the High Court in Dublin an application for a writ of habeas corpus was made. Mr Justice Powell issued a conditional writ of habeas corpus, pending full argument from both sides. By leave of the court the order was 'telegraphed' to Major General Strickland in Cork.

Moylan was brought up for trial on 30 May at Victoria Barracks. The prisoner later described the trial:

> There was a loaded revolver in front of the Chairman of the bench. The gallery was crowded with a number of curious onlookers – all British Officers – and soldiers stood round the chair where I sat with drawn revolvers. The lawyers arrived and the charge was read out to me.[627]

The prisoner was charged with levying war and, secondly, being improperly in possession of arms, ammunition and explosives.

Albert Wood KC led for the defence. Junior counsel for Moylan was John Bourke, who had acted for John Allen. Albert Wood opened the argument with old-fashioned courtesy: there was no objection to his being tried by the individual members of the court but the prisoner 'took exception to their jurisdiction'.

The procedure utilised by Wood was known as a special plea in bar, which challenged the jurisdiction of the court.[628] The order made by the High Court and the supporting affidavits setting out the objections to jurisdiction were submitted to the court. The argument amounted to this: that the Military Court lacked jurisdiction to try the case and should in any event take no step pending the determination of the writ of habeas corpus. This argument was rejected by the court. Counsel responded by announcing their decision to withdraw from the trial, and accordingly did so.[629]

The record shows that the court entered a plea of not guilty in respect of both the charges. In accordance with what had become standard practice in the Military Court, the accused was offered the assistance of an officer, which was declined. The relevant parts of the evidence are set out below.

Private Baker, C Company, stated:

> On 16 May 1921 I was on duty with a party of military near Knocknagree and Kiskeam … At about 07.00 hours I noticed about 100 yards on my right that there was a movement amongst the bushes on a hedge. I went towards the place … I then saw a man lying on his back who appeared to be asleep. It was the accused. I told the accused to get up. As he did not get up I kicked his foot. Before accused got up I took hold of the revolver (produced) and a detonated bomb … which the accused held in his right hand.

Company Sergeant Eyers told the court: 'The accused was brought to me by Private Baker. I proceeded to search accused and in his right-hand breeches pocket I found the seven rounds of .45 ammunition (produced). Accused made no statement.'

In answer to questions put by the court, C.S.M. Eyers said: 'The horn sounded about three miles around. From the noise I judged there were about 100 men ahead of the troops. Later in the day I saw four or five armed men moving away. I also saw two men blowing horns on a hill. We took twelve prisoners that day.'

Company Sergeant Major Reece told the court:

> Just before 04.00 hours I heard a shot up a lane near a house I was searching. I went up the lane towards where I heard the shot, and found a party under Lieutenant Temple, I got into the lane and a few minutes later I heard a signal whistle from the top end of the lane and it was repeated, then someone walked down the lane towards me, and then I said, 'Halt, hands up!' I could see that he was wearing an overcoat and a light cap. The man answered, 'All right, I have got them up.' Then I could see he had his hands above his head. I covered the man with my rifle and told him to come on. Immediately, he dropped his hands and bolted up the lane. I fired at him with a rifle. At about 04.30 hours we started to search the country and houses. At the top of the lane I saw the bank and then I proceeded to a farm on the right. A great coat, Sam Browne belt and a holster were brought to me. The great coat is the one the accused is now wearing. Accused was brought into the lane by the first and second witnesses, and they handed him over to an officer, together with the revolver and the bomb produced. The officer asked accused if the revolver and bomb belonged to him and the accused replied 'Yes'. This reply was quite voluntary. I saw the accused searched … and I saw several rounds of revolver ammunition (.45) taken from the right-hand breeches pocket of the accused. This was in the vicinity of the farm. Accused asked me if he could proceed down the lane to find a pair of glasses he had lost. I went down the lane to the spot where I had fired. I had noticed that the accused had on a light cap and spoke like the man I had heard when I fired. So I asked him if anyone had shot at him during the morning. He said 'Yes' and that it was down the lane. I said it was I who had fired at him, and he said, 'it was a pretty near one …'

The record shows that the prisoner declined to cross-examine, give evidence or make a statement.

The President announced a verdict of not guilty on the charge of levying war. Nothing was said about the verdict on the second charge, which implied conviction.

As to sentence, the President announced that the communications received were 'favourable', and therefore the court adjourned for the prosecution to call evidence of character. The issue of whether a death sentence might yet be passed and even carried out before the High Court ruled on the legality of the trial was real. *Hansard* records that at Westminster, Sir Hamar Greenwood, Chief Secretary for Ireland, was questioned about the trial.

> Captain Benn: Will the right honourable gentleman say whether the writ of habeas corpus which has been issued will be obeyed by the Military Court or does it not run?
>
> Sir H. Greenwood: That is one of those very difficult legal questions which I cannot answer off hand ...[630]

The Military Court reconvened on 5 June when the prosecutor set out the findings regarding the character of the accused. The evidence was mixed. The accused had a conviction for making seditious speeches for which he had been sentenced to one year's imprisonment with hard labour.[631] There was other evidence. Here is an extract:

> The accused was in charge of a party of rebels who ambushed the late Divisional Commissioner Holmes and a party of police near Kingwilliamstown on 28 January last. Divisional Commissioner Holmes was wounded and later succumbed to the injuries he had received. Certain of the rebels wanted to shoot some members of the RIC who were lying on the road. These members of the RIC were saved by the intervention of Moylan, the accused, who I understand said to his own men, 'If you shoot them, I will shoot you.'[632]

The President indicated that the court would give 'full consideration to the statement of the prosecutor'.[633] The court then adjourned again.

It appears that Barry Sullivan had every expectation that execution would follow, not least because the day before Thomas Keane had been executed at Limerick. Sullivan therefore pressed for a full hearing on the writ of habeas corpus. On 9 June at the High Court in Dublin, Mr Justice Powell heard counsel for the prisoner in support of a motion to make the writ of habeas corpus absolute.[634] The authorities were against the prisoner, and, as Mr Justice Powell pointed out: 'You are asking me to reverse myself and the full court of the King's Bench.' Henry Hanna

KC opposed the application: 'Was every person who was brought before a military court to be allowed to come in here and make applications of this kind?'

After further inconclusive legal argument, the conditional order was continued pending the decision of the House of Lords in Clifford and Sullivan, which was due the following week. Until then, Justice Powell concluded: 'I hope that no irremediable step will be taken.'[635]

As it turned out, Sullivan's fears were not made out. General Macready put out a press release the same morning before Justice Powell sat: it is unlikely the timing was co-incidental. On the charge of improper possession of arms and ammunition, fifteen years' penal servitude was ordered.

Writing over thirty years later, the prisoner's view was that the army considered it impolitic to execute an elected representative when peace talks were in the offing.[636]

CHAPTER THIRTY-FIVE

Patrick Loughlin, Cashel, County Tipperary

Patrick Loughlin was tried at Victoria Barracks on 2 June. He was charged with being improperly in possession of seven rounds of ammunition and a revolver loaded with five rounds. He was secondly charged with being improperly in possession of documents prejudicial to the Restoration of Order in Ireland Regulations. He pleaded not guilty to both counts.[637] He was represented by C.K. Murphy, solicitor.

An army officer gave evidence that on 10 May he had been leading a patrol. They visited a house and during an inspection of an outhouse, he saw the accused kneeling by an attaché case containing documents. The accused was taken outside. Almost immediately after this, one of the soldiers found the loaded revolver in the outhouse. The officer told the court that the ammunition was found in the attaché case and the accused made no admission about the gun. An army notebook was found on the accused.

The accused gave evidence that he had seen the patrol coming along the road. He had stepped inside the outhouse to avoid it. He had been found there. He denied having anything to do with the gun, the ammunition, the attaché case or the documents. In cross-examination he admitted that he had taken refuge in the outhouse because he had been 'wanted' since the previous October. The army notebook, he conceded, was his.

Loughlin was found guilty and sentenced to death by shooting.[638] Review took place by the JAG[639] and sentence was confirmed by General Macready. Loughlin avoided execution by a very narrow margin. By the time the case papers went from GHQ Dublin to the JAG in London and back to Macready the executions had been suspended.[640]

It is worth noting that the second offence charged was contrary to the ROIR and provides an example of the way in which the jurisdiction of the Military Court was extended by degrees.

CHAPTER THIRTY-SIX

Patrick Cronin, Finuge, County Kerry

Patrick Cronin was tried at Victoria Barracks on 8 June. He was charged with being improperly in possession of a revolver and improperly in possession of eleven rounds of ammunition. Cronin was represented by Joseph McCarthy, counsel. A very brief account of the trial survives.[641]

The first witness, the head constable, stated that he was leading a convoy of three lorries towards Tralee on 1 May. He saw the accused on the road and halted him and ordered him to put his hands up. The accused put his hand into his hip pocket and pulled out a revolver which he put into his trousers pocket. The head constable pulled out his own revolver. He searched the accused and found a fully loaded revolver. He was arrested and cautioned but said nothing.

The prisoner lived close by. The Register shows his home to be Finuge, a village at the crossroads a couple of miles south-west of Listowel on the Tralee Road.

The head constable told the court that the prisoner's home was searched and eleven rounds of ammunition were found in a bag of flour. On cross-examination it transpired the revolver was rusty, although it had been sandpapered. Cross-examination continued:

> Q: 'Was this boy beaten by anybody on the lorry?'
> A: 'He was not beaten nor interfered with in any way after arrest or while on the way to Tralee.'
> Q: 'Do you know his cap, collar and shirt were all bloodstained?'
> A: 'No.'
> Q: 'This comes as a surprise to you?'
> A: 'Yes.'

Two more police witnesses gave supporting evidence. One said he had seen the accused in the guard room at Tralee and he did not seem to be 'knocked about'.

The accused, in answers to the court, said that the revolver had been found upon him. It was not loaded. He never had any ammunition. He had found it in the road about a fortnight previously. He had told the head constable this. It was rusty. A fishing net had been stolen from him the night before and since he knew who the thieves were he had taken the revolver out to frighten them.

The accused told the court that the head constable had not told him that he had found ammunition at the house. We do not know exactly in what circumstances the accused alleged that he was beaten. The report cryptically reports that 'here the accused repeated certain allegations'.

In cross-examination the accused could not say why he had kept the revolver, simply that he 'kept it in a ditch'. He agreed that he had not made allegations of ill-treatment prior to the trial. This was because, he said, he had been threatened.

The mother of the accused, Lizzie Cronin, was called and said she was present when the house was searched but the head constable did not mention finding any ammunition (and therefore by implication his evidence was untrue). She added that she had seen the gun in the house. She regarded it as useless and had seen the children playing with it some days before the arrest of her son. The head constable was recalled to the witness stand and he insisted that the accused had not been ill-treated.

The prisoner's case, which amounted to being framed by the head constable and, at the very least, being beaten up on the way to the barracks, was an uphill one. No evidence of ill-treatment of the accused was called apart from what he told the court.

Patrick Cronin was convicted on both charges and sentenced to penal servitude for life.[642] He was released in January 1922. Nothing is known about him save that he was twenty-four years old, a single man who lived with his parents, younger brothers and sisters. It is entirely possible that the prisoner sustained a beating at the hands of the head constable. Context, of course, is everything. Some weeks before, Major McKinnon of the Auxiliaries was shot dead on the third green at Tralee. Three weeks before Cronin's arrest, the head constable of Tralee, Francis Benson, was shot dead on his doorstep. He left a wife and five children.[643] His successor, who must have been a friend and a close colleague, was the officer who arrested Cronin. Anyone found in possession of a gun, even unloaded, could expect a difficult reception.

Whether Cronin's account about the gun was true or not cannot now be determined. No other information has come to light about the prisoner.

CHAPTER THIRTY-SEVEN

Jones Bridge

WILLIAM DALY (SHANNONVALE),
TIMOTHY KEOHANE (RICHFORDSTOWN),
JOHN DRISCOLL (RICHFORDSTOWN),
CORNELIUS DRISCOLL (BALLYMACWILLIAM)

The trenching of roads was actively pursued by Volunteers in the Martial Law Area since December 1920.[644] The purpose was to prevent the army reinforcing ambushed troops or to facilitate an ambush or simply disrupt communications.[645] Trenches were easily filled in and so the focus shifted to the destruction of bridges. The paucity of explosives meant that bridges had to be dismantled at night, stone by stone. The process was noisy and time-consuming. The army and the police responded vigorously and in the spring of 1921 there were a spate of night-time shootings at bridges.[646]

We are concerned with Jones Bridge in west Cork. Just after midnight on 9 March 1921 a patrol of the Essex Regiment came upon a group of men near the bridge on the old Clonakilty to Ballinascarty road. Preparations for the demolition of the bridge over the river were in hand. Four men were captured.[647] One, William Daly, was wounded.

The trial was delayed for some weeks while Daly recovered from his wound. The four men were tried by a military court at Victoria Barracks on 13 June 1921.[648] They were charged that on 9 March 1921 they did levy war against His Majesty the King, by taking part in preparations for the demolition of a bridge. The accused were represented by Joseph McCarthy.[649]

An army officer gave evidence that on the night of 9 March he was leading a patrol from Clonakilty. About 150 yards from the bridge he came across three of the accused by the roadside. He arrested them and put up a Verey light in the direction of the bridge. He then saw a man crouching between him and the bridge. He saw the man throw something over the hedge. It looked like a revolver case and belt. A shot was fired at the man. The officer went forward and found the man was Daly. He was wounded.

On the bridge, the officer found a number of picks, shovels and crowbars and a loaded shotgun. There were barrels on the bridge supporting planks. Holes in the structure of the bridge had been chiselled out. The prisoners were taken back to barracks at Clonakilty. The next morning the officer went back to the bridge and found a pool of blood where Daly had lain. On the other side of the hedge he found a revolver, four bullets and a holster and belt. A rifle was also found.

It was suggested on behalf of Daly that the motion the officer had seen was Daly putting up his arms. This was denied. A lance corporal gave corroborating evidence and identified the four accused. A police sergeant gave evidence that he had searched the area and found a rifle. Another RIC man found bloodstains and a loaded revolver. In a disused house 400 yards away he found a motorbike.

William Daly gave evidence. He told the court that he had put up his hands when challenged near the bridge. He was shot. He did not have a revolver and he was not asked any questions about a revolver when he was captured. There had been other civilians at the bridge who had got away. He told the court that he had served in the British Army. He said he had been threatened by unknown men and forced to go to the bridge. He had been afraid to refuse.

> 'Who came for you that night?'
> 'A man.'
> 'Did you know him at all?'
> 'No.'
> 'Was he masked?'
> 'No. He was a stranger to me.'
> 'Had he a gun?'
> 'Well he spoke as if he might have.'

When he got to the bridge he saw twelve to fifteen men there. He did nothing and was sent home. At this point, it seems, the army arrived. He denied being a member of the Volunteers or Sinn Féin.

The other three accused also gave similar accounts and advanced the defence of duress. They each denied having a gun and each denied being a member of the Volunteers or Sinn Féin. All four men were found guilty. As a matter of law, duress was a defence to the charge of levying war. It follows that the basis of the conviction rests on the finding that each man had voluntarily taken part in the demolition of the bridge, which the court found amounted to levying war against the King.

No evidence has emerged to suggest that the Volunteers used impressed labour to destroy bridges. The prosecution and the defence might be seen in that context.

All four men were sentenced to death by being shot.[650] The trial and convictions were reviewed by the Judge Advocate General[651] and proceedings were confirmed. Two days later an announcement was made at Westminster that no more executions would take place pending the resolution of an appeal to the House of Lords, a reference no doubt to Clifford and Sullivan.[652]

CHAPTER THIRTY-EIGHT

Garryricken House, County Kilkenny

JOHN LUTTRELL, PATRICK LUTTRELL, JAMES LUTTRELL, THOMAS LUTTRELL AND JAMES McKENNA

Garryricken House stood five miles from Callan in County Kilkenny. Built on the site of an earlier property, Garryricken was one of those fine old Georgian residences that graced southern Ireland at the beginning of the last century. The house and grounds were part of a larger estate owned by the Marquis of Ormonde, head of the Butler family that had rendered long service to the Stuart Kings. At the great battle of 1690 Butlers fought on both sides and afterwards, James Butler, second Duke of Ormonde, who had commanded King William's English Horse, recovered his lands. Garryricken House stood at the heart of a large estate and enjoyed a long association with the Kilkenny Hunt. Pheasant were reared and in the winter the gentry from Kilkenny came down 'to shoot Garryricken'.

In 1920 on the death of the Marquis of Ormonde the estate passed to the Earl of Ossory but Garryricken House remained empty. There were no more shooting trips or house parties and the grand ballroom gently decayed. Most of the furniture was removed from the house and the estate was put up for sale.

Next to the main house was the caretaker's lodge, connected to the ballroom by a door held shut by a hasp. For many years the Luttrell family lived in the lodge. The men worked as gamekeepers or labourers and it is probable that some of the women worked at 'the big house'.[653] By 1921 the caretaker was John Luttrell, who lived in the lodge with his wife and children. On 12 March 1921 the army raided Garryricken House. A number of men escaped after a shootout. One policeman was killed and the District Inspector was wounded.[654]

The five men left at the house were held and tried by military court at Waterford Barracks on 14 June.[655] The accused were charged that, on

12 March, they did levy war by attacking a detachment of His Majesty's troops; second, being improperly in possession of arms, namely two rifles and four revolvers; third, being improperly in possession of ammunition; fourth, that, knowing armed rebels were at Garryricken House, they failed to inform the military. John Luttrell faced an additional charge that, knowing there were armed rebels in the house, he falsely told a district inspector that there were no rebels in the house.

The accused denied the charges. They were represented by Patrick Lynch KC and J.J. Mooney.[656]

An army officer told the court that as a result of information received, a joint police and military raid was planned which took place in the early hours of 12 March. The convoy left Callan at 5.30 am and arrived at about 7 am and surrounded the house. An officer and the District Inspector knocked on John Luttrell's door. He came down. He was questioned as to why he had allowed men to stay at the house without informing the military.[657] He replied: 'I would be afraid to with no military or police protection.' He was pressed about whether men were staying and replied: 'There may be; as far as I know there is no one.'

They went upstairs and inspected John Luttrell's bedroom and then walked down a corridor where they saw three or four men. The men were called on to halt but they fired on the District Inspector, Hubert Baynham. They retreated to the caretaker's bedroom and District Inspector Baynham leaned out of the window to give instructions to his men but 'immediately sank back wounded'. There was considerable firing going on and the officer said that John Luttrell, the caretaker, seemed un-inclined to help the wounded inspector 'until I pointed my gun at him'. The firing continued and after a while another man came down the passage: 'I fired at him and he went back.'

District Inspector Baynham, who had recovered from his wound, was the next witness. He described how he came to be wounded: 'I put my head out of the window and shouted to one of my constables. I had just attracted his attention when a shot rang out close to me. I was shot on the back of my spine and fell on the window sill.' He also told the court that as he lay back on the bed he reproached John Luttrell for not telling him there were armed men in the building. To which John Luttrell replied that he had received some 'terrible threatening letters'.

A corporal searching the building came upon a party of men on the stairs. They fired on him and he fired back but it was 'only dimly lit'. He went outside the house and was fired on again from the house. In the distance he saw an armed man running through an archway and disappearing. He was directed to bring up a Lewis gun and did so. He opened fire on the top storey of the house. A single shot was fired in reply. After that there was intermittent firing from the house. This lasted about an hour and a half when reinforcements arrived. They then rushed the house. Later he saw a dead policeman lying outside the house under a blanket. He also saw the five accused being held outside the house.

Another soldier who arrived later on the scene gave evidence that when he arrived he was directed to the side of the building and there found James and Thomas Luttrell in a house, a converted barn. They were arrested. Reinforcements having arrived, they rushed the house and there in a passage he saw McKenna and Patrick Luttrell being herded along by a soldier. In a bedroom close by he found caps and leggings and a loaded .38 revolver. Later that day the County Inspector and a number of RIC men arrived and a full search took place. Under the floorboards of a top middle room he found two rifles, a loaded revolver and a loaded automatic. It appeared that they had been 'hastily put away'. He also found ammunition and a bandolier.

Another witness gave evidence that in the final search and clear-up he found a .38 revolver with dum-dum bullets in one of the bedrooms.

Four of the prisoners were taken away in lorries. John Luttrell was released but later charged.

The Defence Case

John Luttrell

John Luttrell told the court he was thirty-six. He was born and raised on the Garryricken estate. He had worked there since he was nineteen. He was the gamekeeper and caretaker. He lived in the caretaker's portion of the house. The property had been empty for some time. It was up for sale and he had been asked to assist with the sale but there had been local agitation concerning the disposal of the estate. He had received a threatening letter which read: 'Prepare for death. The day of the landlord is over.'

On the morning of 12 March he had been disturbed by knocking. He looked out the window and saw the army officer and police. He went down in his night shirt and spoke to the officers. He was asked if there were strangers in the house and he told them: 'I would not be able to tell you that. I could guarantee there were none in my portion of the house.' He did not know about the main house. The officers came inside.

The army officer opened a door leading onto the main portion of the house and there followed a burst of shots. They went into Luttrell's bedroom. 'The DI then asked me if I thought there was anyone in the house and I replied I did not know, which was the truth.' The District Inspector leaned out the window and immediately 'dropped' onto the window sill having been shot. Luttrell heard his wife and two children 'roaring' and then he heard his wife say: 'Don't shoot.' He looked at the army officer who was pointing his gun at him. The officer told him to look after the District Inspector. He went to the District Inspector and helped him onto the bed. He and his wife removed his waistcoat and shirt and found a bullet hole on top of his left shoulder. With his wife's help they cut up linen and bandaged his wound. 'He was bleeding very hard for ten minutes.' There was a lot of shooting outside for some time. At some point the officer in the bedroom left and went into the passage. There was a shot and the officer returned. After some time other soldiers arrived with his brother Patrick and McKenna. He was asked to identify them and did so. He was questioned but let go. His brothers and McKenna were removed in a lorry. He had seen men crossing the lawn in the early morning some weeks before.

Cross-examined, he said that McKenna and his brother had slept in the main house on the night in question but he did not know this at the time. He agreed the District Inspector had reproached him after he was shot but Luttrell told the court that he did not know there was anyone in the house. He told the court the windows were insecure. He also maintained that he told the inspector about the threats that he had received. He added that his wife took those threats very seriously. He was asked:

> 'If you informed the police, would you not get protection?'
>
> 'I would be in a bigger hole then.'

He said his brother Patrick used to sleep over occasionally and there was a spare bed for men who might be 'threshing' and need to stay over. But this had not occurred to him when the District Inspector asked him who was in the house.

John Luttrell's case was supported by a character reference from Lord Ossory and the steward of the estate.

James Luttrell

James Luttrell told the court that he and his brother Thomas were sleeping at their father's house in the Garryricken estate. On the morning of 12 March they were awoken by gunshots. They went downstairs to kindle the fire. They were arrested by the military 'before the kettle had boiled'. They were questioned and taken outside and searched. They were asked if 'they knew anything about those damned murderers in the house'. They were held outside the main house. They saw no shooting from the house but 'the soldiers fired a few bursts from the Lewis gun.'

He told the court he had seen his brother Patrick and McKenna the night before at his father's house. They 'had some drink taken'. He was cross-examined briefly. He told the court he had been alarmed by the shooting but did not go outside. He had never seen any strange men 'knocking around Garryricken'. He had seen the threatening letter received by his brother and told him 'not to mind it'.

Thomas Luttrell

Thomas Luttrell gave evidence and corroborated the account given by James. When he was cross-examined he told the court that he had lived at Garryricken all his life. He added that James McKenna often stayed at his father's house. McKenna 'used to drink very much', he said. McKenna was going to a funeral on the 12th and he had arranged to go with him.

Patrick Luttrell

Patrick Luttrell told the court that he was a ploughman on the estate. That he had spent the evening of 11 March at his father's house with James McKenna. Later they decided to go up to 'the big house' to sleep. Sometimes workers on the estate used that room to sleep whenever they needed to. At about 2 am or 3 am three men entered through the window. They were armed. They took the bed and ordered Patrick and McKenna to sleep in the armchair. If they moved they would get 'a spy's death'. In the morning they were awoken by noise. One of the men went to investigate and soon after they heard firing. Patrick and McKenna crawled towards John Luttrell's portion of the house. But there were shots fired from the direction of his brother's room and they retreated.

They then went downstairs and went to a door which joins the main house to the caretaker's lodge. They broke the hasp on the door and went through into the caretaker's kitchen. 'At about 10 o'clock we heard a whistle and glass breaking all over the place.' The military came in and questioned them and they were taken up to his brother John's bedroom where they were identified.

Cross-examined, Patrick Luttrell said that he was a ploughman on the estate. He often stayed over in the room at 'the big house'. He said that James McKenna had come down 'specially' for a funeral of a man called Clancy who had been shot by the army. He did not know that Clancy was a member of the IRA. They had travelled seven miles to the funeral. These remarks provoked some cross-examination about their friends and associates. They had been drinking that night, he told the court and McKenna, who lived about a quarter of a mile away, was too drunk to go home.

James McKenna

James McKenna gave evidence that he was the son of a farmer who lived close by. He had served in the army from 1916 to 1919 and then transferred to the reserve. His discharge certificate was produced and it showed him to be 'good, honest and trustworthy'. He had been wounded on the Somme.

On the day before the raid he had been to a funeral and then came back to Garryricken House. He had often stayed over at 'the big house' and he was 'intimate' with one of the Luttrell sisters. He went to sleep and was awoken by intruders, who took the bed. In the morning he awoke to see the last of the men leaving. He heard shooting and at some point he and Patrick Luttrell left the bedroom and went into the ballroom and down the passage to John Luttrell's part of the house. He led the way. They were shot at and retreated and got to John's part of the house by a different route. His account broadly supported Patrick Luttrell's account. When cross-examined he said he did not know Clancy was a member of the IRA and 'he did not notice the coffin covered by a tricolour'. He could not remember going to bed; he was 'fearfully drunk' that night.

A local farmer who had served with the British army and sustained a serious head wound during the war also gave evidence. He said that on the morning of the raid he had heard shooting and later seen a number of men walking through the fields, '9 or 10 of them walking parallel to the public road'. Most of them held something which 'might be rifles'. The evidence of this witness was supported by another local man.

Mrs John Luttrell and her sister-in-law both gave evidence that on the evening after the raid two men had come to the house. They had gone into the big house and went upstairs. They remained there for ten or twelve minutes before coming down and leaving. They asked the witnesses not to mention their visit. The implication of this evidence is that these men were the owners of the firearms found upstairs and they were returning to take possession.

Verdict and Sentence

John, Thomas and James Luttrell were acquitted on all charges. Patrick Luttrell was convicted of levying war, failing to give information and improper possession of arms. He was sentenced to penal servitude for life. James McKenna was convicted of levying war and sentenced to penal servitude for life.[658] They were released in January 1922.

The name of the officer who lost his life is not known. Inspector Baynham, on the other hand, overcame his wounds and received compensation of £5,000 at the July Assizes.[659]

The full truth as to what happened at Garryricken House did not emerge for many years. It appears that the object of the raid was to capture Volunteers who were believed to be using Garryricken House. Edmund Aylward and four other Volunteers slept at Garryricken on the night of the raid.[660] They were disturbed the following morning by a woman shouting that the house was surrounded. The room was pitch black. As they dressed, a shot was fired at them and fire was returned. Aylward and two others managed to get out of the house while it was still not quite dawn. They turned at some point and saw the District Inspector leaning out the window. They shot him. Aylward and the other two directed their fire at a machine gun crew which caused them to take cover. They then shot a police officer guarding the perimeter before making their escape. According to Aylward, two of their number did not manage to escape from the house and were captured. Presumably these two were McKenna and Patrick Luttrell, who were of course the only two convicted.

James O'Connell, Ballinleenty, County Tipperary

On 12 March 1921 two unarmed military policemen were on duty at Limerick Junction station. At about 8.10 pm they were fired on. One soldier was wounded. The attackers made off.[661] It should be added that the accused lived about eight miles from Limerick Junction. He was arrested whilst attending a local funeral.

The prisoner was tried at Victoria Barracks on 16 June 1921.[662] He was charged that on 12 March at Limerick Junction he joined with two others unknown and attacked with firearms a detachment of His Majesty's forces. He was also charged with improper possession of arms on the same date.

O'Connell entered not guilty pleas. He was represented by R.J. Kinahan and James Meagher, led by James Sealy KC who later became one of the very first circuit judges appointed by the new state.[663]

The issues in the case were identification and alibi. Evidence was given by a soldier that he had been on duty at Limerick Junction railway station. At about 7.50 pm he saw 'the accused walk up and down on the platform with another civilian'. The accused spoke to someone on a stationary train on the platform and then he went and joined two men and they walked up the platform. He then heard shots and saw a lance corporal fall to the ground. He 'saw the accused and another man with revolvers in their hands'. They 'fired two more shots' at him and one at his comrade who was lying on the ground. The witness said that neither he nor the lance corporal were armed. He made a phone call for help. He then 'lifted the lance corporal onto the train and took him to Tipperary'. This rudimentary but sensible step probably saved the lance corporal's life. Tipperary was the nearest large town, only a few miles by train. There was also a garrison there.

On 23 March the witness picked the accused out at a parade at Cork detention barracks. The line-up consisted of twenty-five men, although it appeared that he had viewed an earlier parade and failed to pick out the accused.

Cross-examined by Mr Sealy, he said part of the station was covered. The station 'was lighted by gas'. The accused wore a big heavy coat with the collar turned up. He had seen the accused walking on the platform a number of times and had remarked on that fact to the lance corporal. He had not known his name and he was nearly always alone when he saw him.

The lance corporal who had been wounded gave evidence. He told the court that he had been standing on the platform between the Cork train and the Tipperary train. The first witness was close by. He heard a volley of shots and was wounded in the left hip and thigh. As he went to ground he was shot again in the wrist. He crawled under a train. He only saw one assailant who wore a mask. This man was 5 feet 8 inches. He wore a macintosh and a soft hat. He also told the court that while in hospital a number of men were brought in for identification but he had been unable to pick anyone out. He had not seen the accused before and could not remember the other military police officer pointing him out on any other occasion.

At this point junior counsel Meagher, whose wig was resting on the desk, attempted to address the court. This set in motion a small spat and a rebuke from the Judge Advocate: 'I am surprised that any member of the Bar, to which profession I belong myself, should address the court improperly dressed.

There is a small irony here: that a military court exercising a jurisdiction not sanctioned by law should become excited about the etiquette of court dress. It may be that wigs and gowns were insisted upon because it lent an air of legality to the process. In any event, Mr Meagher's wig went back on his head with an abject apology and the trial continued.

Another soldier gave evidence that he had attended a parade and recognised the accused as a man he had seen at Limerick Junction railway station on various occasions. When he saw him he was wearing a soft hat and a long coat and muffler. He accepted in cross-examination that he had failed to pick out the accused at an earlier parade.

The prosecution called evidence about the taking of the summary of evidence and elicited the fact that the accused had said 'he was innocent of the charge.' That ended the prosecution case.

James Sealy KC then made a submission. He argued that levying war was an offence by reason of statute: Poyning's Law of 1494. Parliament had also provided that treason must be proved by an 'overt act' proved by two or more witnesses.[664] In this case the overt act was the shooting and there was only a single witness called in support of that act. The accused was therefore entitled to be acquitted on that charge. Counsel's argument amounted to this: if the court was to prosecute the accused for treason then it must also apply those parts of the Treason Acts which conferred protections upon the accused.

This argument was rejected by the Judge Advocate on the ground that trials under martial law were entirely independent of common law. That was so, but it should be pointed out that the rule under which the military courts were constituted required strict adherence to the rules of evidence.[665] Sealy advanced a second argument, namely that the evidence was so weak that the case ought to be stopped. This argument was also rejected.

The accused gave evidence that he was twenty years old. His father was dead and he helped out on his mother's dairy farm. He told the court he had been studying for a bank clerkship. He was not a Volunteer. He had never had a firearm and did not know how to use one. On 12 March he had supper at home with his mother and two brothers and then he had gone to a neighbour's house where he spent a while talking to his neighbour and his wife about the forthcoming Grand National at Fairyhouse. He remembered it because he 'lent' his newspaper to his neighbour and 'had to go back for it'. The neighbour gave evidence supporting the alibi. They had been talking about 'good things' for the National. His wife and a friend all gave evidence in support of the alibi.

The record suggests that the defence evidence was undented in cross-examination. Although the alibi was a little odd, being based on a conversation about the Grand National, the race was not run until the end of the month. This was, however, an identification case where there was a single witness whose identification of his attacker had taken place in difficult circumstances and there was no supporting evidence. Looking at the case in the round, the evidence was not strong. O'Connell was acquitted on both charges.

No information has come to light since which bears on the identity of the men who carried out the attack. One final point deserves mention. The accused referred to his brothers in evidence. But neither brother was called to substantiate his alibi. A census check reveals that the accused had a twin brother.[666] Given that the issue in this case was whether the accused was correctly identified, it is curious to say the least that he did not mention this in evidence.

CHAPTER FORTY

Patrick Higgins, Ardra, Rostellan, County Cork

Higgins was one of the survivors of the engagement at Clonmult in February. He had sustained a bullet wound in the mouth and was taken with the others to the hospital wing at Victoria Barracks. He was not fit to be tried with the others because of his wound; when this had resolved, a long-standing complication of an appendicitis condition intervened and he seems to have become lost in the system for a time.

Higgins was tried at Victoria Barracks on 21 June. He was charged with levying war against the King. He was represented by George Daly, counsel.[667]

The trial[668] started with an application for one of the officers of the court to stand down. He had been identified as an officer who had sat on the trial of the other men captured at Clonmult. The officer stood down and was replaced by another.

The facts of the siege are set out in the chapter on Clonmult and need not be repeated here. Suffice to say there was evidence that the cottage was surrounded by troops and a siege took place during which there was 'intermittent firing' from the cottage and resistance was broken after the roof was set on fire.

The principal issue in the Crown case was finding satisfactory evidence that Higgins was captured at Clonmult. One witness gave evidence that he had seen Higgins after the siege with a 'bandage on his head'. The witness accepted that 'the accused was not one of those who had tried to escape', as he put it.

An RAMC corporal told the court that Higgins and the other men captured at Clonmult were brought into the hospital wing at the barracks on the night of the siege and that Higgins was wounded.

The prosecution, having proved that Higgins was captured at Clonmult, the defence case opened and the focus shifted to the explanation given by Higgins for his presence at the farm. Higgins gave evidence that he had previously been a member of the Volunteers but had resigned due to ill-health occasioned by an inflamed appendix. He had gone on the run after his home was raided but he had been forced to return home due to ill-health. He then met his old school friend Richard Hegarty on the Saturday night before the engagement. He denied knowing any of the men at the farmhouse except Hegarty. They had spent the night at the farmhouse near Clonmult and he was there the following afternoon when the military arrived and went into the house with the other men. He had lain on the floor and took no part in the shooting. Later when the surrender took place he emerged from the house with his hands up and went across to the barn where he was wounded.

Higgins called his uncle, a cousin and his mother to substantiate his account. A magistrate gave evidence of good character, although this evidence was diminished when it became apparent that the witness was unaware that Higgins had ever been a Volunteer.

George Daly's closing remarks laid stress on the fact that Higgins had been wounded after the surrender, and not therefore in the course of a fight. He also stressed that Higgins had been wounded by 'a stray bullet'. This suggestion differed from the account that Higgins later gave to the Bureau of Military History.[669] It is likely that counsel took this tack to avoid any suggestion of impropriety by Crown forces and by so doing give the court the opportunity to acquit without seeming to give credence to allegations against the army or the police. If that is so, the tactic failed.

Higgins was convicted of levying war and the following day was informed that he had been sentenced to death by being shot. The trial proceedings were reviewed by the JAG[670] and confirmation followed.

While Higgins was being tried and sentenced, Patrick Lynch and Hugh Kennedy had successfully applied to the Master of the Rolls for a conditional writ in the case of J.J. Egan, who had been sentenced to death by military court. This fact was not lost on William Barry, solicitor for Higgins, who instructed John Costello, who with Kennedy and Lynch then applied for and obtained a conditional writ for Higgins pending full argument. Higgins' case was then linked to that of Egan v Macready, which later resulted in the release of Higgins.

CHAPTER FORTY-ONE

Patrick Casey, Milford, County Cork

The prisoner was tried at New Barracks, Limerick on 24 June. He was charged that on 4 June he was improperly in possession of a revolver and ammunition at Milford.[671] Casey pleaded not guilty. He was represented by R.J. Kinahan, counsel.[672]

Milford is close to the border between Cork and Limerick, a few hundred yards from Kilbolane Castle which was famously reduced to ruins by Cromwell's troops. In 1921 Milford was a small but thriving village with a school, a post office, barracks and a creamery. The barracks was abandoned in the autumn of 1920. A number of local Volunteers then tried to burn it down, resulting in a shootout in which a Volunteer and a Black and Tan were wounded. The barracks was burned down a few days later[673] and soon after the creamery was destroyed as a reprisal.[674] After the destruction of the barracks, the village lost any strategic value and Milford seems to have returned to a peaceful existence untroubled by the conflict until the summer of 1921 when this prisoner was captured and taken for trial at Limerick.

An army officer told the court that he was travelling in a Crossley tender towards Milford. He saw three men by a gate. When they saw the tender the men ran into a yard. The officer pulled up and the men were chased by the officer and two soldiers. The accused was captured by an outhouse. Nothing was found on him except an empty notebook.

A soldier came over and showed the officer a Mauser pistol which he had found. The pistol was loaded. The prisoner was asked if the pistol was his and he denied it. He was asked why he ran and he said he was afraid of the military. Five more rounds of ammunition were found in the yard. The gun and ammunition had the appearance of having been put there very recently.

In cross-examination the soldier accepted that the accused had been out of his sight for twenty seconds. He was asked if he had seen some 'stampeding horses' and said no. He accepted there was a large crowd in the village but it melted away.

A private gave evidence that he had chased the accused and caught up with him in the yard. The pistol was found lying on a sack on the window sill of the outhouse. Cross-examined, he said he did not notice any excitement in the village. He said that the accused was out of his sight 'for half a second'. Another soldier gave evidence that he had been sitting on the back of the Crossley tender and saw the accused run into the yard. As the Crossley pulled up he jumped out and ran after him into the yard. He found the accused standing with his back to a small outhouse.

The owner of the property was called and he gave evidence that there were no arms on his property that day and that he did not know the accused. In cross-examination he said that he had heard there had been some excitement in the village that evening caused by runaway horses. He said that there were a heap of stones by the outhouse in the yard and that in order for someone to put the gun on the sill, they would have to 'stretch'.

A civilian witness gave evidence for the defence. He told the court that he had been in the village that evening. Some horses had bolted and the accused had tried to catch one. The accused, who was in the street, was captured. The witness related that he too had been arrested but released the next day.

The accused elected not to give sworn evidence on which he could be cross-examined. He made an unsworn statement to the court. He said that he had been cycling to Newcastle West on business. He had dismounted and tried to catch a runaway horse but failed. A military tender had come into view. Thinking they were Black and Tans, he stepped into the yard and out of view. He was arrested there.

The accused was sentenced to death by shooting. Sentence was commuted to fifteen years' penal servitude.[675] There is no information as to why sentence was commuted; it may well have related to reservations about the strength of the evidence.

CHAPTER FORTY-TWO

Adam Jones, Rosslare Strand, County Wexford

Adam Jones was tried at Waterford Military Barracks on 27 June 1921. He was charged with two offences. First, levying war against His Majesty by taking part in an attack on Rosslare police barracks. Second, that on the same day he had in his possession, at Mauritiustown, Rosslare, a number 4 shotgun cartridge.[676]

Jones pleaded not guilty. He was represented by John O'Byrne, counsel,[677] who was later Attorney General and a judge of the Supreme Court.

The evidence showed that on the night of 14 May gunfire was opened on the barracks at Rosslare which were then located behind the old coast road at the top of the cliff overlooking the sea shore. The assault involved sustained firing which lasted about ten minutes but it seems there were no casualties. Immediately after the attack a party of soldiers and police went to the home of Adam Jones at Mauritiustown, arriving just as dawn was breaking.

An RIC officer found the accused at home in bed. He was asked to hand over his clothes and he did so. The clothes were wet and the trousers smelled of sea water. The coat was damp with sand adhering to the sleeves and his boots were wet. A shotgun cartridge was found in his coat. He was asked: 'Is that your cartridge?' He replied: 'Yes' and was immediately arrested.

In answer to a question from the President of the court, the witness stated that the clothing had been put into the lorry after the raid and kept in the office at the barracks. It had not been bagged up until the summary of evidence was taken.

The officer recounted that a number of shotgun cartridges were found by the barracks and that a gun had been found at the rear of the barracks and one on the strand. This last piece of evidence resulted in an objection by John O'Byrne: 'I have not got notice of the gun ... it is not in the summary of evidence and no notice has been served on the prisoner that additional evidence would be produced.' The objection was overruled.

It transpired that the cartridges found matched the size and make of the cartridge found on the accused. Mauritiustown was about two and a half miles from the barracks via the sea shore and four miles by road.

An army officer told the court that when he came to the house of the accused he had noticed 'there was dew on the grass' and there were 'footprints coming from the shore' through the field at the back of the house, which suggested that the accused may have recently returned home. There were cattle in the field but the footprints did not lead towards them.

A submission by defence counsel that there was no case to answer on the charge of levying war was rejected, on the advice of the Judge Advocate. He did not say why, but it must amount to a chain of circumstantial evidence: the proximity to the barracks, the cartridge, the footprints in the field and the state of the accused's clothing so soon after the attack.

The defence case opened with an unsworn statement from the accused. He told the court he was a signalman on the Great Southern and Western Railway. He also kept cows. On the night of 14 May he was working in the early evening. He then called on Mrs Elizabeth Barry's house at Maytown some miles south of Rosslare. He then 'went to tend a sick calf' and became muddy and wet when dealing with the animal. He walked to Rosslare to buy cigarettes but found the shop shut. He spent some time with a group of men playing 'toss'. He then went home to check a cow that was about to calf, after which he went back to work and relieved a signalman. He 'passed the train for him' and closed up the signalbox at about 10.30 pm. He then walked home along the railway bank. He was home by 11 pm. He had supper and went to bed. The cartridge had been found by him some days before on the links.

A number of witnesses were called for the accused. A former soldier, who had served with the Munster Fusiliers, supported the account given by the accused that he visited Mrs Barry who ran a farm near Maytown: 'He came in with some cabbages.'

Other witnesses supported his account about the trip to the shop and the game of 'toss'. His brother-in-law gave evidence that he lived with the accused and his wife and four children and elderly mother in a small two-bedroom house. The witness had come home on the night in question around 10.30 pm. The accused was already at home. They had supper and went to bed. The witness then locked the house. Mrs

Jones, wife of the accused, also gave evidence that he had come home, had supper and gone to bed. The house had been locked and they were disturbed by the military in the morning. The witnesses were cross-examined in the usual way but appear to have been consistent and detailed.

Adam Jones was acquitted of levying war. He was convicted of possession of the cartridge. He was sentenced to a term of three years' imprisonment.[678]

One matter which calls for comment is that there is an odd hiatus in the proceedings just before the defence case opens. Defence counsel John O'Byrne appears unsure of the rules governing the procedure for calling of witnesses and the Judge Advocate embarks on a courteous and detailed explanation of the rules. It should be said that O'Byrne was an able lawyer. What transpired, as has been suggested elsewhere, is that the rules governing the procedures of the Military Court were never published or disseminated to defence advocates.

CHAPTER FORTY-THREE

Thomas Looby, Irishtown, Clonmel, County Tipperary

The prisoner was brought to Victoria Barracks on 30 June 1921. He was tried on a single charge, namely that on 22 May 1921 he was improperly in possession of a revolver and ammunition.[679] The prisoner pleaded not guilty. He was represented by Joseph McCarthy.[680]

Counsel Joseph McCarthy submitted that he was not ready to go on with the case owing to 'insufficient knowledge of the evidence to be presented to the court'. There were also, he told the court, witnesses who were coming down from Clonmel. He asked for an overnight adjournment. The prosecutor replied that there was 'nothing in the regulations to warrant the adjournment applied for'.[681] He also pointed out that the accused had ample time to prepare his defence: Looby had been captured some six weeks previously. McCarthy again submitted that it would be 'extremely inadvisable to proceed'.

The court retired to consider this application and on returning granted defence counsel half an hour 'to make himself acquainted with the facts of the case'. Half an hour is hardly sufficient time to take instructions in a capital case and this aspect of the trial makes uncomfortable reading.

After this adjournment evidence was called. A soldier gave evidence that on the night of 22 May at about 1.15 he was on patrol from Clonmel barracks. His patrol were crossing a field when he heard another soldier shout a challenge. He ran to the side of the road and saw a man running towards him. The patrol 'opened fire' and the man fell. He saw another soldier seize from the man a belt and revolver and a revolver holster. The man had with him a push bicycle and saddle bag.

He accepted in cross-examination that he had not been close enough to hear the shots but saw the flashes of gunfire through a hedge. He was about 200 yards away. 'Accused was lying on the ground. Witness asked him if he was able to get up and walk, and he said he was. Accused was taken back to barracks.'

An army sergeant gave evidence that he had seen two men on the road. He challenged them to put their hands up. One did. The other ran. He fired at this man, who fell wounded. He covered the man with a revolver. While he did this another soldier searched him and recovered the revolver, which was loaded, and a pouch. He identified the accused as the man.

The record is limited but it shows cross-examination by defence counsel was cursory.

The case was then stood over until the next day. There is no record of what transpired on the second day, by which time the trial had become overshadowed by the impending peace talks. It is known from other sources that Thomas Looby was convicted and sentenced to 'death by being shot'.[682] His conviction was reviewed by the JAG[683] and confirmed by General Macready.

A notable aspect of this case was the refusal of the application to adjourn to allow defence counsel to prepare the case. We cannot know all the details of the case and we should perhaps be cautious in making conclusions based on such a short report. However, Looby had been wounded when captured, which may have taken up his attention. It may also be that the prisoner had difficulties getting or funding representation.

The application to adjourn requires one further comment. The prosecutor contended that 'the Regulations did not provide any warrant for the adjournment that was applied for'. This misstated the Regulations.[684] The cumulative effect of Regulation 18 and 23 entitled the accused to require the court to take 'all reasonable steps' to allow him prepare his defence and secure the attendance of witnesses.

This error was not pointed out by defence counsel and this may be because the Regulations were not published and he did not have access to them.

CHAPTER FORTY-FOUR

Michael Purcell, Kildringagh,[685] *County Kilkenny*

The prisoner was aged twenty-one. His father had a blacksmith's forge in Kildringagh, where he and his wife raised ten children.

The circumstances in which the prisoner was captured and tried arose out of an engagement on the Slieveardagh Hills near Tubbrid. On Friday 13 May a party of soldiers and Auxiliaries encountered a group of rebels en route to attack Urlingford Barracks.[686] The army appear to have attempted an encircling movement which was partly successful. According to army records, one unnamed army officer was slightly wounded and a rifle, a shotgun and two revolvers were seized.[687] According to statements made to BMH, two Volunteers sustained wounds, from which they died.[688]

The accused was tried at Waterford Barracks on 29 June on a single charge, that on 13 May 1921 he levied war against the Crown by participating in an attack on His Majesty's forces. The trial was delayed for some weeks and the record that survives is silent as to why. Almost invariably the delay resulted from the fact that the prisoner was recovering from wounds.

The surviving record of this trial is brief.[689] Other events dominated the news, including the impending Mansion House Conference with the Unionists and Sinn Féin attending. In addition, Jack Dempsey's heavyweight title defence against Georges Carpentier was in the public eye and there was little interest in the trial of Purcell. The prisoner was unrepresented at his trial.

The report of the trial shows that joint army and police units were on patrol near Tubbrid. The prisoner was seen on the crest of a hill signalling with a large white handkerchief to 'other civilians' on nearby hills overlooking the road from Kilkenny to Tullaroan. Purcell was captured and dropped a large parcel of sandwiches. He was found to have a number of lemonade bottles in his pockets and a large white handkerchief. After his capture the army and Auxiliary units engaged a number of rebels in an exchange of fire which lasted half an hour.

The accused gave evidence and told the court that he had been waving a handkerchief but he was simply waving to a 'chum' on another hill. The accused was convicted. He was sentenced to life imprisonment.[690]

No evidence emerged subsequently which casts any further light on the accused's involvement in the events that led to his capture.

CHAPTER FORTY-FIVE

Michael O'Callaghan, Ballyhone, Emly, County Tipperary

The accused was tried at New Barracks, Limerick on 30 June 1921. He was charged that on 4 May 1921 he was improperly in possession of a shotgun and a bomb. He was also charged with being improperly in possession of ammunition.[691]

The accused was then twenty-three, the eldest son of a local farmer. He pleaded not guilty. He was represented by R.J. Kinahan, counsel.[692]

An RIC man gave evidence that he was involved in a search near Kilteely. A number of men were seen at a farmhouse nearby. They were reading papers. When they became aware of the presence of the police they began to run. The police officers crossed a ploughed field and saw three men making for the hills. The officer told the court that he called on them to halt but they took no notice. The witness opened fire with the result that 'two of the men fell and were assisted by a third and disappeared over a wall'.

The officer was joined by another policeman and they advanced 500 yards where they found the accused lying by a hedge. Close by lay a double-barrelled shotgun, field glass case containing a bomb, and cycle toolbag containing shotgun ammunition. The accused was 'bleeding freely'. The prisoner was not cautioned but denied when questioned that the items were his. He admitted being 'a despatch rider'. Cross-examined, the officer said that the men were wearing satchel bags. Three satchel bags were later recovered. He was sure they heard the warning to surrender. 'There was a blood trail from the gear to the accused.'

Another police officer gave evidence that while the other officer gave chase he had searched some nearby cottages and found leggings, a haversack containing clothes, dressings and a splint. He heard shooting and rushed out. In the distance he saw the accused being arrested. In a statement made on oath to the court, the accused said that he was twenty-three years old, a farmer, that he was given a despatch and told to take it to a house in Kilteely. This he did and handed the despatch to the two men who were later seen with him. They were armed and carrying haversacks. When he got to Kilteely 'the hour was late' and he stayed over. In the morning someone shouted a warning that the military were coming and he ran with the other two men. In due course he was wounded. This was his 'first and only despatch'.

In cross-examination he said that he had become a Volunteer in February. He had joined the Emly company. This was the first time he had been asked to carry a despatch. The man who gave him the despatch was a stranger. He gave the surname of the man but was able to give no other details. He told the court that Kilteely was three and a half miles from his home at Emly. He denied having arms in his possession.

Two witnesses gave evidence as to the movements of the accused earlier that day and confirmed that he had not been armed.

Robert Kinahan, counsel for the accused, invited the court to acquit the prisoner of the charge of improper possession of arms and to have him charged with being a member of the Volunteers. The court declined to accede to the submission and O'Callaghan was convicted on both counts. He was sentenced to ten years' penal servitude. His counsel was less fortunate. Within a few days the young and very able Robert Kinahan was taken ill while on circuit in Maryborough and died soon after.[693]

CHAPTER FORTY-SIX

Waterfall, County Cork

TIMOTHY HEALY, PATRICK DWYER, JOHN RYAN, JAMES MURPHY, THOMAS RIORDAN, JOHN HORGAN, JOHN DRISCOLL, PATRICK McAULIFFE, PATRICK LANE, TIM DESMOND, DAN FORDE, GEORGE MURPHY, EUGENE RIORDAN, DENIS LANE, JOHN FINN, JEREMIAH FORDE, JOHN DINEEN, JOHN COLLINS, TOM MURRAY, DANIEL O'KEEFE, TIM SULLIVAN, WILLIAM DWYER

We are concerned with events in the village of Waterfall on 27 June 1921. Waterfall was then a village about four miles south-west of Cork city. The trial came about as a result of 'information received' by the Manchester Regiment that Walter Leo Murphy was in the habit of holding battalion meetings at a pub in Kilumney, a few miles from the army barracks at Ballincollig. The meetings were held in the evenings but the dates were not known. There was other information that Murphy was planning an action for the following day.

The Manchester Regiment faced a problem in travelling unobserved because the signalling system used by the rebels was highly effective. For this reason Lieutenant Colonel Evans used a small number of officers travelling in civilian clothes. The regimental record shows that: 'Lieutenant Colonel Evans CMG DSO and Lieutenant Vining proceeded across country to Inniscarra Bridge at 20.00 hours, and picked up four officers from Cork in two Ford motor cars. Proceeded to Kilumney.' [694] The cars were stopped short of the village and the officers walked across the fields. They found the village quiet, with no young men in the public house. The absence of young men in Kilumney persuaded Colonel Evans that there was a meeting taking place close by. He took his party on to Donovan's pub, a small end-of-terrace house on the edge of Waterfall. He stationed men by each of the exits.[695] At the time of their arrival it was approximately 10.30 pm.[696]

One officer went to the rear of the pub. According to evidence given at the Court of Inquiry, Colonel Evans stood at the front door. A man ran out into the street. He was called upon to halt and was fired upon. He began 'zig zagging down the road'.[697] He was fired upon again by Colonel Evans. He fell to the ground and died. This man was Walter Leo Murphy.[698]

A press release by Dublin Castle shows that forty-five men were detained[699] but only twenty-three men were kept in custody. A quantity of arms were seized and the prisoners were brought back to Victoria Barracks. The next day one of the prisoners, Charles Daly, was taken out to identify the location of an arms cache. The findings of the Military Court of Inquiry were that he was shot dead trying to escape.[700]

There remained twenty-two prisoners and the trial of these men commenced at Victoria Barracks a few days later on 1 July.[701] All the accused faced two charges. First, that they were unlawfully and jointly in possession of arms and ammunition, namely two rifles, one revolver, one Mauser pistol, fifty-three rounds of ammunition and twenty-three rounds of revolver and pistol ammunition. Second, that at Waterfall on 27 June 1921 they did consort with rebels.

The accused, who were all local men, were described in press reports as being 'of the farm labourer class'. They were 'aged about 19–30'. All the accused entered not guilty pleas. All were represented by counsel.[702]

Lieutenant Vining gave evidence that he went with a party of eight soldiers to Waterfall. Arriving outside a pub he jumped out and ran to the back door. There was 'a wild rush of civilians' trying to get out but he 'pointed his revolver at them and ordered them back into the bar'. There were about forty to fifty men in the room. Some wore bandoliers or belts and some carried revolvers. He ordered them to put their hands up. There was a loud clatter as revolvers, belts and bandoliers slid to the ground. One of the men had a waist belt on with a holster on the right side. Vining 'particularly noticed him' and the butt of a revolver was sticking out of the holster and the belt was fastened with a 'very noticeable brass buckle'. Vining identified this man as Murray. He recognised him having seen him twice before. He found a loaded Lee-Metford rifle and two loaded Webley revolvers. He found a loaded Mauser revolver, two bandoliers, fifty-one rounds of .303 ammunition and various belts. The belt he had seen worn by Murray had with it a loaded revolver. Some of the bullets had been 'nipped at the top'.

Lieutenant Colonel Evans gave corroborating evidence. He also told the court that as the raid began a man had 'dashed' against him and run down the road. He shouted at the man to stop and fired at him. He was shot and died. This, he learned later, was Walter Leo Murphy. Lieutenant

46.1 Round up of suspects, Martial Law Area 1921. Courtesy of the Trustees of the Imperial War Museum.

Colonel Evans ordered the release of some of the prisoners and held the others for trial.

All the accused gave evidence. All said they were at the pub for a drink or to watch 'the score of bowls'. None admitted to having or seeing weapons or being involved in the Volunteers. Few admitted to knowing Walter Leo Murphy. One or two tried to make light of their situation. Patrick Lane told the court that he had 'no arms or ammunition in his hands but he had a gallon of porter (laughter)'. A great many supporting witnesses were called including the landlady Mary Donovan, who told the court that she was a widow, a publican and ran a 70-acre farm. She had been working in the bar that night and there were forty to fifty men there. She did not see any arms. She told the court that the accused Eugene Riordan was her cousin and was employed by her and lived at the house. On the night in question she heard a shout of 'Black and Tans' and men rushed 'in all directions'. Some years previously Mary Donovan had been a domestic servant with no particular prospects. She worked for a well-to-do widower. They married but he died and she prospered as a publican and farmer. She emerges as a formidable landlady and it is likely that she would have been aware of all that went on in her pub.

Thomas Murray gave evidence. Immediately after he started to give evidence, the prosecutor announced that there was a further charge against the prisoner, namely possession of a handgun and six rounds of ammunition. Murray entered a not guilty plea. He told the court he was seventeen. He had known Leo Murphy 'but not too well'. He also admitted that he 'knew the officer who picked him out and the officer knew him'. Murray suggested the officer might have mixed him up with someone else at the bar. He was cross-examined:

> 'The officer said you were wearing a holster and belt. Do you suggest this officer was making a mistake?'
> 'I do.'
> 'Do you suggest that some other man was wearing that belt?'
> 'Yes. The officer could not have seen my waist at the time.'

Murray's sister told the court that he lived only 100 yards from the pub. He had worked that day and had eaten his supper at home and gone on 'to the score'. She added that he was not 'a Volunteer'. This evidence was supported by a railway man. He had been at the pub but was one of those released without charge.

Verdicts and Sentence

Murray was convicted of improper possession of a gun and ammunition and consorting with rebels. He was sentenced to death by shooting.[703] Nothing is known about this prisoner save that he was then seventeen, from Waterfall. William Dwyer and Patrick McAuliffe were acquitted of both charges.

The court rejected a plea by the prosecutor to convict all the prisoners on the basis of 'joint possession' and all others were acquitted of improper possession of arms and ammunition but convicted of consorting with rebels. Eugene Riordan, Daniel O'Keefe and John Driscoll were sentenced to six months' imprisonment. The rest were sentenced to one year's imprisonment.[704]

Whether the Military Court made a correct factual determination is entirely uncertain. The fact that the arms and ammunition were found in the pub was not disputed at the trial. Nor was it disputed that Walter Leo Murphy had been shot trying to escape. BMH statements make it clear that there was a bowls match at the pub that evening and also a battalion meeting.[705] Beyond this, the record of the trial does not provide sufficient detail to understand why the court drew distinctions on verdict or culpability.

An odd feature of the case was that a large number of men who had been at the pub were released immediately after the raid and no charges were brought against them. The evidence called at the trial does not reveal any distinction between them and most of those put on trial.[706] The entire trial is redolent with ambiguity. There are grounds to suspect that some of the men gave false names when arrested and maintained this fiction throughout the trial.

In relation to Murray there is one point which requires mention. The raid took place at 10.30 pm in a small, crowded country pub of the kind often filled with cigarette smoke and never well lit. No view is expressed on the correctness of the findings made by the court, it is simply observed that the evidence against Murray rested entirely on the identification made by Lieutenant Vining in the circumstances outlined.

The Truce came about a week after the trial. The case papers were reviewed by the JAG two weeks later. The review, which consists of a single line, confirms the proceedings were regular and the conviction and sentence in respect of Murray might be confirmed by General Macready.[707] Conviction and sentence of death were duly confirmed.

The Register shows that all the convicted men were released in January 1922.[708] The fate of the two men acquitted is less clear. At the end of the trial the record shows that 'no order was made regarding the release' of the men acquitted.[709]

46.2 Officers of the Auxiliary Division RIC (ADRIC). Courtesy of the Trustees of the Imperial War Museum.

CHAPTER FORTY-SEVEN

Denis Driscoll, Coolgarriv, Killarney, County Kerry

The prisoner was tried at Victoria Barracks on 6 July 1921. He was charged that at Coolgarriv on 1 July he was improperly in possession of a revolver, two rounds of revolver ammunition and two rounds of rifle ammunition.[710] The accused pleaded not guilty. He was represented by Joseph McCarthy.[711]

Evidence was given that a military and police party left Killarney on patrol at about 12.15 am on 30 June. At about 1 am they saw the accused in the townland of Inchicullane. He was cycling. He was halted and searched and in his coat pocket was found a revolver loaded in two chambers. Also found in his coat pocket were three revolver bullets with the tops cut off and a paper pattern of a firing target. The accused was cautioned and said he was 'in a bog all day'.

Cross-examined, the army witness stated that he thought the accused appeared 'a little simple'. A second witness corroborated the evidence given by the first and added that rifle ammunition was also found on the accused. The prosecution also adduced in evidence a statement made by the accused when the summary of evidence was taken. In reply to caution the accused said: 'I cannot recognise this court.' He stated that he was 'a soldier of the Republican Army and claimed the treatment of a prisoner of war'.

No evidence for the accused was called. Press reports refer to the accused as a young man. His counsel referred to him as a 'little boy', which may have been stretching the facts. The evidence was not disputed by counsel, who referred to the remarks made by the accused and described the accused as easily misled, 'unable to realise the gravity of the issues involved'. Counsel related that the accused had only been seen by his solicitor two days previously. He asked for time to put character statements before the court.

The prosecuting officer observed that the accused's comment about 'being in a bog' might mean a great deal more than his counsel had said.

The case was adjourned for character evidence to be placed before the court. The accused was sentenced to death by being shot.[712] The case papers were reviewed by the JAG. Conviction was approved.[713] Sentence was confirmed.[714]

CHAPTER FORTY-EIGHT

Grenagh House, Killarney, County Kerry

FRANK MORGAN, PETER O'CONNOR, THOMAS O'CONNOR AND JOHN O'CONNOR OF GRENAGH HOUSE

Grenagh House was a fine old Georgian residence overlooking the north shores of Lough Leane at Killarney. In 1921 it was owned by the O'Connor family, known locally as the Ponter-Connors on account of the father acquiring a sick panther from a travelling circus. The panther was restored to health and walked on a chain by the father, who became known locally as 'the Panther' and later Ponter-Connor. He ran a successful cattle business supplying beef to the army.[715] By 1921 Old Mr O'Connor had died and passed the farm to his four sons. In the summer of that year the Royal Fusiliers acquired information that wanted men sometimes sheltered at Grenagh House.

In the War of Independence the terrain shaped the conflict and this was very much the case in Killarney. The army barracks was in the town, flanked by the lake and overlooked by the mountains. The army could not move without being seen. As one officer later wrote: 'Whenever a party left barracks, smoke fires would go up on the hills.'[716]

In order to effect a raid, the Royal Fusiliers waited until late at night before setting off from Killarney in boats. Rowing with muffled oarlocks they crossed the lake[717] and landed near Grenagh House in the early hours. The raiding party achieved complete surprise. They seized a quantity of arms and ammunition and arrested three of the O'Connor brothers and Frank Morgan.

These accused were tried at Victoria Barracks on 6 and 7 July 1921. They were charged with a single offence, namely that at Grenagh House on 30 June 1921 they were improperly in possession of arms, ammunition and explosives, viz two service rifles, one revolver, one fully loaded revolver, ninety-six rounds of ammunition and two live grenades.

All four pleaded not guilty. Morgan stated he was a soldier of the

Irish Republic and refused to recognise the court. Joseph McCarthy[718] of counsel appeared for John O'Connor. Martin O'Connor[719] of counsel represented Peter and Thomas O'Connor. The record shows that Morgan was not 'professionally represented' but that the court assigned counsel to Morgan[720] although the record suggests the prisoner did not welcome this.

The first witness told the court that he had entered the house and found Peter O'Connor, who demanded to know what business he had coming into the house. In an upstairs room a service rifle was found and in a nest of drawers a revolver and belt and documents. Some women and John O'Connor were found upstairs together with Morgan. According to the witness, Morgan immediately took responsibility for all guns and documents in the house. Two more belts, one with ammunition, were found upstairs and a bandolier with ammunition and two haversacks were found. Each haversack contained a grenade. In a coat that was hanging up, twenty rounds of ammunition were discovered. A Webley revolver was found mixed up in blankets in a bedroom. In that bedroom there were three unmade beds. Thomas O'Connor was found standing at the door of a barn where he had apparently been sleeping.

An RIC district inspector gave evidence that he had known the O'Connor family for many years. They were a respectable farming family. They were 'young men who minded their own business'.[721]

Morgan was called for the defence of the O'Connors, despite an objection by the officer assigned to look after his interests. Morgan gave evidence that he was not related to the O'Connors. They were not Volunteers. The documents found in the house belonged to him. He said the guns and haversacks had been taken by himself and one other to the house at around 1 am on the night of the raid. They had climbed through the window and in doing so had been challenged by John O'Connor. He was not dressed. They were armed and told O'Connor they intended to sleep at the house. They told O'Connor to go to bed and he did so. There was no electric lighting in the house and they made their way to bed with the help of a torch. Morgan and his friend went to sleep and were woken by the military the next morning. Morgan said he prevented anyone going downstairs at the point of a revolver. The equipment was then spread out around the upper part of the house by him.

Morgan was asked for the name of his friend but declined to disclose it. Despite being pressed by the prosecuting advocate he maintained it was not 'necessary' to name his companion. He told the court that they had brought the equipment to the house with the aid of a bicycle. He stated that he had known Peter O'Connor twelve months. He knew John O'Connor slightly but did not know Thomas O'Connor. He told the court that he was from Killarney. He had been on the run. He was a Volunteer, a battalion engineer. He chose not to try and escape from the property because he did not wish to place responsibility on the O'Connors. He told the court that it had been his intention to clear out that morning and go 'to the mountains'.

Peter O'Connor gave evidence that he was the householder. He ran a substantial farm and dealt in cattle. He had not been involved in any illegal organisation and he had never allowed any Volunteer to come to his house. He had been awoken by the arrival of the military and had been arrested coming down the stairs.

Thomas O'Connor gave evidence that he had been drinking the night before and had arrived home at 11 pm. He was 'afraid' to knock at the door. He slept in the barn. John O'Connor denied being a Volunteer or bringing equipment to the house.

Counsel for Peter and Thomas O'Connor then announced that he had a professional commitment in London. Would the court kindly adjourn the case until his return? This was probably a ruse to buy time; the papers were full of the peace talks and a truce would bring a reprieve. The court ruled that the case could not be put back. In any event the case was stood over until the next day, when counsel appeared.

Helena O'Connor gave evidence. It appears she lived with her brothers and had 'supervision' of Grenagh House. She told the court that her brothers were not members of the IRA or the Volunteers. They had not gone drilling since 'the Arms Act'. This was a reference to the Firearms Act which came into force the summer before.[722] The Act increased penalties for possession of firearms and allowed the state greater power to stamp out drilling.

Helena O'Connor's evidence was slightly double-edged because it implied the men had been Volunteers at least until the summer before. Although it should be said that many young countrymen drilled in the summer of 1920 but took no part in the conflict. Whether the officers trying the accused appreciated this nuance is uncertain.

She maintained she had not seen guns in the house or correspondence relating to the Volunteers. She maintained that the guns could not have been at the property without her knowledge. She accepted that she was not at home on the night the army raided the house but maintained that she had not been told to stay away from the house that night. Her brothers spent most of their time 'playing cards at home'. None of them were away from home without her knowledge. One of them, Thomas, had been 'addicted to drink' for some years despite their efforts to help him.

The question of how Morgan's associate might have escaped the round-up seems to have occupied the court for some time. The logic seemed to be this: if there was an explanation for the disappearance of Morgan's unnamed friend, then Morgan's evidence might be true. If not, then his evidence was untrue.

In summing up, the Judge Advocate told the court that if they believed Morgan then that would be grounds to convict him but if they could not accept the evidence of this man then they would have to review the three cases individually. Morgan, he added, was 'a self-confessed criminal'.

The court closed for half an hour and reconvened and asked to hear character evidence, and was informed that nothing was known against the men.

Counsel for the O'Connors laid responsibility on Morgan. Morgan, when asked if he had anything to say, demanded to be treated 'as a prisoner of war'.

All four accused were convicted. The court, of course, had the opportunity of hearing and seeing the witnesses but the evidence against Peter O'Connor (the cattle dealer) appears slim. The evidence against Thomas, who on any reasonable view of the evidence had been sleeping off a hangover in the barn, was tenuous.

The case was reviewed by the JAG, who concluded that the convictions against the three O'Connors could not be regarded as 'safe' and should not be confirmed. His concern was shared by General Strickland.[723] The ground which caused the JAG to have concerns related to the joint trial of the O'Connors with Morgan, who admitted being actively involved in the rebellion whereas the others did not. This factor, the JAG reasoned, might have caused one or more of the O'Connor brothers to be circumspect in advancing their case.

Despite this clear direction, the Register at the National Archive shows that all the convictions were confirmed and all the prisoners were sentenced to death by shooting save for Thomas O'Connor, who was sentenced to life imprisonment.[724]

All four men were released in January 1922. The O'Connor fortunes took another bad turn around this time. The family, which had been prosperous and employed a number of servants, quickly went bankrupt and the farm was sold off. John O'Connor, who had been ill-treated in prison, emerged in 1922 minus an eye and a testicle. He emigrated to Canada and died a few years later, still in his twenties.

Peter O'Connor, still young at twenty-six, became a solicitor in London.[725] There is no information in relation to Thomas O'Connor or Frank Morgan.[726]

CHAPTER FORTY-NINE

William Ryan, Ballinroe, County Tipperary

The prisoner was tried at New Barracks, Limerick on 6 July. He was charged with levying war against the King in that on 23 June he and other civilians attacked an RIC patrol. He was represented by Edward McGelligott, King's Counsel.[727] He pleaded not guilty.

McGelligott objected to the jurisdiction of the court. No details are given but by this date Clifford and Sullivan was before the House of Lords and legal argument in Egan v Macready was taking place in the High Court in Dublin that very day. We can infer that counsel was advancing the same challenges to the jurisdiction.

A police sergeant gave evidence[728] that at about 8.15 pm on 23 June a police patrol operating in the townland of Ballinroe observed a party of nine civilians some distance away. They saw a man crossing the field towards them. This turned out to be the accused. He was called upon to halt but did not do so. Fire was opened on the civilians, who fired back from 'the cover of the furze'. The other civilians disappeared into a nearby wood.

A police constable gave evidence that when he first saw the accused he was about 80 yards away. He could not see if he was armed because he could only see his head and shoulders.

A civilian gave evidence identifying the prisoner who worked on his farm but had disappeared shortly before his capture.

Ryan gave evidence. He told the court he was a farm labourer and that he worked for a farmer about five miles from the scene of attack. On 22 June he worked as usual and left work at 5.30 pm. He went to Moyne and then returned. He was seen by a party of armed men who asked him if he was a member of the Republican Army. He said he was not. He was kept blindfolded. He said they brought him to Ballinroe where an order was given to halt. He was told to run by some men. He was frightened by the firing and did so. He denied being a member of the IRA or any secret society. He had never drilled or taken part in any ambush or act of violence. He told the court he had spent twenty-four hours in custody before being liberated.

The accused was acquitted and discharged. His account was an odd one but on the Crown evidence he was some distance from the civilian party when he was seen. There was no evidence he was armed or that he had taken part in the firing. How he came to be caught up in this way may be speculation. However, the most likely explanation is that he came upon an ambush party unexpectedly. They were reluctant to let him go in case he gave away their whereabouts and took him along.

CHAPTER FIFTY

Lieutenant Hanley Hunt, RNVR

Hanley Hunt was tried by a military court at New Barracks, Limerick on 7 July 1921. He faced two charges. First, questioning a soldier about troop movements at Tarbert on 9 June. Second, being improperly in possession of ammunition.[729] The accused, who was a lieutenant in the Royal Naval Reserve, was represented by Michael Binchy of counsel.[730] He pleaded not guilty.

A private soldier gave evidence that he had met the accused at Tarbert. They had moved from one pub to another. The accused had questioned him about the name of his commanding officer, the strength of his unit and matters relating to deployment. The soldier accepted in cross-examination that he had not mentioned in the summary of evidence that the accused had asked about troop strengths.

A military officer stated that he met the accused in Glin on 13 June. The accused had objected to a curfew imposed on the town because, as he put it, the place is 'quiet'. The following day he had declined to observe the curfew. The officer made inquiries of the accused and visited his hotel room. He searched his belongings and found four bullets with the nose cut through. Also found were two powder horns, some air pellets and a sporting cartridge.

The accused gave evidence and told the court that he was a member of the Royal Navy Reserve and had served in the navy during the war. He had served on HMS *Blake* with Commander Kenworthy, who had gone on to become a member of Parliament at Westminster. Hunt's only son had been killed in the Great War. He told the court he had been given the cartridges by another naval officer some time before. They were used for hunting game, such as deer. He gave up all ammunition after the proclamation but the four bullets escaped his notice.

He accepted that he had shared a drink with a private soldier. He had just come off ship. He probably had asked the name of his commanding officer with a view to calling on him. And, he added, he had called upon the commanding officer and had been treated most discourteously by a junior officer who had threatened to shoot him in the street. To which he had replied: 'Fire away, you ain't fit to pull the trigger.'

The accused's reliance on his friendship with Commander Kenworthy may not have helped his cause. Kenworthy had been a most trenchant critic of the army campaign in Ireland. He despised Lloyd George and this appears to have given his campaign an extra piquancy. The result was that Kenworthy was loathed by the military. Despite this connection, the Military Court acquitted the accused of the first charge: asking about troop movements. The court convicted the accused on the charge of possessing ammunition. He was fined £15.[731] Possession of ammunition was effectively an offence of strict liability but it might be inferred from the sentence that the Military Court accepted Hunt's explanation.

CHAPTER FIFTY-ONE

Father Noonan, Ballina and Boher, County Tipperary

Reverend James Noonan, parish priest of Ballina and Boher, was tried by military court at Limerick on 30 June. He was charged that on 26 June, at Ballina, he incited one James Hogan to disregard an order given by the military to remove an obstruction on the road. He was also charged with obstructing an Auxiliary by shaking his fist in the officer's face.

Father Noonan was not represented. He entered not guilty pleas.

An Auxiliary gave evidence that the roads around Ballina had been 'trenched'.[732] He had orders 'to round up all men of military age'[733] to repair the roads. Instructions were given to Hogan, who was then driving cattle belonging to Father Noonan. Hogan was ordered to join a work party to fill in trenches. He did not obey the order because at this point Father Noonan appeared and stated that it was very 'unjust' to order Hogan to carry this out as he was driving cattle from the field. The Auxiliary gave evidence that the cattle were safe in the yard and that Father Noonan's demeanour was very hostile: he 'shook his fist'. According to another account he shook his fist in the face of the officer.[734]

A second Auxiliary gave evidence that he told Father Noonan that 'no exceptions would be made' and that if the accused used his influence the 'road cutting' would cease. The accused then became 'noisy and abusive' and said that he could not stop the trench cutting and 'you people would not be able to do so'.

The Auxiliary then left but saw Father Noonan at his house later. He witnessed a conversation between an officer and Father Noonan in which the accused refused to let Hogan go and took full responsibility. The Auxiliary told the accused he would have to explain himself to the commanding officer. The accused said he would not go to the commanding officer. If he wanted him he would have to come and see the accused.

A third officer described Father Noonan as 'excited, insolent and abusive and shaking his fists'. The scene is not hard to imagine: red faced, eyes bulging fist shaking, Father Noonan comes across as an old-fashioned parish priest not used to being challenged.

In an unsworn statement Father Noonan told the court that the cattle were to be driven from the yard to the field where they would remain overnight. When he went out he was unable to find Hogan and found the cattle straying in the village. Curfew was approaching. It was some time later that he found Hogan. The cattle were 'dry' and he asked Hogan to give them water. He could not remember giving any other orders. He denied that he had any intention of interfering or obstructing the Auxiliaries in the course of their duty. His mind was 'fixed on the cattle'.

The prosecutor stated that he was glad Father Noonan expressed regret and would not press the case further. The prosecution came to an end on that note. The court imposed a £20 fine for threatening the officer.

This was probably one of the more ludicrous confrontations of this conflict, although it illustrates issues of wider importance. Father Noonan's conduct might ordinarily have merited an appearance before the justices. Because he was in the Martial Law Area he found himself before a court with unlimited powers. Inciting a civilian to defy an order given by the military was regarded as a serious matter which could not go unchallenged. It was probably for this reason and perhaps the position held by a parish priest in the community that this case was heard by the Military Court rather than the Summary Court. This is the context in which this bizarre prosecution was brought and tried.

The case is also noteworthy because of the use of forced civilian labour which was used mainly to combat the practice of trenching roads and demolishing bridges which had become widespread during the conflict. This issue has been explored elsewhere in this work.[735]

Proclamation No. 1 issued on 12 December 1920 required all citizens 'to obey and conform to all orders' given by the military.[736] In the Martial Law Area instructions governing the use of forced labour were issued by Brigade Major B.L. Montgomery.[737] Forced labour was confined to filling trenches, repairing bridges, removing obstacles erected by rebels or improving army defences. The instructions emphasise that the burden of doing such work should fall, where possible, on people with 'rebel sympathies'. Forced labour was not to be used for 'fatigue work in barracks'.

Sometimes the desired result was achieved by prohibiting fairs and markets until the roads and bridges were restored by the local people.[738]

In other instances local people were rounded up and compelled to fill in trenches, re-build bridges[739] or assist in the destruction of homes as part of official reprisals.[740]

In west Cork troops also used 'local civilian labour' to fill the trenches, but according to Major Percival of the Essex Regiment 'they would invariably be opened again within the next few days – probably by the same labour'.[741] In north Cork the Gloucester Regiment adopted a less confrontational approach; they seized the wheels of farmers' carts which were held in the barracks until trenches were filled in.[742] In rare instances the use of forced labour went further, for example cleaning Auxiliary headquarters at Macroom Castle.[743]

PART IV

CHAPTER FIFTY-TWO

Analysis of Trials by Military Court

Any analysis must start and end with a reference to the judgment of the Master of the Rolls in Egan v Macready, which found that the military courts were unlawful. The scale of what took place should also be acknowledged. The Military Court sentenced thirty-seven men to death, of whom fourteen were executed. Sentence was commuted to penal servitude in five cases,[744] and of the other eighteen, two successfully sought writs of habeas corpus[745] and sixteen remained under sentence of death until early 1922.[746] There were, in addition, approximately thirty-three other men serving sentences of life or ten years or more and a much larger number serving short sentences. These men were of course part of a wider pool convicted and sentenced under the ROIA or interned under statutory powers.

There are limitations on what can be said. In some cases the trial papers have not been preserved. In the case of fourteen prisoners it has not been possible to trace any record of the trial. This analysis of the Military Court and the Register[747] is subject to those limitations.

A starting point might be to dispel a perception that has grown up over the years: that all or most of the prisoners tried by the Military Court were actively involved in the rebellion. It was certainly intended that military courts would be used for exactly that purpose and as the year wore on this class of prisoner became the focus of the system. The evidence clearly suggests that many of the prisoners were active Volunteers but in fact the system did not target suspects with precision. It was pointed out at the outset of this study that the prisoners tried included one Auxiliary, three RIC men, three domestic servants, a housewife, a parish priest, an officer of the Royal Naval Volunteer Reserve, a Unionist landowner, and two men with learning difficulties, one of whom was severely disabled.[748] It also included the Waterfall trial in which nineteen men were convicted, not of being involved in the rebellion but of 'consorting with rebels'. It is tentatively suggested that a significant number of the men and women tried had no active involvement in the rebellion.

The types of cases dealt with by military courts were dictated by an odd mix of circumstances and army resources. When martial law was implemented in December 1920 the RIC had almost ceased to act as a police force and to a significant extent their policing functions had been taken over by the army. The 6th Division had no training in a policing role and the army's experience of prosecutions was confined to the courts martial of soldiers and latterly of civilians under the Defence of the Realm Regulations and the ROIA. The 6th Division legal branch based at Victoria Barracks comprised of only half a dozen officers. By December 1920 their caseload was a difficult one and it grew quickly.

A review of the trials shows that the prosecution did not rely on forensic evidence such as fingerprinting. It is doubtful if the 6th Division even possessed that expertise. It is also clear that there were no cases where forensic evidence was called by the defence. The 6th Division also lacked experience in conducting identification parades and received no training in this area. This was a remarkable omission because even in that time it was recognised that the conduct of identification parades required skills that were subtle and not obvious. Nor was there any organised attempt to secure confessions for use as evidence.

The caseload of the Military Court was also shaped by the fact that the army was usually unable to call civilian evidence in support of prosecutions. Witnesses were unwilling to come forward because their loyalty lay elsewhere or because they feared the consequences of giving evidence. In the trials reviewed in this study there were only four in which a civilian witness gave evidence for the Crown. In three of these cases the civilian witness was plainly reluctant and favoured the defence. There is also the trial of Michael Casey (Newmarket on Fergus) where the widow of the deceased withdrew the statement she had given to police.

No cases came about as a result of prolonged observation or investigation. Typically these cases came about as a result of a raid where men were captured resting up: Clonmult is one example, Rahanisky House and O'Brien's Castle are others. Occasionally information received allowed the army to surprise Volunteers preparing an ambush: Dripsey is one example. Much more unusually men were captured while in ambush: Mourne Abbey is one example and Patrick Casey (Ballybricken) another. One other source of arrests was motorised patrols. Clifford and Sullivan were captured in this way, as was John Allen. Each was found to be armed and the prosecution was confined to that narrow factual issue.

Referral For Trial by Military Court

The process by which prisoners were selected for trial by the Military Court (as opposed to courts martial under the ROIA) is worth examination.

First, soldiers were dealt with by military law. Second, after an initial flurry of cases, including Hart and three other constables, RIC men charged with serious offences[749] were always diverted towards courts martial under the ROIA. The Military Court was intended to focus on those actively involved in the rebellion.

According to the case papers that survive, the process involved the Military Governor satisfying himself that trial by ROIA court martial was 'impracticable'. A proforma setting out the test can be found in some of the earlier trial papers.[750] No reasons were given as to why trial by the method sanctioned by law was not practicable. The trial of Cornelius Murphy, for instance, took a little over an hour and the question arises: why was it impracticable for that case to be tried by court martial under the Restoration of Order in Ireland Act? There is no logical answer to this question save that trial by the Military Court was quicker and it was General Strickland's preferred forum. The proclamations of martial law converted a number of criminal offences into capital crimes and also created military courts to try these cases and impose capital sentences. This analysis is supported by a memo circulated by General Strickland: 'Military courts are as a rule kept for those offences where a death sentence is likely to be awarded which cannot be awarded according to the ordinary law.'[751] That in essence is how these cases came to be tried by military courts.

It is tentatively suggested that the primary factors in determining trial by the Military Court involved an assessment of the circumstances of capture. Where there was an inference that the prisoner was actively involved in the rebellion, then this pointed towards trial by military court. Intelligence about the offender might also influence the decision. In the case of Clifford and Sullivan where the case papers are very full, there is an inference that intelligence about the men dictated the decision to try them by military court. A review of the trials suggest a final yardstick, namely that the facts of the case were straightforward.

The Charges

Most of the accused were tried for possession of arms and/or levying war or conspiracy to levy war against the King. A handful were charged with possession of explosives, military equipment or documents prejudicial to martial law. Two prisoners were tried for murder and one for shooting with intent to murder.

Other charges were directed to those who gave assistance to the rebels: harbouring rebels, aiding insurrection, consorting with rebels, failing to give information or giving false information or asking questions about troop movements or in one case disobeying an order.

Legal Training for Officers Trying Cases before Military Courts

It was a necessary condition of trials under the ROIA that one of the tribunal members be certified 'as a person of legal knowledge and experience'.[752] In trials before the Military Court there was no such requirement. There is a question as to whether officers serving on military courts had significant legal training and experience. Lieutenant Colonel Meyler, head of the 6th Division legal branch, was a solicitor. He probably had extensive experience of the courts martial process but a review of his career suggests it is unlikely he had any significant experience of conducting serious prosecutions. Lieutenant Colonel Vandeleur, who sat as president of many of the trials which resulted in executions, also had no legal training. Many of the officers trying these cases did have courts martial experience in the Great War but that is not reassuring having regard to the literature on this subject.[753]

Judge Advocates

The pool of army lawyers available was a small one. The *Record of the Rebellion* candidly recounts that after the Great War any lawyers of 'standing or ability' left the service and returned to private practice.[754]

The JAG ran a ticketing system in which officers of sufficient legal training were placed on a panel which authorised them to sit as judge advocates in ROIA trials. A smaller panel was authorised to sit on ROIA courts martial where the charge carried the death penalty. By the spring of 1921, Captain Branston and Captain F.E. Young, who were part of the 6th Division legal branch, were ticketed to sit as judge advocates in ROIA courts martial where the death penalty could not be imposed.[755] No such ticketing system existed in relation to military courts. Captain Branston and Captain Young sat as Judge advocates in a number of military court cases where the death penalty was imposed.

Even those authorised to sit as Judge Advocates were capable of making basic errors. An example is the trial of Joseph Murphy for the murder of Private Squibbs. This was a prosecution under the ROIA but the principle raised is of general application. In that case the Judge Advocate declined to allow cross-examination of witnesses about prior inconsistent statements. This error was recognised by the High Court, although it declined to intervene.[756] There are other examples, in the case of Mulcahy and Ronayne it was acknowledged by the JAG that the Judge Advocate had wrongly allowed cross-examination of an accused about a confession which he had ruled to be inadmissible.[757] In the Clonmult case, in which Captain Young was Judge Advocate, he gave an erroneous ruling on an elementary point of admissibility.[758]

The picture, however, is a mixed one. In some trials the focus of the court reporter has fallen to a significant extent on the Judge Advocate. In these cases, notably O'Brien's Castle, Adam Jones and Mallow Barracks, the remarks of the Judge Advocate indicate competence and detachment.

Prosecution Advocates

In serious or capital ROIA trials prosecution counsel was often brought over from England, usually on the Holyhead ferry and then by destroyer to Cork. These advocates were brought over primarily because trials and pre-trial procedures under the ROIA were complex.

The Military Court procedures were more straightforward and therefore all these trials were prosecuted by officers drawn from the 6th Division legal branch. Major Gover, who was a barrister by training, prosecuted a number of the multi-handed trials, such as Dripsey, Clonmult and Rahanisky House.

The officer who probably prosecuted most of the Military Court trials was Captain Young, who was the courts martial officer for the 6th Division. Young prosecuted John Allen, Ronayne and Mulcahy and Patrick Casey. He was also Judge Advocate in the Rahanisky House and Clonmult trials. He featured, therefore, in a significant number of the trials in which records survive at the National Archive and by inference many more.

Captain Young was described in the JAG's files as a solicitor. He was then a young man in his late twenties who had spent most of the Great War in France. It has already been suggested that his experience of legal practice must have been slight. It should be said that the experience and training necessary to conduct serious prosecutions ought not to be underestimated.

Captain Young's conduct of the prosecution of men accused of the Mallow Barracks raid fell far short of the necessary standard.[759] Two criticisms were not disputed at the trial: breaching an undertaking given to a defence solicitor and the destruction of part of the summary of evidence which may have assisted the accused.

Captain Young also prosecuted Ronayne and Mulcahy, where he persuaded the Judge Advocate to allow him to cross-examine the accused about a confession which had been ruled inadmissible.[760] Young also prosecuted Patrick Casey (Ballybricken) in which he successfully opposed the prisoner's application to adjourn to get legal representation. These would constitute significant failings in a professional advocate but Young was an officer in an army, with limited experience of law. He had become part of the process.

Legal Representation of Prisoners

The evidence suggests that those prisoners who wanted to be legally represented were represented. A single exception was Patrick Casey (Ballybricken), whose case we shall turn to in due course. In those cases where prisoners appeared at their trial unrepresented they were offered the assistance of an officer acting as 'prisoner's friend'. In cases where records survive, this was usually declined.[761]

The *Circular Memoranda* required that where a prisoner declined representation, an officer should be appointed to watch his case and report back to the Military Governor.[762] There is no evidence as to whether this happened or to what extent it served any purpose. The representation of prisoners was undertaken by a small number of solicitors,[763] who often instructed counsel or King's Counsel. Although some of the advocacy is a little quaint by modern standards, there is no doubt the work was done well.

There was of course no system of publicly funded representation. There is evidence that the families of prisoners often paid for representation.[764] There was a large and active legal profession and counsel fees were modest. In the appeal to the Lords in Clifford and Sullivan, King's Counsel's fees were collected by public subscription in the Mitchelstown area. In some cases the lawyers acted out of conviction[765] or waived or reduced fees because they were moved by the plight of the prisoner or his family.

Preparation for Defence While Awaiting Trial

The shortest period between capture and trial was a single day.[766] The usual duration between capture and trial was about two or three weeks. This figure was occasionally longer where the accused or a witness was recovering from wounds. All trials before the Military Court commenced with certain formalities, one of which was an inquiry as to whether the accused was ready for trial. The trial records show that usually counsel indicated they were ready. Four exceptions can be identified where the accused were self-evidently not ready for trial but applications to adjourn were refused.[767] These cases make uncomfortable reading.

Trial Issues

Challenging the jurisdiction of the court was still a common stance in courts martial under the ROIA even in the summer of 1921. This was because the death sentence was confined to cases of murder and levying war. The sentencing powers of the Military Court were not limited and therefore the practice of denying jurisdiction was less common.

A significant number of prisoners challenged the legal jurisdiction of the Military Court at their trial, usually through counsel. The dilemma for the prisoner arose when the challenge was overruled. Two prisoners took no part in their trial and pursued their challenge through the High Court.[768] Much more commonly, prisoners who challenged the jurisdiction of the court went on to defend the case on the facts.

There were a number of cases in which the prisoners were captured with arms in a house: Rahanisky House, the Clonmult siege, the Waterfall raid and O'Brien's Castle are examples. The cases turned on whether the accused had an innocent explanation for presence at the scene.

Confession evidence was rarely relied upon by the Military Court. An important distinction needs to be made here. There is ample evidence of casual brutality, or worse, particularly at the point of capture[769] or in outlying barracks.[770] In general, however, the Military Court cases reviewed suggest that there was no system of interrogation to secure admissions for use in evidence. Nor were the Military Court trials characterised by disputed admissions or allegations of violence used to secure admissions. There are a few exceptions: Thomas Mulcahy, who was wounded and captured at Mourne Abbey, was asked two critical questions after capture,[771] namely whether he had taken part in the ambush, and where his gun was. In the case of Cregan, an RIC officer readily agreed that the accused was hit with a rifle butt during questioning. In both of these cases the confession was excluded by the court. The only case in which the accused were subject to a formal interview was that of Punch and Murphy. In that case also, the interviews were excluded by the court, there being evidence of maltreatment while in custody. In the case of Egan, a disputed admission was given in evidence after a voire dire.[772] In the case of O'Callaghan,[773] the accused was questioned when wounded and confessed to being a courier rather than a combatant, which was consistent with the case he advanced at trial, and for this reason, one suspects, no application to exclude was made. In the O'Brien's Castle case, allegations of ill-treatment were made but not found to be proved.

The question needs to be asked as to why there was no concerted effort to secure admissions. The answer may be that the ability of the RIC to carry out policing functions had been greatly compromised. Second, most of the prisoners were in the custody of the army or were quickly transferred to the custody of the 6th Division, which did not engage in the process of interviews for use in evidence. The trials focused on what could readily be proved about the conduct of the accused at the point of arrest. Therefore, in many trials the dispute was whether the prisoner was armed and, if so, could he provide an innocent explanation. In other cases the issue was confined to what the accused could be proved to have done, for instance taking part in an ambush, the destruction of a bridge, harbouring rebels or possessing seditious documents.

A number of cases involved disputed identification and/or alibi. Identification parade procedures in the Martial Law Area were not well conducted by contemporary standards and this was recognised by the JAG in one of his many advices.[774] Examples include Punch and Murphy, the case of Dennehy and Cunningham and the Mallow Barracks raid. Visual identification is now recognised as an inherently unreliable form of evidence.[775] Juries are always reminded of the special need for caution when the case depends largely or wholly on the strength of visual identification. They are also reminded that there have been many instances of wrongful identifications and the fact that a convincing witness may be mistaken. These directions are the product of the hard-earned experience of the criminal courts, which are alert and receptive to these issues. But they were also well known to the criminal courts in 1921. At the turn of the twentieth century a series of highly publicised miscarriages of justice based on flawed identification evidence led to the setting up of the Court of Appeal.[776] It is likely, however, that these issues were not at all well known in the army.

Nearly every case of disputed identification also involved an alibi advanced by the accused. This gave rise to other difficulties because many officers who served in the 6th Division were inclined to believe that prisoners would go to great lengths to construct false alibis. There is evidence they were briefed to that effect.[777] The view expressed by Lieutenant Grazebrook about the trial of Dennehy and Cunningham echoed the feelings of other officers: 'Many witnesses went down from Kanturk and Kilbrin to swear black was white.'[778] In general terms there is evidence that some witnesses gave untrue alibi evidence or conspired to do so.[779] There is also evidence that some defence solicitors tried to subvert the trial process in any way they could.[780] That is not surprising, but it was an added complication to the fact-finding process. As the Mallow Barracks case demonstrates, officers were sometimes unable to discern a bona fide alibi.

Observations About the Trial Process

The picture is not straightforward. As we have seen, prisoners were represented if they wished and were able to pay. Trials were open to the press and the public.

The evidence shows that prisoners were able to cross-examine witnesses. There is evidence in a few cases of witnesses being obstructive or unhelpful to defence counsel and being called to account by the court.[781]

Most of the prisoners tried by the Military Court gave evidence, a privilege that was denied those being tried under the ROIA. Those who did not were exposed to an adverse inference not available under civil law.

One account of the Military Court trials suggested that trials were rushed. A contemporary account of the trial of Patrick Higgins implied that he was tried, convicted and sentenced to death in the space of fifteen minutes and that other prisoners were dealt with in a similar manner:[782] 'He and I were called out, and marched across the square to the court martial quarters. He was led in while I was kept outside the door. He was in for less than fifteen minutes when he came out, and was put aboard a lorry bound for Cork jail: he had been sentenced to death.'

A consequence is that other historians have, quite understandably, taken up this criticism and concluded that some trials 'were conducted in a very rushed manner'.[783] There are many significant criticisms of the Military Court but this one cannot be sustained.[784] Higgins was represented by counsel at his trial. During the trial six witnesses gave evidence for the Crown. Higgins himself gave evidence and called four witnesses. The trial lasted over a day. None of this proves that the trial was fair or unfair but it disposes of a small myth attaching to these trials. There is other evidence on this point. In the case of O'Brien's Castle, the court adjourned and visited the scene to evaluate defence submissions about lines of sight. In the case of Dennehy and Cunningham, the court adjourned and the army provided assistance in tracing defence witnesses who had gone missing.

A question does arise as to whether military courts abided by the rules set up for trial. The answer is a mixed one. The rules governing the Military Court were created by the army to meet the prevailing conditions and were amended where necessary in the face of a rebellion that was continuing to present new problems. As a consequence, the rules evolved swiftly. For instance, the presence of the accused at the taking of the summary of evidence was soon dispensed with. There were compelling pragmatic reasons for this but it should be remembered that the presence of the accused at the taking of the summary of evidence was regarded as an important protection for the accused and this was demonstrated in the Mallow Barracks trial where evidence which was potentially helpful to an accused was destroyed.

By the summer of 1921 an odd hybrid system had emerged in which trials were still being conducted by reference to the rules of procedure governing Field General Court Martial[785] and also by the *Circular Memoranda*. Even when the rules governing the Military Court were finally drawn together in the *Circular Memoranda*, these provisions were departed from when it was thought necessary, as in the so-called drumhead trials, to which we will return.

A linked issue related to compliance with the Treason Acts which provided for sentence of death but which also conferred certain protections on the accused, the most notable of which was the requirement that there be evidence 'upon the oath of two lawful and credible witnesses'. The *Circular Memoranda* stipulated that the Military Court should observe the rules of evidence 'as strictly as any other court'[786] but there are a number of cases in which the protections of the Treason Acts were ignored.[787]

There are other factors which bear on the fairness of the trial process. By late spring the *Circular Memoranda* came to govern, at least in theory, the procedure in the Military Court, although the evidence suggests that this document was never made public or circulated to advocates defending these trials. There are a number of indicators. A close reading of some of the trials makes it clear that the advocates were not just unfamiliar with the forum, they were not privy to the rules under which the trial was being conducted.[788] A review of the cases discloses a single oblique reference in the course of legal argument to the *Circular Memoranda*, where prosecuting counsel misquotes the Regulations without contradiction by his opponent.[789] In this regard it should be noted that the *Circular Memoranda* contained a number of provisions relating to severance, adjournments, representation, rules of evidence and an entitlement for time to prepare a defence and matters of that kind. But the case papers do not show any attempt by counsel to utilise these provisions to the advantage of the accused and there is therefore an inference that counsel were not privy to this document. A final and obvious point is that the memoranda is marked 'Confidential' and 'For official use only'. If this analysis is correct, it is a striking example of procedural unfairness.

There were other, more profound shortcomings in the trial system. The army was acting as complainant, prosecutor and judge. The head of the 6th Division legal branch sometimes sat on military court trials as judge advocate and those who prosecuted were his immediate subordinates.[790] The relationship was uncomfortably close.

In an effort to meet some of these concerns, orders were given that officers who sat on military courts did not go out on patrol.[791] This step was taken to ensure that officers were not prejudiced by reason of their experiences. But many of the officers who sat on these courts were drawn from regiments that were suffering significant casualties and they shared living accommodation with others who were in the front line.

In these circumstances, even the decision by General Strickland to order trial by military court carried with it unspoken implications about the gravity of the case and the culpability of the accused which cannot have been lost on junior officers trying these cases.

The officers who sat on these courts also served on ROIA courts martial and courts of inquiry into the deaths of civilians caused by the military. This pool of officers shared many duties. To take one example: Cornelius Murphy was prosecuted by Captain Branston. A few days later the records show the same officer sitting on a court of inquiry considering the causes and the legality of Murphy's execution.[792] This small group of officers rotated duties when necessary. They had become part of a process and nothing could rescue the Military Court from the accusation of partiality.

There was one particular difficulty that did apply to the Military Court and ROIA trials with particular force: the gulf in class, lifestyle and custom between the officers trying these cases and the prisoners was substantial. One senses that the life experience of the officers was so remote from the men they were trying that they often struggled to evaluate evidence.

It should also be said that the atmosphere in which these cases were conducted was not conducive to impartial reflection. These circumstances were brought about by the rebellion itself. Thus names of witnesses and the names of officers were withheld from the public because of the very real threat to the lives of those involved in running military courts. The accused were also under heavy guard throughout the trial and it was the practice of the President of the court to place his revolver on the table close to hand.[793] None of this helped achieve a dispassionate consideration of the evidence.

In one case there is evidence the court was manifestly hostile – the Clonmult case gave rise to a famous rebuke by Michael Comyn, King's Counsel: 'Shoot them if you must but try them first.'[794] The evidence on this issue is necessarily anecdotal. There are other indicators. In the Clonmult case the court deliberated for twenty minutes before returning convictions for levying war against six of the accused. It is difficult to see how the court could have given separate consideration to the case for and against each accused in this short time. In the Mallow Barracks case five prisoners were convicted of murder after deliberations lasting only forty-five minutes. It is suggested that, having regard to the number of witnesses called, this was insufficient time to even read through the note of evidence.

Balanced against this are a significant number of other cases in which trials were conducted in the spirit of fairness.[795] There are also very occasional examples of the prosecuting officer taking steps which are only consistent with a desire to be fair.[796]

A small number of men who were tried by military court later made statements to the Bureau of Military History.[797] All of them challenged the jurisdiction of the Military Court but none of them complained that the officers conducting the trial were overtly partisan. In fact, Malone, for one, seemed quite impressed with the colonel who conducted his trial.[798] Perhaps not much weight should attach to this point because it is apparent from a close reading of the statements that the men regarded their trial as an incidental part of their account. The real areas of concern are more fundamental.

Did Verdicts Accord with the Evidence?

Before answering this question it is necessary to recognise that a trial which is unlawful can never be fair. Second, the protections present under civil law or under ROIA courts martial were not present in military court trials. Third, in the Military Court trials the frequent consequence of conviction was to expose a prisoner to a capital sentence which was not available under civil law. Any inquiry on this issue is subject to those limitations.

It should also be remembered that the Military Court had the advantage of seeing and hearing the witnesses. Second, many of the case papers have been destroyed. We are therefore doubly handicapped in making an assessment.

Of the 128 men and women tried, nearly 25 per cent were acquitted. This statistic may be significant, but without knowing more about the quality of evidence called, it is not possible to draw safe inferences. In any event only three prisoners made a formal admission of guilt or entered a guilty plea[799] and in cases where prisoners were at risk of execution, a not guilty plea was always entered by the court. Having regard to these factors and the relatively small number tried, no safe conclusions are possible on this account.

A review of statements made to the BMH does not reveal any obvious errors made by the Military Court.[800] Thomas Malone, for instance, denied the right of the court to try him but he evidently accepted that the verdict reflected the evidence.[801]

There are some trials where serious doubts were expressed at the time by General Strickland or the JAG. In the case of Daniel O'Callaghan, General Strickland entertained grave doubts about the conviction but this did not stop execution.[802] Strickland also expressed the view that the convictions of the O'Connor brothers should be set aside but they were not. Similar concerns were raised by the JAG following the trial of John O'Sullivan.

There remain significant doubts in relation to the convictions of the younger prisoners in the Clonmult case. There are also a smattering of other cases which give rise to serious doubts. Hassett (O'Brien's Castle) is one. Thomas Keane is another. A question mark hangs over the conviction of a number of men in the Waterfall trial. There is also the Mallow Barracks trial, which provides a unique insight into the shortcomings of the trial system. In many other trials, the case papers do not survive, and there is simply insufficient information on which to form a judgment. It should not be forgotten that the lower tier of the Military Court, the Summary Court, imposed 549 sentences of imprisonment. The Summary Court is outside the scope of this inquiry. All that can be said is that no records were kept, and most prisoners were unrepresented; in view of this analysis there was ample scope for error and unfairness.

Sentence

Again, caution must be exercised because in many cases the original case papers do not survive and we are not privy to the full facts. Subject to that qualification, a number of points may be made.

A criticism advanced in the spring of 1921 was that the justice system discriminated in favour of loyalists. It was certainly the policy to draw a distinction between loyalists and those known to be disaffected.[803] Very few loyalists came before the Military Court, probably only two: William Gabbett, a landowner, former army officer and supporter of the Union, was convicted on charges of possession of ammunition and fined £75. Hanley Hunt of the Royal Navy Volunteer Reserve was convicted of possession of ammunition and he too was fined. These men did not pose a threat to the Union and were dealt with accordingly.

There are more cogent criticisms of the sentencing practices of the Military Court. The main purpose of the military courts was to impose capital sentences for those in possession of arms but the disparity in sentencing was remarkable. In the Rahanisky House trial, eleven men were convicted of conspiracy to levy war and sentenced to long terms of imprisonment. The decision not to sentence the men to death was greeted with dismay at the headquarters of the 6th Division.[804] There are a number of such cases. Whether this was because the officers trying these cases had reservations about the quality of the evidence or were out of step with High Command is open to question.

In the case of Cornelius Murphy, convicted of possessing a handgun and ammunition, the Military Court imposed the death sentence but made a strong recommendation for mercy. He was executed. There are a number of comparable cases where the death sentence was not imposed for arms offences. And there were a number of cases of men convicted of the much more serious offence of levying war who escaped the death penalty. It is difficult to discern an intelligible pattern. For instance, five men convicted of participating in the Dripsey ambush were sentenced to death and executed. In respect of one, Daniel O'Callaghan, the Military Court made a recommendation for mercy but he was executed. The following month Denis Murphy, having recovered from his wounds, was tried, convicted and sentenced to death for participating in the same ambush. No recommendation for mercy was made but his sentence was commuted.

It may be that in the minds of the officers trying these cases, the charge on which a prisoner was convicted was the primary measure of culpability but not the only one. The inconsistencies are still remarkable. Something may be gleaned from Judge Babington's study of courts martial in the Great War.[805] These trials took place only a few years earlier and are comparable for that reason. Judge Babington's conclusion was unflattering: that many officers lacked the skills and experience to try serious cases. Particularly on the issue of passing capital sentences, they were simply 'out of their depth'.

Review and Confirmation

The process of confirmation had two elements. First, the Military Governor in Cork (General Strickland) or the Military Governor in Limerick (Brigadier Cameron) would send the case papers to GHQ Parkgate in Dublin. In cases not attracting the death penalty there would usually be a brief endorsement recommending confirmation of sentence. Where the death penalty had been imposed there would be a short note which usually read: 'Recommend that the sentence be carried out.'[806] In a few cases there might be a longer endorsement; for instance, in the case of Keane,[807] Brigadier Cameron forwarded a petition to Macready with a note stating that the petition for reprieve was supported by individuals of substance who were known to be loyal to the Crown.

In the case of Clifford and Sullivan, General Strickland wrote a short note confirming the sentence of death for each man based on intelligence about their involvement.[808] By the prevailing standards of criminal law and the courts martial process, the practice was not unusual, although it was unsatisfactory because the prisoners had no opportunity of commenting on the reliability of that material. In fact for reasons set out in the chapter on Clifford and Sullivan, the intelligence on those two men was substantially inaccurate and overstated their involvement but it probably influenced the key decisions, namely trial by military court and, following conviction, confirmation of sentence of death.

The case papers were usually reviewed by the office of the Judge Advocate General in Dublin but in cases where the death penalty had been imposed, excepting so-called drumhead trials, the papers were reviewed by the JAG in London. The JAG would provide a short advice to General Macready, who would then make a decision to confirm the conviction and sentence or not.[809]

There is no doubt that Jack Shine, John O'Sullivan, Diarmuid O'Leary, Punch and Murphy owe their lives to the intervention of the JAG. The early advices written by the JAG show detailed consideration of the evidence. As the months passed the advices shortened to five or six lines and a few no more than a single line: a case in point is that of Thomas Murray, aged seventeen, sentenced to death for possession of arms on the strength of a single disputed identification.[810]

Cassel's view appeared to be that his role was not to act as a court of appeal or to second guess the tribunal that saw and heard the witnesses. He took the view that his role was confined to ensuring the charge was known to law, supported by evidence and that the proceedings were otherwise regular and his advices reflect this.

One final observation on the process of confirmation. A feature of the 1921 trials was the petitions launched to save prisoners. In a number of these cases, extensive petitions were put before General Macready. Representations were made by a variety of interested parties, mainly backbenchers at Westminster and senior clergy. The case papers which survive suggest that General Macready was entirely uninfluenced by external pressures such as these and this is well illustrated in the case of J.J. Egan and Thomas Keane, where General Macready confirmed sentence despite such pressures.

Drumhead Trials

It may be appropriate to conclude this analysis by reference to the so-called 'drumhead' trials. How many took place during the War of Independence? It is necessary to define the term 'drumhead', which is not an easy task, since it had no legal status. In the context of this conflict, however, the description may be applied to a trial where the prisoner was denied representation and/or the usual process of review by the Judge Advocate General was avoided. In his memoirs, General Macready wrote of three[811] and O'Malley suggests at least two.[812] It now seems clear that there were only two instances when this procedure was used. The first was Patrick Casey, who was captured on 1 May and tried and executed the following day. The second case was that of Daniel O'Brien, tried two weeks later. O'Brien is in a slightly different category because he declined the opportunity to be represented and offered no defence. Patrick Casey, on the other hand, was denied the opportunity of being represented. In his case it is clear that the military abandoned their usual procedures in order to avoid the prisoner being represented and bringing a legal challenge.

Both of these cases took place in May 1921 when the army was losing the initiative in the conflict. The available evidence shows that the executions took place in contravention of standing orders given by the Army Council in London. They demonstrate a particular feature of this era: that as the conflict wore on, the army was given or assumed increasing powers. In the summer of 1921, plans were laid to extend martial law to the twenty-six counties. Those plans (reviewed in Chapter 16) included mass internment, a suspension of habeas corpus and a dramatic increase in the use of 'drumhead' trials to try and execute those caught with arms. By reason of Proclamation No. 8, the plans also included a major extension of the military courts to try those who were essentially bystanders. Mercifully the Truce held and the plans were never put into operation. This episode remains a salutary lesson in the dangers of departing from due process.

CHAPTER FIFTY-THREE

Postscript

The army began a withdrawal from the twenty-six counties in early 1922 and the campaign in Ireland became the subject of lectures at staff college. Even the use of martial law came under scrutiny, although the analysis was disappointingly banal: 'cavalry are useless in a city against armed insurgents' was one of the gems offered to up and coming officers.[813]

General Macready retired, he was created a baronet and wrote his memoirs. General Strickland returned to England and was later appointed general officer commanding Egypt. Both men lived to their eighties. Lieutenant Colonel Vandeleur retired in 1922. He also lived well into his eighties. His son, J.O.E. Vandeleur, commanded the Irish Guards at Arnhem.

Lieutenant Colonel Meyler, the legal officer for the 6th Division, was appointed CBE for his services in Ireland. He retired from the army in 1922 and was elected to Westminster as a Liberal member of Parliament but quickly lost his seat. He then ran a small legal practice in London until 1929 when financial difficulties resulted in a court order for the seizure of his assets. The Sheriff attended his offices to enforce the court order. The colonel's secretary later told the coroner there was a brief confrontation with the Sheriff before Meyler appeared in the doorway, 'white, distressed and upset'. He went to an office and shot himself dead.

Henry Hanna KC served as a judge of the High Court for many years. Tim Healy KC became the first Governor General of Ireland.

Three other advocates call for mention. First, Patrick Lynch and Michael Comyn emerge as probably the most formidable advocates of their generation. Mention must also be made of Joseph McCarthy, who represented many of the prisoners, notably those without money or connections. McCarthy emerges as a thoughtful and compassionate advocate. He went on to serve on the Circuit Bench.

Patrick Lynch KC enjoyed a long and successful career at the Bar. The quality of his advocacy was long remembered.[814] Lynch went on to serve in Seanad Éireann and was later Attorney General. Michael Comyn KC practised for many years before going up to Seanad Éireann and later to the Bench where he presided over the Eastern Circuit. In later years he was remembered as both just and kind, a rather stout figure with a fondness for snuff. He sat for many years after the compulsory retirement age because his birth had never been registered and the Department of Justice were unable to force his retirement.[815]

As to the prisoners, Cadet Hart, who had been fortunate to escape with his life, was released from Broadmoor in 1922. He appears to have been reunited with his wife Bessy. They emigrated. The other prisoners, those that survived, were released in early 1922 to pick up the threads of their lives as best they could. Many were caught up in the Civil War that followed.

As to the wider picture, the War of Independence in Ireland was followed by civil war and military courts sat frequently: there were seventy-seven executions. The few that sought legal redress found that the courts of the Irish Free State followed the line of decisions established by ex parte Marais[816] and that of John Allen.[817] One, Erskine Childers, a former clerk of the House of Commons, was executed while his application for a writ of habeas corpus had yet to be determined.[818] Others were executed without trial. This was one of the unpalatable legacies of 1921, a perception that the rule of law was a tool, to be ignored or manipulated.

This review, however, would not be complete without a reminder that military courts were not specific to Ireland or even the Empire. Military courts were deployed in the United States during the Indian Wars to try native Indian combatants: in the American Revolutionary War, the American Civil War[819] and many other wars and conflicts. They still appear at times of crisis, in different parts of the world. In common law jurisdictions, the remedy for the prisoner, if there is one, is still a writ of habeas corpus.

APPENDIX 1

Proclamation of Martial Law, 10 December 1920

Whereas certain evilly disposed persons and associations with the intent to subvert the supremacy of the Crown in Ireland have committed divers acts of violence whereby many persons including members of the forces of the Crown and other servants of His Majesty have been murdered and many others have suffered grievous injuries, and much destruction of property has been caused;

And whereas in certain parts of Ireland disaffection and unrest has been especially prevalent and repeated murderous attacks have been made upon members of His Majesty's forces, culminating in the ambush, massacre and mutilation with axes of sixteen Cadets of the Auxiliary Division, all of whom had served in the late war, by a large body of men who were wearing trench helmets, and were disguised in the uniforms of British soldiers, and who are still at large:

Now I, John Denton Pinkstone, Viscount French, Lord Lieutenant General and Governor General of Ireland, do hereby proclaim, by virtue of all the powers me thereunto enabling, that the following counties, namely the County of Cork (East Riding and West Riding); the County of the City of Cork; the County of Tipperary (North Riding); the County of Tipperary (South Riding); the County of Kerry; the County of the City of Limerick – are, and until further order shall continue to be, under and subject to martial law.

And I do hereby call on all loyal and well affected subjects of the Crown to aid in upholding and maintaining the peace of this realm and the supremacy and authority of the Crown, and to obey and conform to all orders and regulations of the military authority issued by virtue of this proclamation.

Given at His Majesty's Castle at Dublin this 10th Day of December 1920.

Proclamation No. 1,[820] *12 December 1920*

By the general officer commanding in chief, The Forces in Ireland

Martial law has been declared in the Counties of Cork, Tipperary, Kerry and Limerick.

Irishmen! Understand this: Great Britain has no quarrel with Irishmen; her sole quarrel is with crime, outrage, and disorder; her sole object in declaring Martial Law is to restore peace to a distracted and unhappy country; her sole enemies are those who have countenanced, inspired and participated in rebellion, murder and outrage. It is to put an end, once and for all, to this campaign of crime that Martial Law has been declared.

The Authorities named in the First Schedule[821] hereto annexed are hereby appointed Military Governors for the administration of Martial Law in the above counties, and all persons will render obedience to their orders in all matters whatsoever.

Note this:
(a) All arms, ammunition and explosives in possession of any person not a member of His Majesty's Naval, Military, Air or Police Forces or who is not in possession of a permit, will be surrendered by the 27th December 1920 to such persons and at such places as are named in the Second Schedule hereto annexed.[822]

(b) After the 27th December 1920, any unauthorised person found in possession of arms, ammunition or explosives will be liable, on conviction by a military court, to suffer death.

(c) Any unauthorised person wearing the uniform or equipment of His Majesty's Naval, Military, Air or Police Forces, or wearing similar clothing likely to deceive, will be liable on conviction to suffer death, and any person in unauthorised possession of such uniform, clothing or equipment will be liable on conviction by a military court to suffer penal servitude.

(d) Note well:
That a state of armed insurrection exists, that any person taking part therein or harbouring any person who has taken part therein, or procuring, inviting, aiding or abetting any person to take part therein, is guilty of levying war against His Majesty the King, and is liable on conviction by a military court to suffer death.

(e) All Law Courts, Corporations, Councils, and Boards are hereby directed to carry out their functions until otherwise ordered.

(f) The Forces of the Crown in Ireland are hereby declared to be on active service.

Signed this 12th day of December 1920

CFN Macready

APPENDIX 3

Proclamation No. 3

By the General Officer Commanding-in-Chief, the Forces in Ireland

Whereas by Proclamations dated the 12th December 1920, and the 1st of January 1921, respectively, issued in pursuance of the declaration of martial law, in certain parts of Ireland, it was directed by me as GENERAL COMMANDING IN CHIEF, THE FORCES IN IRELAND, that all law courts should continue to carry out their functions until otherwise ordered, I now hereby order that within the areas in which martial law has been declared the jurisdiction of all courts of justice, in all matters whatsoever relating to any claims whatsoever in respect of any damage or injury alleged to have been done by the Forces of the Crown or by any member thereof, save in so far as any proceeding may have been sanctioned by the Military Governor, is hereby suspended until further orders.

Signed this 14th Day of April 1921
CFN Macready
Commanding in Chief, the Forces in Ireland
(See: PRO/WO/93/39)

APPENDIX 4

Military Court Trials Not Covered in this Work

In respect of the following prisoners, it has not been possible to trace any record of trial by Military Court. The author would like to hear from anyone who can provide information on these trials. The place names are reproduced as they appear in the Register and it is likely some place names are misspelled.

The author also wishes to hear from anyone who has information in respect of the Military Court trials covered in this book and courts martial under the Restoration of Order in Ireland Act.

Michael Duane, Ballylanders. Tried 24 February 1921 for improper possession of arms and equipment. Found not guilty.

John M. Buckley, Bishopstown, County Cork. Tried 29 March 1921 on a charge of improper possession of firearms. Found not guilty.

Thomas Flavin, College Road, Cork. Tried 4 March 1921 for improper possession of arms. Found not guilty.

William Boland, Youghal, County Cork. Tried 25 June 1921 for improper possession of ammunition. Sentenced to five years' penal servitude.

Christopher Sullivan, Boherbue, County Cork. Tried for improper possession of arms and aiding and abetting the insurrection. Found not guilty.

James Nolan, Cork. Improper possession of arms and ammunition. Sentenced to ten years' penal servitude.

Jack Hayes, Tipperary. Tried for improper possession of ammunition.

George Lemon, RIC, Cork. Tried 30 December 1920 for robbery. Sentenced to eighteen months.

Herbert Brown, RIC, Cork. Tried 30 December 1920 for two offences of robbery. Sentenced to two years' penal servitude.

Patrick Maxwell. Tried 30 December 1920 for robbery. Found not guilty.

Alexander Lavery, RIC. Tried for shooting with intent to murder. Found not guilty.

Michael O'Keefe, Freemount, County Cork. Tried 28 May 1921 for improper possession of ammunition, explosives and documents. Sentenced to death by being shot.

Maurice O'Loughlin, Killinane, County Tipperary. Tried 22 and 23 March 1921 for improper possession of arms, ammunition and levying war. Found not guilty.

Michael Ryan, Dromina, County Cork. Tried 22 and 23 March 1921. Tried with the above for improper possession of arms, ammunition and levying war. Found not guilty.

Select Bibliography

Abbott, R. *Police Casualties in Ireland, 1919–22* (Cork: Mercier Press, 2000)

Archbold, *Criminal Pleading Evidence and Practice*, 25th Edition (London: Sweet & Maxwell, 1918)

Augusteijn, J. *From Public Defiance to Guerrilla Warfare* (Dublin: Irish Academic Press, 2002)

Babington, A. *For the Sake of Example* (London: Pen & Sword Books, 1993)

Borgonovo, J. *Spies, Informers and the 'Anti-Sinn Féin Society': The Intelligence War in Cork City, 1920–1921* (Dublin: Irish Academic Press, 2007)

Callwell, C.E. (ed.), *Field Marshall Sir Henry Wilson*, Vol. II (London: Cassell & Co., 1927)

Campbell, C. *Emergency Law in Ireland 1918–25* (Oxford: Clarendon Press, 1994)

Carroll, A. *Seán Moylan: Rebel Leader* (Cork: Mercier Press, 2010)

Chacksfield, K.M. *The Dorset and Somerset Rebellion* (Wincanton: Dorset Publishing Company, 1985)

Clode, M.F. *The Military Forces of the Crown* (London: J. Murray, 1869)

Cockburn, F. (ed.), *R v Nelson and Brand* (London: William Ridgeway, 1867)

Comyn, J. *Their Friends At Court* (London: Barry Rose Publishers, 1973)

Comyn, J. *Summing It Up* (Dublin: Roundhall Press, 1992)

Coogan, T.P. *Long Fellow, Long Shadow* (London: Hutchinson, 1993)

Costello, C. (ed.), The Four Courts: 200 Years (Dublin: The Incorporated Council of Law Reporting for Ireland, 1996)

Deasy, L. *Towards Ireland Free* (Dublin and Cork: Mercier Press, 1973)

Dicey, A.V. *The Law of the Constitution*, 8th edition (London: Macmillan, 1915)

Dutton, G. *The Hero as Murderer: The Life of Edward John Eyre* (London: Collins, 1967)

Dwyer, T. Ryle, *Tans, Terror and Troubles* (Cork: Mercier Press, 2001)
Ferguson, K. *King's Inns Barristers, 1868–2004* (Dublin: The Honourable Society of King's Inns, in association with the Irish Legal History Society, Irish Academic Press, 2005)
Fitzpatrick, D. *Politics and Irish Life, 1913–21* (Cork: Cork University Press, 1998)
Forsyth, W. *Cases and Opinions in Constitutional Law* (London: Stevens, 1869)
Foxton, D., *Revolutionary Lawyers* (Dublin: Four Courts, 2008)
Griffith, K. and O'Grady, T.E. (eds), *Curious Journey* (London: Hutchinson, 1982)
Hall, E.G. *The Superior Courts of Law 'Official' Law Reporting In Ireland 1866–2006* (Dublin: The Incorporated Council of Law Reporting for Ireland, 2006)
Hamilton, N. *The Full Monty. Vol. 1: Montgomery of Alamein 1887–1942* (London: Penguin, 2001)
Hanna, H. *The Pals at Suvla Bay* (Dublin: Ponsonby Ltd, 1916)
Hart, P. *The IRA and its Enemies: Violence and Community in Cork, 1916–1923* (London: Oxford University Press, 1999)
Hart, P. *The IRA at War, 1916–23* (New York: Oxford University Press, 2003)
Harvey, D. and White, G. *The Barracks: A History of Victoria/Collins Barracks, Cork* (Cork: Mercier Press, 1997)
Healy, M. *The Old Munster Circuit* (Dublin and Cork: Mercier Press, 1986)
Hibbert, C. *The Great Mutiny: India 1857* (London: Penguin Books, 1978)
Hopkinson, M. *The Last Days of Dublin Castle: The Diaries of Mark Sturgis* (Dublin: Irish Academic Press, 1999)
Hopkinson, M. *The Irish War of Independence* (Dublin: Gill & Macmillan, 2004)
Hussein, N. *The Jurisprudence of Emergency* (Ann Arbor, MI: University of Michigan Press, 2003)
Jeffery, K. (ed.), *Field Marshal Sir Henry Wilson: A Political Soldier* (New York: Oxford University Press, 2006)
Kilfeather, T.P. *The Connaught Rangers* (Tralee: Anvil, 1969)
Kostal, R.W. *A Jurisprudence of Power: Victorian Empire and the Rule of Law* (Oxford: Oxford University Press, 2006)
Lentin, A. *The Last Political Law Lord* (Newcastle: Cambridge Scholars Publishing, 2008)
Lynch, P. *Some Members of the Munster Circuit* (Cork: Woodlands Press, 1946)

Mackenzie, P., *Lawful Occasions* (Cork: Mercier Press, 1991)
Macready, C.F.N. *Annals of an Active Life*, vol. 2 (London: Hutchinson and Co., 1925)
Micholls, G. *A History of the Seventeenth Lancers*, vol. II (London: Macmillan, 1931)
Middlemass, K. (ed.), *Thomas Jones: Whitehall Diary*, vol. III (London: Oxford University Press, 1971)
Murphy, G. *The Year of Disappearances: Political Killings in Cork, 1921–22* (Dublin: Gill & Macmillan, 2010)
Ó Broin, L. *W.E. Wylie and the Irish Revolution* (Dublin: Gill & Macmillan, 1989)
O'Callaghan, J. *Revolutionary Limerick* (Dublin: Irish Academic Press, 2010)
O'Callaghan, S. *Execution* (London: Frederick Muller Ltd, 1974)
O'Donoghue, F. *No Other Law* (Dublin: Irish Press Limited, 1954)
O'Malley, E. *On Another Man's Wound* (Dublin: Anvil, 2002)
O'Neill, T. *The Battle of Clonmult: The IRA's Worst Defeat* (Dublin: Nonsuch Publishing, 2006)
ÓRuiarc, P. *Blood on the Banner: The Republican Struggle in Clare* (Cork: Mercier Press, 2010)
Oram, G. *Death Sentences Passed by Military Courts of the British Army 1914–24* (London: Francis Boutle Publishers, 1998)
Power, P.C. *The Courts Martial of 1798* (Dublin: The Irish Historical Press, 1997)
Radzinowicz, L. *A History of English Criminal Law from 1750*, vol. 4 (London: Sweet & Maxwell, 1948)
Sheehan, T. *Lady Hostage* (Cork: Lee Press Ltd, 2008)
Sheehan, W. *British Voices* (Cork: The Collins Press, 2007)
Spilsbury, J. *The Indian Mutiny* (London: Weidenfeld & Nicolson, 2008)
Toomey, T. The War of Independence in Limerick 1912–1921 (Limerick: Privately published, 2010)
Townshend, C. *The British Campaign in Ireland, 1919–21: The Development of Political and Military Policies* (London: Oxford University Press, 1975)
Weiner, F. *Civilians Under Military Justice* (Chicago: Chicago University Press, 1967)
White, G. and O'Shea, B. *The Burning of Cork* (Cork: Mercier Press, 2005)
Witton, G. *Scapegoats of the Empire* (Melbourne: Angus & Robertson, 1982)
Wylly, H.G. *The History of the Manchester Regiment*, vol. 2 (London: Foster, Groom & Co., 1925)

Reports

Arrangements Concerning the Cessation of Active Operations in Ireland (Cmd 1534) *Hansard*

Report on the Concentration Camps in South Africa (the Fawcett Report) 1902 Cd 893

Report of the Jamaica Royal Commission, 1866

Report of the Commission of Inquiry into the Present Conditions in Ireland (The Labour Party, London, 1921)

Report of the Committee on Evidence of Identification, 1976 (Cmd 338)

Who Burnt Cork City? (The Irish Labour Party, 1921)

Proclamations Issued by Field Marshal Lord Roberts in South Africa (Cd 426 of 1900)

Papers Relating to the Administration of Martial Law in South Africa (Cd 981 of 1902)

Articles

Ainsworth, J. 'British Security Policy in Ireland, 1920–21', *The Australian Journal of Irish Studies*, vol. 1 (2001), p.176

Dodd, C. 'The Case of Marais', *Law Quarterly Review* (1902), p.143

Keane, R. 'The Will of the General: Martial Law in Ireland, 1535–1924', in C. Costello (ed.), *The Four Courts: 200 Years* (Dublin: The Incorporated Council of Law Reporting for Ireland, 1996)

Harvey, A.D. 'Who Were the Auxiliaries?' *The Historical Journal*, 35, 3 (1992), p.665

Holdsworth, W.S. 'Martial Law Historically Considered', *Law Quarterly Review*, vol. 18 (1902), p.117

Earle Richards, H. 'Martial Law', *Law Quarterly Review*, vol. 18 (1902), p.133

Townshend, C. 'Martial Law: Legal and Administrative Problems of Civil Emergency in Britain and the Empire, 1800–1940', *The Historical Journal*, 25, 1 (1982), p.167

Primary Sources

Archives of the Judge Advocate General, Royal Courts of Justice, London

Imperial War Museum

Irish Military Archive, Cathal Brugha Barracks, Dublin

National Archives, Dublin (Census of Ireland, 1901/1911)
National Archives, Kew, London
National Library of Ireland
Parliamentary Archives, Westminster, London

Army Records

Camberley Staff College Archives
Essex Regimental Diary, 1921
Lincolnshire Regiment Archives, Lincoln
Hampshire Regimental Journal, 1921
Hampshire War Diary, 1921
Manchester Regiment Register of Arrests, 1921
Manchester Regiment Record of Service in Ireland, 1921
Manual of Military Law, 6th edition, 1914
Minute Books of the Judge Advocate General, PRO/WO/83/40–41
The Record of the Rebellion and the Part Played by the Army in Dealing With It. Vol. 3: Law, PRO/WO/141/94
Regimental Archives of the Royal Fusiliers
Soldiers of the Gloucestershire Museum
Strickland Papers – *The Irish Rebellion in the Sixth Divisional Area From After 1916 Rebellion to December 1921* (Referred to in this text as the *Sixth Division Record of the Rebellion*)
The White Lancer (the journal of the 17th Lancers)

Selected Cases

A and Others v Secretary of State for the Home Department [2005] 2 AC 68
Attorney General v De Keyser's Royal Hotel [1920] AC 508
R v Allen [1921] 2 IR 241
Attorney General for the Cape of Good Hope v Van Reenan AC [1904] 114
Clifford and Sullivan [1921] 2 AC 570
John J. Egan v General Macready and Others [1921] 1 IR 265
In Re the Queen v Marais ex parte Marais [1902] AC 51
DF Marais v GOC Lines of Communication and the Attorney General of the Colony [1902] AC 109
R v Fitzgerald Edwards and Hooper [1921] 55 ILTR 60
Hamdan v Rumsfeld 548 US 557 (2006)
Higgins v Willis (1) [1921] II IR 383
R v Murphy [1920] II IR 190

Mgomini and Others v Attorney General for the Colony of Natal TLR, vol. xxii 413
R (Childers) v Adjutant General of the Provisional Forces [1923] 1 IR 5
R (Ronayne and Mulcahy) v Strickland and Another [1921] IR II, 333
Tilonko v Attorney General of the Colony of Natal [1907] AC 93
The King v Charles Pinney Esquire (1832) 3 Barnewall and Adolphus 947
The King v The Governor of Lewes Prison ex parte Doyle [1917] 2 KB 254
The King (Garde and Others) v Major General E.P. Strickland and Others [1921] IR II, 317
Wolfe Tone 27 State Trials 613
Wright v Thomas Judkin Fitzgerald 27 State Trials 759
R v Nelson and Brand (William Ridgeway, 1867)
Report of the Case of The Queen v Edward John Eyre, W.F. Finlason (London: Chapman & Hall, 1868)
Ex parte Milligan 71 US 2 (1866)
The King (O'Brien) v Military Governor of the Military Internment Camp North Dublin Union and Minister for Defence [1924] 1 IR 32
R v Wall 28 St Trials 51

Selected Statutes

The Bill of Rights 1 W & M s 2, c.2
The Defence of the Realm Consolidation Act, 1914 5. Geo. V, c.8
The Firearms Act 1920 10 & 11 Geo 5, c.43
The Government of Ireland Act 1920 10 & 11 Geo V, c.67
The Habeas Corpus Act 1679, 31, Cha 2. 2
An Act for the Suppression of the Rebellion 39 Geo 3, c.11
The Indemnity Act 1920 10 & 11 Geo 5, c.48
The Mutiny Act 1 William & Mary s.2, c.5
The Restoration of Order in Ireland Act 1920 10 &11 Geo 5, c.31
The Riot Act 1 Geo 1, Stat 2, c.5
The Treason Act (1695) 7 & 8 Will III, c.3
The Treason Act (1708) 7 Ann, c.21
The Treason Act (1795) 36 Geo 3, c.7

Also:
The Hague Convention 1907

Newspapers and Periodicals

Clare Champion
Clonmel Chronicle
Cork Constitution
Cork Examiner
Freeman's Journal
Irish Law Times
Irish Times
Kerryman
Limerick Chronicle
Limerick Leader
New York Times
Saturday Record and Clare Journal
Waterford News and Star

Notes

PREFACE

1. See, for instance, Hamdan v Rumsfeld, 548 US 557 (2006).
2. A and Others v Secretary of State for the Home Department [2005] 2 A C 68.
3. A distinguished exception might be C. Campbell, *Emergency Legislation In Ireland, 1918–25* (Oxford: Clarendon Press, 1994). Professor Campbell's book provides a scholarly overview of the complex emergency powers legislation and case law which includes a significant section on the martial law period.
4. Jack Shine and John Duane, PRO/WO/35/208.
5. L. Deasy, *Towards Ireland Free* (Cork and Dublin: Mercier Press, 1973), Appendix D, p.340.
6. Campbell, *Emergency Legislation In Ireland*, pp.94–5.
7. D. Macardle, *The Irish Republic* (London: Corgi, 1968), p.426.
8. J. Comyn, *Their Friends At Court* (London: Barry Rose Publishers, 1973), p.52.

CHAPTER 1

9. During 1921 approximately 1,890 people were tried by courts martial under the ROIA and the DORA nationwide. Military courts accounted for another 128. See *The Record of the Rebellion and the Part Played by the Army in Dealing With It. Vol. 3: Law*, p.16. To this figure should be added 549 people sentenced to imprisonment by the Summary Court. The number of internees rose to 3,458 nationwide: see *House of Commons Debates* 14 April 1921. Approximately 790 of these were interned under martial law: see PRO/WO/48/148, letter 1 November 1921, General Macready to War Council.
10. PRO/WO/35/208.
11. R v Allen [1921] 2 IR 241; Egan v Macready [1921] 1 IR 265; In re: Clifford and Sullivan [1921] 2 AC 570.
12. The raid on Caherguillamore House, near Bruff, County Limerick took place on 26 December 1920. Sixty-six men were tried under the ROIA and received substantial sentences of imprisonment.
13. PRO/WO/35/208.
14. PRO/WO/48/148, letter 1 November 1921. The letter is typed but the figures have been inserted by hand, presumably after checking.
15. Cornelius Murphy, John Allen, Daniel O'Callaghan, John Lyons, Timothy McCarthy, Patrick Mahony, Thomas O'Brien, Patrick Ronayne, Thomas Mulcahy, Maurice Moore, Patrick Sullivan, Patrick Casey, Daniel O'Brien and Thomas Keane. The trial and execution of these men is detailed in the chapters that follow.
16. J.J. Egan and Patrick Higgins.
17. The analysis receives some indirect support from General Macready's memoir which suggests that thirty-seven men were sentenced to death by military court: C.F.N. Macready, *Annals of an Active Life*, vol. 2 (London: Hutchinson and Co., 1925), p.586.
18. This analysis is also supported by *Record of the Rebellion. Vol. 3: Law*, p.4 which gives almost identical numbers; PRO/WO/141/94.
19. The BMH statements identified are O Maoileoin (No. 845), O'Leary (No. 1589), MacNamara (No. 1135) Moylan (No. 838), Patrick Clifford (No. 946), Patrick Higgins (No. 1476), Dan Forde (No. 810), Michael O'Sullivan (No. 1186).
20. Personal communication, PRO, January 2010.
21. *Record of the Rebellion. Vol. 3: Law*, p.12.

22. R v Edwards, Fitzgerald and Hooper [1921] 55 ILTR 60. The owners and editor were court martialled for publishing seditious material contrary to Regulation 27 of the ROIR.
23. The clearest examples are the trial of Punch and Murphy and that of Cronin, which are dealt with in the body of this study.
24. This was the analysis of Lord Cave in Re: Clifford and Sullivan [1921] AC 570.

CHAPTER 2

25. K.M. Chacksfield, *The Dorset and Somerset Rebellion* (Wincanton: Dorset Publishing Company, 1985), p.75.
26. The Assizes were presided over by Judge Jeffreys and became known as 'the Bloody Assizes' and the prisoners were hardly any better off.
27. For a historical analysis, see *Law Quarterly Review*, vol. 18 (1902), p.117 et seq and for the position in Ireland see R. Keane, 'The Will of the General: Martial Law in Ireland, 1535–1924', in C. Costello (ed.), *The Four Courts: 200 Years* (Dublin: The Incorporated Council of Law Reporting for Ireland, 1996).
28. *Rushworth's Collection*, vol. 3.
29. See, for instance, F. Cockburn, *R v Nelson and Brand* (London, William Ridgeway, 1867).
30. *House of Lords Parliamentary Debates*, 1 April 1851, 3rd series, vol. 115, cols 843–82.
31. 1628.
32. 31 Cha.2 c.2. This Act reinforced the Act of 1640 which enacted that the will of the King or the Privy Council was not of itself sufficient to justify imprisonment.
33. The Bill of Rights 1689 enacted that the maintenance of a standing army in time of peace without the consent of Parliament was contrary to law.
34. 1 William and Mary S.2 c.5. In subsequent Acts the qualification 'in time of peace' was added by what is thought to have been a draftsman's error: see Judgment of the Lord Chief Justice R v Nelson and Brand. And see F. Weiner, *Civilians Under Military Justice* (Chicago: University of Chicago Press, 1967) which traces the development of military law.
35. 1 G, 1 Stat 2 c.5.
36. At St Peter's Field, Manchester in August 1819, troops were deployed by magistrates to carry out an arrest. The troops charged a large crowd, killing fifteen and injuring many hundreds.
37. Cmnd papers 7234. Report of the Committee Appointed to Inquire into the Disturbances at Featherstone in 1893.
38. An example might be the mutiny of the Connaught Rangers in the Punjab in 1920. Letters from home contained news of the excesses of the Black and Tans. A peaceful protest turned into mutiny. One soldier, Daly, was executed. Nine other death sentences were commuted to life imprisonment. See T.P. Kilfeather, *The Connaught Rangers* (Tralee: Anvil Books, 1969). Another example might be the Curragh Mutiny of 1914.
39. 1805 and 1816. These instances of martial law are taken in large part from M.F Clode, *The Military Forces of the Crown* (London: John Murray, 1869), p.481.
40. 1823.
41. 1832 and 1865.
42. 1837–8. In Lower Canada 108 men were convicted by military court. Of the ninety-nine sentenced to death, twelve were hanged and fifty-eight were transported to Australia.
43. 1817 and 48.
44. 1849. In the course of this insurrection forty-four people were sentenced to death, of whom twenty-one were executed. Ninety-two people were flogged and others banished without trial. One backbencher at Westminster pressed for a Royal Commission without success.
45. 1834, 1849–51. The Kat River Rebellion arose out of pressure for land which resulted in the resettlement of the Kat River people. In this instance forty-eight men – the 'Kat River Rebels' – were sentenced to death after trial by military court. Their sentences were commuted after some agonising over whether penalties imposed under martial law could be carried out after the rebellion.
46. 1862. All offenders were tried by due process of law.
47. 27 State Trials 613.
48. Ibid.
49. 39 Geo 3 C.11. These laws were gradually relaxed and martial law was avoided in Ireland throughout the rest of the nineteenth century, although the trial of civilians by courts martial was introduced by statute in 1833 to deal with widespread unrest: 3. Will iv. C 4. Nor was martial law invoked to deal with the Fenian Rising in 1867.

50. A backbencher, Brougham, later Lord Brougham, delivered a powerful indictment of the evidence that led to the conviction of Reverend Smith. *Hansard*, 1 and 11 June 1824. Brougham's attempt to impeach the conviction through Parliament failed on a vote of 146–93.
51. The 1798 rebellion resulted in many courts martial, many fair, others not. See P.C. Power, *The Courts Martial of 1798* (Dublin: The Irish Historical Press, 1997). The repression of the rebellion is better remembered for wanton cruelty.
52. Professor Townshend has pointed out that no one then sought to characterise this episode as martial law: C. Townshend, 'Martial Law: Legal and Administrative Problems of Civil Emergency in Britain and the Empire, 1800–1940', *Historical Journal*, 25, 1 (1982), p.168. This is not entirely so, but in any event it is submitted that the nature of what was done does not change according to the label that one places upon it.
53. C. Hibbert, *The Great Mutiny, India 1857* (London: Penguin, 1978), p.215.
54. J. Spilsbury, *The Indian Mutiny* (London: Weidenfeld & Nicolson, 2008), p.281.
55. *Report of the Jamaica Royal Commission, 1866.*
56. G. Dutton, *The Hero as Murderer: The Life of Governor Edward John Eyre* (London: Collins, 1967), p.220.
57. *Report of the Jamaica Royal Commission, 1866.*
58. Wright v Fitzgerald 27 St Tr 759. In this case Wright, a French language teacher from Clonmel, was flogged by the high sheriff without inquiry as to whether he was a loyalist or a rebel. As it turned out, Wright was a man of unimpeachable character. The jury awarded £500 and costs to the plaintiff.
59. R v Wall, 28 St 51. Joseph Wall was the Governor of Goree. In that capacity he subjected a Sergeant Armstrong to a lashing. The unfortunate sergeant lost consciousness and died after some 700 lashes. Governor Wall was tried for murder. At his trial he asserted that what was done was necessary to suppress a mutiny. His defence was rejected by a jury. He was convicted and hanged.
60. W.F. Finlason, *Report of the case of The Queen v Edward John Eyre* (London: Chapman & Hall, 1868).
61. In fact Justice Blackburn's analysis of the law contradicted the charge delivered to the grand jury by Lord Chief Justice Cockburn in the case of Nelson and Brand. Lord Chief Justice Cockburn then initiated through the press a series of spiteful rebukes against Justice Blackburn. The law was rendered even less clear.
62. This aspect of the Jamaica Affair has been charted by R.W. Kostal, *A Jurisprudence of Power: Victorian Empire and the Rule of Law* (Oxford: Oxford University Press, 2006).
63. PRO/CO 323/287, 26 January 1867.
64. This was the view of Lord Coke, who was prominent in framing the Petition of Right. 'A rebel may be slain in the rebellion; but if he is taken, he cannot be put to death by the martial law', Rushworth's Collection, vol. 3, Appendix p.81. This was also the view of Lord Chief Justice Rolle, who was also involved in framing the Petition of Right.
65. It is not clear when the Guidance ceased to have effect but it is mentioned in Tilonko v the Governor General of Natal AC [1907] 93 in circumstances which make it plain that it still had force of law.
66. This episode was drawn to my attention by R.W. Kostal's study, *A Jurisprudence of Power*.
67. Cd 981 of 1902. To which should be added many other unofficial executions. See the trial of Breaker Morant and others in G. Witton, *Scapegoats of the Empire* (Melbourne: Angus & Robertson, 1982).
68. In re: The Queen v Marais ex parte Marais AC [1902] 51.
69. Van Reenan's Case AC [1904] 114.
70. Ex parte DF Marais [1902] AC 109.
71. Mgomini, Mzinelwa and Wanda (by their next friend Alfred Mangena) v His Excellency the Governor and the Attorney General for the Colony of Natal 22 TLR 413.
72. Tilonko v Attorney General of Natal [1907] AC 93.
73. Professor Campbell has pointed out that no precedent was cited by the court. See Campbell, *Emergency Law in Ireland, 1918–25*, p.130. And see Civilians under Military Justice.
74. G. Oram, *Death Sentences Passed by Military Courts of the British Army, 1914–24* (London: Francis Boutle Publishers, 1998). This statistic does not include figures from the Indian Army, pp.19–65.
75. Ibid. p.29.
76. Ibid. pp.19–65.

77. The figure of those sentenced to death and executed excludes a number of German spies, camp followers and members of labour battalions who might ordinarily come within the ambit of military law.
78. The King v The Governor of Lewes Prison ex parte Doyle [1917] 2 KB 254.
79. PRO 30/89/36 The Hon William Wylie KC.
80. PRO/WO/71/348.
81. *Hansard*, 6 August 1919, vol. 36, cols 490–504.
82. Act of Indemnity 1920 10 &11 Geo V c.48, section 5.
83. This was a consequence of the Petition of Right, the Mutiny Act 1689 and also the fact that in 1798 martial law had been given effect by statute 39 Geo III c.11, the preamble of which referred to a prerogative power to invoke martial law.
84. The King v Charles Pinney Esquire (1832), Barnewall and Adolphus 947.
85. A.V. Dicey, *The Law of the Constitution* (London: Macmillan 1915 [8th edn]), p.283.
86. Marais v The General Officer Commanding [1902] AC 109.
87. Although it has been argued that it is artificial to expect the law to 'appear at its own vanishing point to determine the rules of its own failure'. N. Hussein, *The Jurisprudence of Emergency* (Ann Arbor, MI: University of Michigan Press, 2003).
88. See the trial of Wolfe Tone 1798, 27 St Tr 613.
89. For the sake of completeness, reference should be made to the Hague Convention of 1907 which formalised the concept of ' unlawful combatants' who might be tried and punished on capture for failure to conform to 'the customs and usages' of war. The Convention was the subject of discussion in Whitehall and among senior army officers but it was not relied upon by the Crown to resist applications for habeas corpus. There were two matters which prevented the Crown relying on the Convention. First it only applied where both sides in the conflict were contracting parties. Second, the Crown could not show complete compliance with the Convention: Article 46 (confiscation of private property), Article 50 (collective punishments).
90. The motion of censure on the trial and sentence of John Smith after the Demerara Rebellion. *Hansard*, 11 June 1824.
91. The Royal Commission into the arrest and subsequent treatment of Mr Francis Sheehy-Skeffington, Mr Thomas Dickson and Mr James McIntyre (cmd 8376) [1916].
92. It was not case law but the public outcry about the internment camps that alleviated conditions for internees. The conditions in the camps were first publicised by Emily Hobhouse and later Lloyd George. Their efforts resulted in a government inquiry – the Fawcett Report – which resulted in substantial improvements in the camps.
93. An example might be General Dyer, who ordered the firing at Amritsar in 1919.
94. The prosecution of Captain Bowen Colthurst, in 1916, for the murder of Sheehy-Skeffington and two others might be an example.

CHAPTER 3

95. *House of Commons Debates*, 6 May 1920, vol. 128, cols 2206–7.
96. *House of Commons Debates*, 2 December 1919, vol. 122, col. 241.
97. *House of Commons Debates*, 18 March 1920, vol. 126, cols 2351–2.
98. J. Ainsworth, 'British Security Policy in Ireland, 1920–1921', *The Australian Journal of Irish Studies*, vol. 1.
99. PRO/CAB/27/108.
100. E. O'Malley, *On Another Man's Wound* (Dublin: Anvil, 2002), p.185.
101. PRO/CAB/27/108, Cabinet Survey for Week Ending 19 December 1921.
102. In the three months ending 31 July 1920, 315 magistrates resigned. See *Hansard*, 9 August 1920, vol. 133, cols 24–5.
103. *Sixth Division Record of the Rebellion*, p.20. It should be recognised that the *Sixth Division Record of the Rebellion* is a partisan account. A rather different account of this process has been written by J. O'Callaghan, *Revolutionary Limerick* (Dublin: Irish Academic Press, 2010), pp.87–91.
104. See, for instance, Alfred Reilly JP, PRO/CO/904/189. The motivation for this killing is a matter of inference. For an alternative view, see J. Borgonovo, *Spies, Informers and the Anti-Sinn Féin Society*, pp.42–3.
105. Robert Love JP gave evidence on behalf of two of the men tried for the raid on Mallow

Barracks. He was a former RIC man. On his account he was the only justice of the peace in Mallow who refused to resign his commission in the face of intimidation.

106. *Sixth Division Record of the Rebellion*, p.19.
107. Cabinet Papers, Irish Situation Committee, 16 July 1920.
108. *Sixth Division Record of the Rebellion*, p.28.
109. *Record of the Rebellion*, p.20. This incident is well described by T. Ryle Dwyer, *Tans, Terror and Troubles* (Cork: Mercier Press, 2001), p.195.
110. R.M. Brady was kidnapped in June 1921 and released after some days. See J.J. Sullivan, BMH witness statement no. 1578, p.21.
111. *Record of the Rebellion, vol. 1*, p.8.
112. M. Hopkinson, *The Last Days of Dublin Castle: The Diaries of Mark Sturgis* (Dublin: Irish Academic Press, 1999), p.3.
113. C. Townshend, *The British Campaign in Ireland, 1919–21: The Development of Political and Military Policies* (London: Oxford University Press, 1975), p.20.
114. K. Middlemass (ed.), *Thomas Jones: Whitehall Diary*, vol. III (London: Oxford University Press, 1971), p.19.
115. Ibid.
116. PRO/WO/35/66, Legal advice received by Macready's HQ, 15 May 1920.
117. Middlemass, *Thomas Jones*, p.21.
118. *Hansard*, 16 August 1920, vol. 133, col. 576.
119. PRO/CAB/24/109, 24 July 1920.
120. See the proviso to section 1 (4) of the Defence of the Realm Act 1914.
121. Archives of the Judge Advocate General, Register of Rulings, 601–751.
122. J. Comyn, *Their Friends at Court* (London: Barry Rose Publishers, 1973), p.121.
123. J. Augusteijn, *From Public Defiance to Guerrilla Warfare* (Dublin: Irish Academic Press, 2002), p.194.
124. The best account of the reprisals issue can be found in the diary of Field Marshall Sir Henry Wilson (IWM). There is also a contemporaneous note written by the government senior law officer William Wylie KC, PRO/39/89/3. See also R. Abbott, *Police Casualties in Ireland, 1919–22* (Cork: Mercier Press, 2000), p.172. And for the British Army perspective, *Sixth Division Record of the Rebellion*, Appendix V.
125. See *Hansard*, 14 July 1920, col. 2386. Also BMH statement of constable Jeremiah Mee, no. 1509.
126. PRO 30/89/3.
127. L. Ó Broin, *W.E Wylie and the Irish Revolution* (Dublin: Gill & Macmillan, 1989), p.108.
128. Diaries of Field Marshall Sir Henry Wilson, CIGS, 29 September 1921.
129. *House of Commons Debates*, 20 October 1920, vol. 133, col. 909.
130. PRO/CAB/23/2253(A)22.
131. Middlemass, *Thomas Jones*, p.40.
132. Ibid.
133. Ibid. The assertions by Churchill have been doubted by Professor Townshend. See Townshend, *The British Campaign in Ireland*, p.122. A body of evidence has subsequently emerged which supports the factual contentions put forward by Churchill. See, for instance, W. Sheehan, *British Voices* (Cork: The Collins Press, 2007), p.187, an account by Major General Wimberley. See also the Archives of the Lincolnshire Regiment, Box 12, 848.
134. Macready, *Annals of an Active Life*, vol. 2, p.515. Macready identified this as the decisive factor in his conversion to the martial law policy.
135. PRO/CAB/23/23/79A, minutes of Cabinet meetings, 29 December and 30 December 1920.
136. Strickland had served in Burma, Sudan and Nigeria. He was colonel of the Manchester Regiment in 1914. He served as a major general without particular distinction in France between 1915 and 1918.
137. Personal Diary, Strickland Papers, IWM.
138. See, for instance, W. Sheehan, *British Voices*, p.187, an account by Major General Wimberley. And see N. Hamilton, *The Full Monty* (London: Penguin, 2001), p.40. 'It developed into a murder campaign, in which, in the end, the soldiers became quite skilful and more than held their own.' See also J. Borgonovo *Spies, Informers and the 'Anti-Sinn Féin Society': The Intelligence War in Cork City, 1920–1921* (Dublin: Irish Academic Press, 2007), p.107.
139. *The Times*, 20 December 1921.
140. PRO/CO 904/149.

141. A.D. Harvey, 'Who Were the Auxiliaries?' *The Historical Journal*, 35, 3 (1992), p.665.
142. PRO/CO 904/149.
143. For a full account, see G. White and B. O'Shea, *The Burning of Cork* (Cork: Mercier Press, 2005) and BMH Statement 719.
144. *Report of the District Inspector of Police*, PRO/C0 904/150.
145. *Hansard*, 13 December 1920, and see extracts from Report of the Inquiry into Cork Fires, PRO/CO 904/150. Captain Hudson of the Cork Fire Brigade alleged his men had been fired on by Auxiliaries, and on one occasion that their hose was cut. This testimony was supported by other fire officers. These allegations were disputed by officers of the ADRIC. K Company were later implicated by the Military Court of Inquiry in some of the fire setting and were soon disbanded. No person was prosecuted for involvement in what took place that night.
146. PRO/WO/141/94, *Record of the Rebellion. Vol. 3: Law*, p.27.
147. The theory had been well tested in South Africa (where Macready had served as Provost Marshal) and in Dublin and Egypt in 1916.
148. Letter by General Macready to the War Office, 22 February 1921, PRO/ WO/141/48.
149. Hopkinson, *The Last Days of Dublin Castle*, p.89.
150. *The Times*, 20 December 1921.
151. PRO/CAB/24/118, Cabinet Survey, 15 January 1921.
152. Martial Law Circular No. 1, *Cork Examiner*, 20 December 1920.
153. 19 January 1921, Strickland Papers, IWM.
154. By the spring of 1921 3,458 people were interned or detained without charge. *House of Commons Debates*, 14 April 1921. This figure varied only a little until the Truce. Approximately 790 were interned under martial law: see Macready to War Office, 1 November 1921, PRO/WO/48/148.
155. The practice of carrying hostages on convoys arose out of difficulties in securing armoured lorries. It followed that convoys were vulnerable to ambush and hostages were carried to ensure safety. As General Macready put it in his memoirs: 'Authority was also given for the carrying of prominent Sinn Féiners on military lorries, which, while it afforded some slight deterrent to outrages, amused the light-hearted soldiery.' Macready, *Annals of an Active Life*, vol. 2, p.503. The practice was widely adopted, although not confined to active supporters of the rebellion. See Willis and Bolster, BMH witness statement no. 808, p.26; Moylan BMH witness statement no. 838, pp.157–8; O'Malley, *On Another Man's Wound*, p.261; PRO/WO/35/66 (order implemented by public notice dated 16 January 1921). See also *Sixth Division Record of the Rebellion*, p.70 and 17th Infantry Brigade, *Summary of Important Instructions*, paragraph 4 (g). The practice originated in the Anglo-Boer War. See Proclamations of Lord Roberts in South Africa, Cd 426 of 1900.
156. See 17th Infantry Brigade, *Summary of Important Instructions*, Regulation 4. See also *Notes on the Administration of Martial Law*, p.6, Strickland Papers, IWM. And see, for instance, *Diary of Lieutenant Grazebrook*, Soldiers of the Gloucestershire Museum, p.25.
157. Macready, *Annals of an Active Life*, vol. 2, p.523. The Procedure is described in some detail in the *Record of the Rebellion*, p.31.
158. Cabinet meeting, 29 December 1920, CAB/23/2379A.
159. Both men were convicted. Lemon was sentenced to two years' imprisonment and Brown received eighteen months, PRO/WO/35/208. The trial record has not survived.

CHAPTER 4

160. *Cork Constitution*, 22 December 1920, courtesy of the National Library of Ireland.
161. National Army Museum, Army List, 1920.
162. Defence counsel's closing submissions during the trial of Hart.
163. PRO/HO/184/50.
164. The Military Court of Inquiry was chaired by Lieutenant Pickard Cambridge MC. The record from which this account is taken can be found at PRO/WO/35/155A.
165. *The Times*, 20 December 1920.
166. This was the first trial conducted by the Military Court. It was not a court martial under the Restoration of Order in Ireland Act because the necessary formalities were not complied with owing to the speed with which the army acted. This analysis is supported by the Register kept by the Judge Advocate General which describes this as a trial by military court: PRO/WO/35/208. It is also clear from the exchanges between counsel and the court on the

first day of the trial that this was a military court. The case papers do not survive and this account is taken from the *Cork Constitution*.

167. Instructed by F.W. Wynne, solicitor.
168. *Cork Constitution*, 6 January 1921, courtesy of the National Library of Ireland.
169. Ibid.
170. Ibid.
171. Ibid.
172. Ibid.
173. Ibid.
174. Dr East, medical officer at Liverpool Prison; Dr Hamblin-Smith, medical officer, Birmingham Prison; Lieutenant Colonel Nicholls, medical officer, Cork Detention Barracks; and Colonel Beyts, Cork.
175. Dr Dyer, medical inspector of prisons and Dr Dawson, medical officer, HM Inspector of Asylums, Ireland.
176. The Royal Commission into the arrest and subsequent treatment of Mr Francis Sheehy-Skeffington, Mr Thomas Dickson and Mr James McIntyre (Cmd 8376).
177. Cabinet meeting, 30 December 1920, PRO/ CAB 23/23 81(20).
178. J.F. Archbold, *Criminal Pleading Evidence and Practice*, 25th edition (London: Sweet & Maxwell, 1918), p.16, the McNaughton Rules.
179. PRO/CAB/24/119.
180. The Trial of Lunatics Act 1883, section 2.
181. *House of Commons Debates*, 17 February 1921, vol. 138, cols 244–6. This was no slip of the tongue. General Macready gave the same account in the *Cabinet Weekly Survey* of week ending 31 January 1921, CAB/24/119.
182. Archbold, *Criminal Pleading Evidence and Practice*, p.16.
183. PRO/WO/81/160.
184. NLI/O'Donoghue Papers, MS 31,226. This Auxiliary has since been identified as Charlie Schulze, the *Irish Times*, 14 December 2010.
185. PRO/WO/35/155 A. The Divisional Commissioner, Holmes, conducted an inquiry into the issue of whether Hart had been drunk and why the other Auxiliaries had failed to intervene to assist Crowley and Canon Magner. The inquiry did not hear from Cadet Milward, Resident Magistrate Brady or Hart himself.

CHAPTER 5

186. Regulation 9. These references are taken from the *Circular Memoranda on Martial Law*, which was created in May 1921 to give effect to a system which was evolving, PRO/WO/35/66.
187. *Record of the Rebellion. Vol. 3: Law*, p.6, PRO/WO/141/94.
188. *Circular Memoranda on Martial Law*, Reg. 10.
189. *Circular Memoranda on Martial Law*, Reg. 12.
190. *Record of the Rebellion. Vol. 3: Law*, p.6.
191. *Cork Examiner*, 28 February 1921.
192. *Record of the Rebellion. Vol. 3: Law*, p.6. The curfew officer assumed the post of summary court officer in March 1921.
193. Born in Somerset in 1875. He qualified as a solicitor but soon after joined the army on the outbreak of the Anglo-Boer War. He served in Natal as a trooper and remained there after the cessation of hostilities and was later a member of the first South African Parliament in 1909–10. He returned to England in 1914 and rejoined his regiment where he served in a reconnaissance role until 1916 when he transferred to the Royal Flying Corps. He was gassed and later wounded. He was awarded the Military Cross, Distinguished Service Order, and the Belgium Order of Leopold. He took over as legal officer for the Sixth Division in March 1921 from Lieutenant-Colonel O.F. Dowson, about whom little is known. Meyler retired from the army in 1922 and briefly served as a member of Parliament at Westminster before returning to private practice as a solicitor.
194. *Record of the Rebellion. Vol. 3: Law*, p.15.
195. A Babington, *For the Sake of Example* (London: Pen & Sword Books, 1993), Chapter 1.
196. The 6th (North Perthshire) Battalion of the Royal Highlanders.
197. A single instance of grave ill-treatment at Cork detention barracks is recounted by O'Leary, BMH witness statement no. 1589, p.9.

198. Comyn, *Their Friends at Court*, p.52.
199. BMH witness statement no. 1589, at p.9.
200. See Chapter 33 this volume, 'Mallow Barracks'.
201. K. Griffith and T.E. O'Grady (eds), *Curious Journey* (London: Hutchinson, 1982), p.207.
202. PRO/WO/83/40, p.339.
203. Rules of Procedure r 114 (A) & r 122..
204. *Manual of Military Law*, 6th edn, Rules of Procedure.
205. PRO/WO/141/48, letter General Macready to War Office, 22 February 1921.
206. Restoration of Order in Ireland Act s1 (2) (b).
207. Restoration of Order in Ireland Act s1(5).
208. In England the law had been amended by the Criminal Evidence Act 1898 to allow an accused the right to give evidence in his own defence. In Ireland a defendant and his or her spouse were unable to give evidence for the defence, a position maintained by the Restoration of Order in Ireland Act s1 (5).
209. *Record of the Rebellion. Vol. 3: Law*, p.6.
210. *Circular Memoranda on Martial Law*, PRO/WO/35/66 Reg. 56.
211. 6th edn.
212. See, for instance, R v Ronayne and Mulcahy. Submissions and ruling on the presence of accused at the taking of summary of evidence, PRO/WO/71/386.
213. *Record of the Rebellion. Vol. 3: Law*, p.6.
214. PRO/WO/35/66 and, for a later version, PRO/WO/141/94, *Record of the Rebellion. Vol. 3: Law*, p.6.
215. Reg. 2.
216. Reg. 14.
217. *Circular Memoranda on Martial Law*, PRO/WO/35/66, Amendments.
218. Letter by General Macready to the War Office, 22 February 1921, PRO/WO/141/48.
219. Hopkinson, *The Last Days of Dublin Castle*, p.89.
220. Reg. 15.
221. Reg. 25.
222. Low Parks Museum, personal communication, 31 August 2010.
223. Sheehan, *British Voices*, p.120, Lieutenant General Percival.
224. Reg. 17.
225. Ibid.
226. Reg. 18.
227. In the case of James O'Connell, tried 16 June 1921, the record shows that counsel was rebuked by the Judge Advocate for removing his wig.
228. Regs 19–22.
229. Reg. 21.
230. Reg. 23.
231. Reg. 68.
232. Regs 69–69a.
233. Reg. 66.
234. Reg. 31.
235. Reg. 29.
236. Regs 38–45.
237. Reg. 25.
238. Regs 44–7.
239. Reg. 47.
240. Reg. 48.
241. This amendment was inserted no earlier than May 1921.
242. Reg. 54.
243. Reg. 55.
244. Reg. 56.
245. In fact the death sentence was only imposed for offences stipulated by proclamation to be capital offences.
246. Regs 73–5. The Military Governor throughout this period was Major General Sir Peter Strickland. The Military Governor General was Macready.
247. *Record of the Rebellion. Vol. 3: Law*, p.18.

CHAPTER 6

248. PRO/WO/83/40, JAG Minute Book, p.555.
249. PRO/WO/83/40 JAG Minute Book, 1921, p.96.
250. PRO/WO/83/40 JAG Minute Book, 1921, p.112.
251. PRO/WO/141/48, letter 9 January 1921, Macready to War Office.
252. PRO/WO/141/48, letter 12 January 1921, Cassel to War Office.
253. PRO/WO/141/48.
254. PRO/WO/141/48, letter 19 January 1921.
255. The case papers from which this account is drawn are in PRO/WO/71/376.
256. 27 State Trials, 613.
257. *Circular Memoranda on Martial Law*, Reg. 31.
258. Legal assistance would usually consist of an officer assigned to represent the accused.
259. It appears from a contemporary press report that his brother Denis was tried by the Summary Court for failing to report the fact that Murphy had a gun and ammunition: *Nenagh Guardian*, 5 February 1921. The result of that trial is not recorded.
260. PRO/WO/71/376, letter to Macready, dated 26 January 1921.
261. This is certainly the view of Anthony Babington. See his *For the Sake of Example*, p.15.
262. Con Meaney, BMH statement 787, p.3.
263. William Reardon, BMH statement 1185.
264. PRO/WO/35/66, *Circular Memoranda on Martial Law*. 'Military Courts are as a rule kept for those offences where a death sentence was likely to be awarded and which cannot be awarded under ordinary law.'
265. The Royal Commission into the arrest and subsequent treatment of Mr Francis Sheehy-Skeffington, Mr Thomas Dickson and Mr James McIntyre (Cmd 8376). Sir John Simon was later Lord Chancellor, Chancellor of the Exchequer and Foreign Secretary.
266. Kathleen Harvey became known as a campaigner for civil rights for black Americans. Her book, *Slavery*, became a minor classic.
267. See, for instance, *Limerick Leader*, 2 February 1921 and *Cork Examiner*, 16 March 1921.

CHAPTER 7

268. The full text of the letter can be found with the Allen case papers at PRO/WO/71/377 or PRO/WO/141/94, *Record of the Rebellion. Vol. 3: Law*, p.34. The letter is initialled M.W. There is no other clue as to the identity of the author. The significance of this document was drawn to my attention by a passage in D. Foxton, *Revolutionary Lawyers* (Dublin: Four Courts Press, 2008). I acknowledge that debt.
269. Moylan, BMH witness statement no. 838, p.251.
270. S. O'Callaghan, *Execution* (London: Frederick Muller Ltd, 1974), p.93.
271. Bourke later practised in Oxford where he became the chairman of quarter sessions and was for many years the Recorder of Shrewsbury. He died in 1967.
272. Longworth served as Judge Advocate in many ROIA courts martial in the period 1919–21, including that of Piaras Beaslaí, Sinn Féin member for East Kerry (the *Irish Times*, 15 May 1919) and J.J. Walsh, Sinn Féin member for Cork (the *Irish Times*, 29 March 1919).
273. PRO/WO/71/377. The account of this trial is drawn from this file and all quotations are from that record.
274. Magna Carta, Chapter XXIX (1297); Petition of Right, Chapter 1 (1628); Sir James Fitzjames Stephens, *History of Criminal Law*, vol. 1, Chapter VII.
275. PRO/WO/35/121.
276. Thomas Molony was the last Lord Chief Justice of Ireland. He served as Solicitor General and Attorney General before going on the bench. His reputation was that of a Home Ruler. He had sat on the Royal Commission into the death of Francis Sheehy-Skeffington and others in 1916. He was known to favour capital punishment.
277. Healy was a well-connected constitutional nationalist. He was also, according to Judge Wyse Power, a member of the IRB (Wise Power, BMH statement 420, p.2). Healy enjoyed success as a journalist, author and an MP. As an MP he had been responsible for the Healy Clause in the Land Act of 1881 which meant that rent increases could not be levied on improvements made by a tenant. He also played a part in bringing down Parnell. He was quick witted, unconventional and regarded as a political maverick but finished his career as the first Governor General of the Irish Free State.

278. P. Lynch, *Some Members of the Munster Circuit* (Cork: Woodhill Press, 1946), p.37.
279. It appears from Healy's submissions that General Macready's affidavit was served on him just a few minutes before the hearing. No adjournment was asked for and no rebutting evidence was obtained. Macready's affidavit would prove decisive in this case.
280. R v Allen [1921] 241, reproduced by kind permission of the Council of Law Reporting for Ireland.
281. Ibid.
282. PRO/WO/83/40, p.121.

CHAPTER 8

283. *Sixth Division Record of the Rebellion*, p.74.
284. O'Callaghan, *Execution*, p.25.
285. H.G. Wylly, *History of the Manchester Regiment*, vol. 2, p.212.
286. *Sixth Division Record of the Rebellion*, p.75.
287. O'Callaghan, *Execution*, p.25. This book draws on local knowledge but does not always identify sources.
288. Moylan, BMH witness statement no. 838, p.160.
289. *Cork Examiner*, Tuesday 1 February 1921.
290. Manchester Regiment, Arrest Register, 1921.
291. The names of prisoners are as recorded in the Manchester Regiment arrest register and the Trial Register.
292. T. Sheehan, *Lady Hostage* (Cork: Lee Press Ltd, 2008), p.111.
293. James Barrett died of his wounds. Denis Murphy recovered and was tried the following month.
294. The case papers can be found at PRO/WO/71/380.
295. O'Callaghan, *Execution*, p.84.
296. J.F. Bourke, counsel, appeared for five of the prisoners: Mahony, Jeremiah Callaghan, Lyons, O'Brien and McCarthy. Wallis Gardiner, solicitor, appeared for Langtry and Sheehan. J.F. Fitzgerald, counsel, appeared for Daniel O'Callaghan.
297. *Cork Examiner*, 10 February 1921. Copyright permission by the *Irish Examiner* is acknowledged.
298. Setting aside, for the moment, fundamental questions about the legality of the process, did the Military Court reach factually correct verdicts? Langtry and Sheehan were not Volunteers and had taken no part in the ambush. The involvement of Jeremiah Callaghan, who was acquitted, and the five men convicted was subsequently confirmed by reliable sources. A raid on Mulcahy's HQ in Dublin in February 1921 resulted in the capture of a number of documents. One was a report written by the commandant of the 6th Battalion recounting the action. The report names six missing men, including three of the men awaiting execution but does not name Lyons (the report is contained in PRO/WO/71/378). Another source of confirmation is an account written from the perspective of the prisoners: O'Callaghan, *Execution*.
299. Ibid.
300. Sheehan, *Lady Hostage*, p.77.
301. Advice by Judge Advocate General to General Macready, 15 February 1921, PRO/WO/141/48.
302. PRO/WO/141/48.
303. Ibid.
304. PRO/WO/71/148 letter from Cassel to Secretary of State, 21 February 1921; and see letter Hamar Greenwood to Worthington-Evans of same date and Cassel's letter of 25 February 1921.
305. It should be pointed out that in the case of Murphy there had been repeated legal delays in respect of execution and Macready had taken it upon himself to commute the death sentence to twenty-five years' imprisonment.
306. R v Allen [1921] 2 IR 241.
307. Ibid. This extract is reproduced by kind permission of the Council of Law Reporting for Ireland.
308. [1902] AC 109.
309. The firing parties were led by Lieutenants Flint, Lambert and Curtis Nuttall of the Hampshire Regiment.
310. Hopkinson, *The Last Days of Dublin Castle*, p.134.

311. Killed were Private Wise and Lance Corporal Hodnet of the RASC. Also killed were Privates Gill and Whitear and Lance Corporal Beattie of the Hampshire Regiment and Signaller Bowden of the Royal Engineers.
312. Hampshire Regiment War Diary, 28 February 1921.
313. O'Callaghan, *Execution*, p.175 contains a harrowing account of the killing of Mrs Lindsay and her butler. She was a widow aged sixty.
314. *House of Commons Debates*, 24 February 1921, vol. 138, col. 1110.
315. *House of Commons Debates*, 3 March 1921, vol. 138, col. 1989.
316. *House of Commons Debates*, 3 March 1921, vol. 138, cols 1992–3.
317. PRO/WO/71/148, Letter from War Office to Macready, 21 February 1921.
318. PRO/WO/71/148, Letter from Macready to Greenwood, 22 February 1921.

CHAPTER 9

319. Manchester Regiment Service Record 1921, p.34.
320. J. O'Sullivan, witness statement no. 1376, p.9.
321. *Sixth Division Record of the Rebellion*, p.81. The information on which the army acted was supplied by Dan Shiels, an ex-soldier. See John Moloney BMH statement no 1036, p.11–17.
322. This account of the trial is drawn from the case notes which can be found at PRO/WO/71/386.
323. The trial proceeded on the first charge sheet. There was a second charge sheet which charged Ronayne with possession of a shotgun and two cartridges and Thomas Mulcahy with possession of a single cartridge. This charge sheet was not pursued following conviction.
324. As the law then stood, a confession was not admissible in evidence if obtained by reason of fear of prejudice or hope of advantage held out by a person in authority. R v Ibrahim 1914 AC 599.
325. Statements made many years later to the Bureau of Military History suggest that Thomas Mulcahy and Ronayne were involved in the ambush. Creedon was not and he was put at risk on a capital charge. Edmund Creedon also was not involved but shot dead on his own land. Cornelius Mulcahy was involved in the ambush but he was acquitted. See Tadhg Looney, BMH witness statement no. 1196 and John Ronayne, BMH witness statement no. 1269, at p.9.
326. The King (Ronayne and Mulcahy) v Strickland and Another [1921] 2 IR 333.
327. Included in the papers to the JAG was a letter from Major Meyler who had acted as Judge Advocate in the trial. The letter shows the most rudimentary grasp of criminal law.
328. PRO/WO/71/386, Advice to General Macready, 9 April 1921.

CHAPTER 10

329. Unless otherwise stated, the account of this trial is taken from PRO/WO/71/380. All quotations from the trial are from that source.
330. The names of those who died were established at a military court of inquiry in lieu of inquest: Joseph Morrissey, William Aherne, David Desmond, Richard Hegarty, James Aherne, J.J. Joyce, Daniel Dennehy, Jeremiah Aherne, Michael Hallahan, Christopher O'Sullivan, James Glavin and Michael Desmond, PRO/WO/35/155A.
331. For an account written from the perspective of the army, see *Sixth Division Record of the Rebellion*, p.83 and for an account written from the viewpoint of the prisoners, see T. O'Neill, *The Battle of Clonmult* (Dublin: Nonsuch Publishing, 2006).
332. Patrick Higgins, BMH witness statement no. 1467, p.6. Higgins was tried in June and sentenced to death. A writ of habeas corpus was successfully sought on his behalf and he was released at the end of July. See chapter 40.
333. Instructed by Maurice O'Connor.
334. Instructed by C.K. Murphy.
335. Unless otherwise stated, the account of this trial is taken from PRO/WO/71/380.
336. O'Leary, BMH witness statement no. 1589, p.8.
337. Comyn, *Their Friends at Court*, p.51.
338. Ibid., p.50.
339. This quotation comes from the *Cork Examiner*, 16 March 1921. The passage quoted does not appear in the official transcript. Having regard to the quality of the reporting by the *Cork Examiner* there is every reason to regard this newspaper as reliable. Reproduced with the kind permission of the *Irish Examiner*.

340. Transcript of evidence, p.109.
341. An analysis of these events by Tom O'Neill (*The Battle of Clonmult*) suggests that these four young men were on the fringes of the Volunteers.
342. *The Saturday Record and Clare Journal*, 2 April 1921.
343. R (Childers) v Adjutant General, Provisional Forces [1923] 1 IR 5.
344. The King (Garde and Others) v Major General EP Strickland and Others [1921] 2 IR 317.
345. With him were Richard Best KC, later Attorney General of Northern Ireland, and Lewis Richard Lipsett, who had appeared as junior for the Crown in the case of Allen. He took silk later that year.
346. These protections were embodied in the Treason Act of 1695, 7 & 8 Will iii, the Treason Act 1708, 7 Ann C. 21 and the Treason Act 1795, 36 Geo 3 C 7. This argument was raised in a number of military court trials, always without success. The JAG had advised on this issue in relation to ROIA courts martial and conferred with the law officers: the result of the discussions is not recorded but it may be readily inferred from decisions made by military courts that it was the view of the JAG and the law officers that the protections of the Treason Acts did not apply to trial by military court. Register of Opinions, the Judge Advocate General, 25 January 1921.
347. R v Allen [1921] 2 IR 241.
348. The King (Ronayne and Mulcahy) v Strickland and Another [1921] 2 IR 333.
349. Instructed by Barry Sullivan of Mallow. Sullivan had just qualified as a solicitor and this was his first capital trial.
350. Relying on Attorney General v De Keyser's Royal Hotel A C [1920] 508.
351. *The Saturday Record and Clare Journal*, 9 April 1921.
352. See, for instance, *House of Commons Debates*, 23 February 1921, vol. 138, col. 938. See also 24 February 1921, vol. 138, col. 1119.
353. *Hansard*, 5 May 1921, Oral Answers, col. 1203. And see Proclamation No. 3, dated 14 April 1921, PRO/WO/93/39.
354. *Cork Examiner*, 12 May 1921, p.7.
355. Higgins v Willis (1) Irish Reports [1921] 386.
356. Also stayed were identical actions brought by Mrs Nellie Vaughan who ran a boarding house on Washington Street and Mrs Bridget O'Shea who ran a grocery shop on Main Street, Midleton, County Cork. In these two cases, the claimants asserted they had received no prior notice of the destruction of their property.
357. Hopkinson, *The Last Days of Dublin Castle*, p.165.
358. *New York Times*, 29 April 1921.
359. O'Leary, BMH witness statement no. 1589 gives a sober account of the action, trial and execution. O'Leary appears to have thought that their cases went on to the Lords which resulted in delays in the executions. It is clear that this was a misunderstanding.
360. Major Compton-Smith of the Royal Welch Fusiliers commanded the military barracks at Ballyvonaire. He was kidnapped while travelling alone on the railway. It is an odd feature of the conflict that many soldiers and officers were allowed to travel on public transport or 'walk out' from barracks. The vast majority were not interfered with and the practice only ceased at this time. Compton-Smith's letter to his wife was published in the *Cork Examiner*, 4 June 1921. It shows a brave and resolute man.
361. IWM Photographic Archive Q107754.
362. PRO/CAB/23/23/79A & CAB/23/23 81 (20).
363. PRO/CAB/24/123, CP 2911.
364. *Record of the Rebellion. Vol. 3: Law*, p.33. PRO/WO/141/94.

CHAPTER 11

365. See Liam Forde, BMH witness statement no. 1710. See also T. Toomey, *The War of Independence in Limerick*, p.581.
366. A record of the trial, from which this account is drawn, can be found in PRO/WO/71/381. Any quotations are from the file.
367. Presumably this was a reference to the general election of 1918.
368. O'Malley suggests that two men were executed after drumhead trial following the engagement near Kildorrery: O'Malley, *On Another Man's Wound*, p.350. It is clear that two men were captured but only Casey was executed. Hennessey, the other man, died of his wounds in custody; see Liam Forde, BMH witness statement 1710, p.22.

369. F. O'Donoghue, *No Other Law* (Dublin: Irish Press Limited, 1954), p.157; See also Liam Forde, BMH witness statement no. 1710, p.17 and Portly Morgan, BMH witness statement no. 1559.
370. Macready, *Annals of an Active Life*, vol. 2, p.518.
371. PRO/WO/ 35/173/1–2.
372. See Chapter 8 this volume and PRO/WO/141/48, letter from War Office to General Macready, 19 January 1921.
373. *Record of the Rebellion. Vol. 3: Law*, p.5.
374. PRO/WO/141/48, telegram, General Macready to War Office, 19 May 1921. Given the dispute between General Macready and the Judge Advocate General, Cassel, in January, the silence from the office of the JAG is inexplicable.
375. PRO/WO/35/66, Cric No. 2/54340.
376. *Hansard*, Army (Annual) Bill, 11 April 1921, Committee Stage.
377. House of Commons oral answers, 5 May 1921, col. 1205. Further acrimonious exchanges followed when the details of the execution emerged: *House of Commons Debates*, motion for adjournment, 9 May 1921, col. 1516.

CHAPTER 12

378. *Sixth Division Record of the Rebellion*, p.104.
379. This account is taken from PRO/WO/71/383.
380. All quotations are taken from PRO/WO/71/383.
381. PRO/WO/35/116.
382. PRO/CAB/124/123 CP/2911, Cabinet Report for Week Ending 30 April 1921.
383. P. O'Brien, BMH witness statement no. 764, at p.43.

CHAPTER 13

384. Luddy, BMH witness statement no. 1151, p.23.
385. The account of the trial of these men is taken from PRO/WO/71/382. All quotations are from that file.
386. Instructed by J.G. Skinner of Mitchelstown.
387. *Circular Memoranda*, WO/35/66, Regulation 31.
388. Patrick Clifford, witness statement no. 946, p.7.
389. Comyn, *Their Friends At Court*, p.52.
390. Sullivan held no rank in the Volunteers. See BMH witness statement no. 1186, p.15. According to the witness statement of Patrick Clifford made many years later, he had orders to destroy the bridge at Ballygiblin. His account is corroborated by P.J. Luddy, who gave the order; see BMH witness statement no. 1151, at pp.22–3.
391. Babington, *For the Sake of Example*, p.16.
392. Prohibition was a discretionary remedy by which the High Court could forbid a lower court or public body from taking an unlawful step.
393. The effect of Section 50 of the Judicature Act was that the Court of Appeal had no jurisdiction to hear an appeal on a criminal cause or matter.
394. J. Comyn, *Summing it Up* (Dublin: Roundhall Press, 1992), p.18.
395. William Roche, BMH witness statement no. 1362, p.5. When the case went to the Lords, the case for the prisoners was argued by Sir John Simon, Michael Comyn KC, James Comyn, J.A. McCarthy and Richard O'Sullivan.
396. The money, about £2,000, was carried at night across country by P.J. Luddy to Mitchelstown where it was lodged with Mr Skinner, solicitor for the accused. See P.J. Luddy, BMH witness statement no. 1151, p.25.
397. WO/83/41, JAG Minute book, 16 June 1921.
398. The judgment of the Lords in Clifford and Sullivan is dealt with in Chapter 16.

CHAPTER 14

399. The case papers can be found at PRO/WO/71/384. This account is drawn from that file.
400. D. Fitzpatrick, *Politics and Irish Life, 1913–21* (Cork: Cork University Press, 1998), p.98.
401. Ibid., p.119.
402. M. Healy, *The Old Munster Circuit* (Dublin and Cork: Mercier Press, 1986), pp.149–51. Lynch served in Seanad Éireann and was later Attorney General.

403. According to an account in the *Limerick Leader*, 4 May 1921, a military court of inquiry found that Clancy had been shot dead trying to escape.
404. The notes of evidence show that counsel referred to Archbold. The 25th edition of Archbold sets out the law as it then was. Levying war in Ireland was treason by reason of Poynings Act 10 H 7 c.22, Ir. A charge of levying war required proof of levying war against the King in his realm. Numbers were not the important issue, it was the intention to levy war that must be proved. It must be proved that the prisoner was actively engaged in levying war or present and aiding and abetting and intending to commit that offence and a tumult or riot is not sufficient.
405. There was an allegation of ill-treatment of Keane which Cassel mentions and suggests should be the subject of investigation. The allegation was strenuously denied by the RIC.
406. *Limerick Leader*, 6 June 1921.
407. There were other executions outside the Martial Law Area: Patrick Maher and Edward Foley on 7 June in Dublin. But Keane was the last man to be executed as a result of a trial by military court. For an account of the circumstances in which Keane was captured, see T. Toomey, *The War of Independence in Limerick*, p.481.
408. There were a spate of such incidents. See P. O'Brien, BMH witness statement no. 764, at p.29.
409. O'Malley, *On Another Man's Wound*, p.371.
410. The Archives of the Lincolnshire Regiment, Box 12.

CHAPTER 15

411. The case papers from which this account is drawn can be found at PRO/WO/71/385. All quotations from the trial are taken from this file.
412. The handwritten type is not legible at this point.
413. O'Malley Military Notebooks, UCD Archives, p17b/130, p.34.
414. Some of the petitions remain with the case papers, PRO/WO/71/385.
415. PRO/WO/83/41, p.133.
416. Hugh Kennedy was appointed King's Counsel in 1920. He became senior legal advisor to Dáil Éireann during the Treaty negotiations and Attorney General of the Provisional Government. He assisted in drafting the new constitution and he became the first Chief Justice of the Irish Free State, a position he held until his death in 1936.
417. *Cork Examiner*, 7 July 1921.
418. R v Allen [1921] 2 IR 241.
419. The King (Garde and Others) v Major General EP Strickland and Others [1921] 2 IR 317.
420. *Cork Examiner*, 7 July 1921.

CHAPTER 16

421. There was no single document bringing the Truce into effect. Both sides entered into an oral agreement and later published their own versions which are silent on military courts and executions. One of the provisions agreed to by General Macready reads: 'Military activity shall be restricted to the support of the police in their normal civil duties. Cmd 1534 of 1921, Cessation of Active Operations in Ireland. In the version issued by Sinn Féin there is a footnote which simply reads: 'There are other details connected with courts martial, motor permits and ROIR to be agreed later.' The author has been unable to discover whether there were any such discussions.
422. The Register, WO/35/208 shows no trials after 8 July 1921. There are no records of such trials held at the National Archive in London or reports of such trials in contemporary sources. There is some evidence the Summary Court continued to function.
423. *Cork Constitution*, 20 July 1921.
424. [1902] AC 109.
425. The argument adopted by the Master of the Rolls reflected the principle laid down in the Lords in the De Keyser Case [1920] AC 508.
426. [1868] Finlason's Report.
427. Report to Cabinet for week ending 30 July 1921, CAB/24/126.
428. Counsel for the prisoners were Sir John Simon KC, Michael Comyn KC, James Comyn, J.A. McCarthy and Richard O'Sullivan of the English Bar. For the Crown, Sergeant Hanna, E.S. Murphy and Lipsett.

429. In re: Clifford and Sullivan [1921] 2 AC 570.
430. The Lords left undecided the question of whether a writ of habeas corpus was open to Clifford and Sullivan and whether the case of John Allen was correctly decided.
431. IR [1921] 280. Reproduced by kind permission of the Incorporated Council of Law Reporting for Ireland.
432. Ibid.
433. *New York Times*, 30 July 1921.
434. PRO/CAB/24/126.
435. See, for instance, PRO/WO/83/41, 352.
436. ILTR [1921] vol. LV, p.202.
437. Report to Cabinet week ending 6 August, PRO/CAB/24/126.
438. PRO/WO/141/94, *Record of the Rebellion. Vol. 3: Law*, pp.32–3.
439. PRO/WO/141/53, Macready, letter to Army Council, 1 August 1921.
440. Special Order of the Day, Parkgate GHQ, Dublin. *Record of the Rebellion. Vol. 3: Law*, p.32.
441. [1921] 2 AC 570.
442. The question of peace talks surfaced repeatedly in the Cabinet minutes in the spring of 1921 and it was public knowledge that emissaries from both sides were engaging in discussions. See Whitehall Diaries, pp.54–68.
443. See, for instance, Comyn, *Their Friends at Court*, p.51. The error has been repeated in D. Macardle, *The Irish Republic* (London: Corgi Books, 1968), p.427 and elsewhere.
444. PRO/WO/35/208.
445. This is the position taken by Dorothy Macardle in her excellent history of the period. See Macardle, *The Irish Republic*, p.427. It was also widely believed by many Volunteers at the time: see William Roche, BMH witness statement no. 1362, p.6.
446. Macready, *Annals of an Active Life*, vol.2, p.564. Macready recalled that executions were suspended pending an appeal to the Lords. *Hansard* provides another point of reference on this issue, at Westminster where in mid-June T.P. O'Connor raised the case of J.J. Egan, who was also under sentence of death. *House of Commons Debates*, 16 June 1921, vol. 143, col. 593. Hamar Greenwood confirmed that no further step would be taken in the case pending the decision of the Lords in a similar case. The only case that went to the Lords was Clifford and Sullivan.
447. CAB/24/123 (CP 2983).
448. Middlemass, *Thomas Jones*, vol. 3, pp.72–3.
449. *Sixth Division Record of the Rebellion*, Appendix V. The actual figure is much higher having regard to unofficial reprisals.
450. Middlemass, *Thomas Jones*, vol. 3, p.72. General Macready argued that the alternative was to rigorously enforce the death sentence for those found in arms.
451. PRO/CAB/27/107.
452. Middlemass, *Thomas Jones*, vol. 3, p 73.
453. Parliamentary Archive, LG/F/25/1/42.
454. A single area where the Committee hesitated and sought legal advice was the question of limiting access to the courts. This issue was referred to the law officers. The record of these discussions cannot be traced.
455. Proclamation No. 5, *Record of the Rebellion. Vol. 3: Law*, p.24.
456. *Record of the Rebellion. Vol. 3: Law*, p.26.
457. Ibid.
458. PRO/WO/35/66, 2 August 1921.
459. PRO/WO/141/55.
460. *Record of the Rebellion. Vol. 3: Law*, p.49.
461. PRO/WO/141/55.
462. A. Lentin, *The Last Political Law Lord* (Newcastle: Cambridge Scholars Publishing, 2008), p.134.
463. Cabinet meeting, 2 August 1921 (62 (21)).
464. PRO/WO/71/382, letter 1 November 1921.
465. Ibid.
466. Ibid.
467. These figures of course do not take account of those convicted under courts martial under the Restoration of Order in Ireland Act or interned outside the scope of martial law.

468. PRO/WO/83/41, 9 November 1921.
469. PRO/WO/141/53, letter, Macready to Lamington Worthington Evans, 9 November 1921.
470. PRO/WO/141/94, *Record of the Rebellion. Vol. 3: Law*, p.5.

CHAPTER 17

471. This account is taken from the *Cork Constitution*, 4 January 1921, and Malone's BMH witness statement no. 845.
472. *Cork Constitution*, 4 January 1921, courtesy of the National Library of Ireland.
473. He was also wanted in the name of Seán Forde.
474. Tomas O Maoileoin, BMH witness statement, pp.76–8.
475. PRO/WO/35/208.
476. PRO/WO/35/208.
477. See Appendix 2, this volume.

CHAPTER 18

478. Census 1911.
479. See PRO/WO/35/208. There is a short report of this case in the *Cork Examiner*, 17 February 1921, from which this account is drawn. Material is reproduced courtesy of the *Irish Examiner* and National Library of Ireland.
480. PRO/WO/35/208.
481. PRO/WO/35/208.

CHAPTER 19

482. The prisoner's name is spelled Renehane in the Register, PRO/WO/35/208. It is suggested that the correct spelling is Renehan.
483. Bridie McKay, forty-four years old, a native of Kerry. She was married to a scrap dealer and built up the business on Pope's Quay after the death of her first husband.
484. *Sixth Division Record of the Rebellion*, p.77.
485. The account of the trial is taken from PRO/WO/71/379. For a different account see G. Murphy, *The Year of Disappearances: Political Killings in Cork, 1921–22* (Dublin: Gill & MacMillan, 2010).
486. James Reardon of counsel represented McKay, Carey and Renehan. J.F. Meagher of counsel represented Fitzgerald, Murphy, O'Driscoll, J. and C. Twomey and Dennehy. J.F. Bourke of counsel represented MacSwiney, Thompson, Conroy and O'Keefe. Mr Gardiner Wallis, solicitor, represented Bowles.
487. Moylan, BMH statement 838, p.258.
488. *Hampshire Regiment Record of Service in Ireland, 1921*, p.9.
489. Hampshire War Diary, 8 February 1921.
490. PRO/WO/35/208.
491. Moylan, BMH witness statement no. 838, p.258.
492. D. Harvey and G. White, *The Barracks: The History of Victoria/Collins Barracks, Cork* (Cork: Mercier Press, 1997), p.72. In this book it is suggested that Baylor took part in the Dillon's Cross ambush in December 1920. Baylor was certainly a local man, then aged twenty-three. He was brought up in Abbey Cottages on the north of Cork city not far from Victoria Barracks.
493. Strickland Papers, Notes on the Administration of Martial Law, Appendix 1.
494. *Sixth Division Record of the Rebellion*, p.77.
495. PRO/CO/762/181. It appears that she had been an informant for some time and had been handsomely paid for her efforts.

CHAPTER 20

496. PRO/CAB/24/109, CP 2504.
497. Michael Connelly, BMH witness statement no. 1618, p.7.
498. The trial was reported in the *Waterford News and Star*, 4 March 1921. Material reproduced is courtesy of the *Waterford News and Star* and the National Library of Ireland.
499. The solicitor for the accused was P.R. Buggy, who was an experienced advocate who had conduct of many serious trials in this period.

500. The Restoration of Order in Ireland Regulations created offences pursuant to the Restoration of Order in Ireland Act 1920 which was passed into law in August 1920. The Military Court asserted jurisdiction over all martial law offences and also offences contrary to the ROIR: *Circular Memoranda on Martial Law*, Regulation 2, PRO/ WO/35/66.
501. The King v Charles Pinney Esquire (1832) Barnewall and Adolphus 947.
502. Reprisals were described by General Macready in his autobiography, *Annals of an Active Life*, vol. 2, p.523. An order for destruction could only be issued by a brigade commander. Notice was served as in 'Form B' PRO/CO/904/114 and destruction followed within the hour. Usually by explosive charge. See also 17th Infantry Brigade, *Summary of Important Instructions*, PRO/WO/141/93.

CHAPTER 21

503. This account is taken from the *Cork Constitution*, 7 March 1921. Material reproduced is by courtesy of the National Library of Ireland.
504. Instructed by Maurice O'Connor of Cork.
505. PRO/WO/35/208.

CHAPTER 22

506. Manchester Regiment, Register of Arrests, 1921.
507. This account is drawn from the *Cork Examiner*, 10 March 1921. Reproduction of any material is courtesy of the *Irish Examiner* and the National Library of Ireland.
508. Murphy was defended by John Bourke BL, instructed by Denis Boudren.
509. O'Callaghan, *Execution*, p.172.
510. Murphy played a full part in the ambush. In O'Callaghan's *Execution*, p.170, he stated that his defence had been made up by his solicitor Denis Boudren and he had been required to rehearse his account.

CHAPTER 23

511. Essex Regimental Diary, 1921, p.20.
512. Recounted by C. Meaney, BMH witness statement no. 787. See also chapter 27.
513. There is reliable evidence that the ambush was planned and led by Charlie Hurley, who was himself killed some weeks later.
514. *Sixth Division Record of the Rebellion*, p.79.
515. A military court of inquiry named the dead civilians as John Spiers, Joseph Byrne, Charles Johnston, John Perrett, Richard Arthur, ticket collector, May Hill, cook, William Finn, seaman. All of the above were found to have been unlawfully killed. William Donoghue and Seán Hegarty were found to have been lawfully killed by the army in self-defence (although a review of other sources strongly suggests they were not part of the attacking party), PRO/CO/904/189. One additional fatality not named by the Military Court of Inquiry was a Mr Galvin, a commercial traveller. An unknown number of civilians were wounded.
516. Volunteers killed included Batt Falvey and Seán Phelan. Daniel O'Mahony and Patrick O'Sullivan managed to get away but died of their wounds. *Kerryman*, 7 October 1967, from an account by T. Kelleher.
517. It has not been possible to trace the names of the army casualties.
518. CAB/24/120, Cabinet Weekly Survey, 19 February 1921.
519. The other man died before coming to trial. It was later said by Diarmuid O'Leary that this man was the stationmaster who had joined the ambush party and been wounded. The circumstances of his death were related by O'Leary in BMH witness statement no. 1589, p.9.
520. The account of the trial comes from the *Cork Constitution*, 22 March and the *Cork Examiner*, 23 March 1921. Reproduction of material is courtesy of the *Irish Examiner* and the National Library of Ireland.
521. By Proclamation dated 21 February 1921, the raising of levies for the Volunteers or payment into such a fund was declared illegal, PRO/W0/93/28.
522. The trial record does not disclose the name of this witness, simply the fact that he was the parish priest. Other records show that Father Desmond was the parish priest of Innishannon and Knockavilla, which included Upton. He was parish priest from 1919 to 1931.
523. It will be remembered that in December 1920 Bishop Cohalan had excommunicated of all those who took part in the 'Ambush War'.

524. PRO/WO/35/208.
525. *Kerryman*, 7 October 1967, an account by T. Kelleher. The role played by the prisoner remains the subject of discussion and conjecture. See Begley BMH statement 1771, p.11. See also W. Sheehan, *British Voices*, p.126.

CHAPTER 24

526. The account of this trial comes from the *Waterford News and Star*, 8 April 1921. Material reproduced is courtesy of the *Waterford News and Star* and the National Library of Ireland.
527. In Kilkenny gelignite was stolen by local miners in small quantities and was passed on to men like Medlar. See Brennan, witness statement no. 1601, p.11.
528. PRO/WO/35/208.

CHAPTER 25

529. This man's name is recorded in PRO/WO/35/208 as John Cote but it appears safe to conclude his name was Coote having regard to the witness statement of MacNamara and the contemporaneous reports of the trial. It appears that on arrest he gave his name as John Moroney, which his counsel accepted was false. Within a week he was prosecuted before the Summary Court for the offence of giving a false name. See *Limerick Leader*, 23 March 1921.
530. The location is described by MacNamara in his witness statement as O'Brien's Castle. It is described in the Register as Kearney's Castle; the exact location is uncertain but it was near Carrahane, County Clare.
531. The account of the trial is taken from the *Clare Champion* and permission to reproduce extracts is gratefully acknowledged. The trial is described in the report as a general court martial but it is plainly a military court having regard to the fact that it is so described in the Register and the fact that a challenge was made in the course of the trial to the martial law jurisdiction asserted by the court. Other sources used include MacNamara's BMH witness statement no. 1135.
532. T.P. Coogan, *Long Fellow, Long Shadow* (London: Hutchinson, 1993).
533. *Limerick Leader*, 23 March 1921.
534. BMH witness statement of MacNamara, no. 1135, at p.35.

CHAPTER 26

535. This account is drawn from the *Cork Examiner*. Material reproduced is by consent of the *Irish Examiner* and courtesy of the National Library of Ireland.
536. Instructed by C.K. Murphy, Cork.
537. PRO/WO/35/208.

CHAPTER 27

538. *Sixth Division Record of the Rebellion*, p.77. And also PRO/WO/35/88B.
539. Con Meaney, BMH witness statement 787, p.17.
540. Sergeant Frederick Boxold was thirty-four, a single man and veteran of the Great War. He was buried at Killarney Cathedral.
541. Holyome was a 23-year old single man from Stepney. He served during the Great War and was wounded in 1916. After his death at Killarney his body was returned to London where he was buried at Tower Hamlets.
542. This account is taken from the BMH witness statement of Con Meaney, no. 787, p.17. It adds detail but is not inconsistent with the account given by the *Sixth Division Record of the Rebellion*.
543. The Grazebrook Diary, p.22; Soldiers of the Gloucester Museum.
544. Strickland Papers, IWM, 'Notes on the Administration of Martial Law', p.3.
545. This account is drawn from the *Cork Examiner*, 10,11 & 12 May 1921 and any material reproduced is courtesy of the *Irish Examiner* and the National Library of Ireland who granted access to the archive.
546. Ibid.
547. Ibid.
548. Ibid.

549. Grazebrook Diary, p.33, 13 May 1921.
550. Grazebrook Diary, p.23.
551. PRO/WO/35/208.
552. The BMH statement of William Reardon, no. 1185 made in 1955 names many of the participants in the ambush but does not mention Cunningham or Dennehy. Nor are they named in BMH statement 787 of Con Meaney who organised and led the ambush. And see O. Doyle, *Journal of the Irish Railway Record Society*, vol. 24, June 2011.

CHAPTER 28

553. The account of this trial is taken from the *Limerick Chronicle*, 19 May 1921. All material reproduced is courtesy of the *Limerick Chronicle* and the National Library of Ireland. The killing of this man was later recounted in a BMH statement by Patrick Reidy (1112) who recorded, somewhat grudgingly, that the deceased met his death in 'a quiet but brave manner'. See also witness statement of James Quinn 1073. And see P. Ó Ruairc, *Blood on the Banner*, p.237.
554. Mulcahy Papers (B8) P.7/A/16.
555. PRO/CO 904/189.
556. Compensation hearing, Ennis Quarter Sessions, Monday 30 May 1921.
557. PRO/CO/904/189.
558. H. O'Brien Moran was famously profiled in Healy, *The Old Munster Circuit*, p.97.
559. *Clare Champion*, 4 June 1921, The sum of £1,200 plus costs was ordered, which under the law applicable at the time was paid from the rates. Material reproduced is courtesy of the *Clare Champion* and the National Library of Ireland.

CHAPTER 29

560. CAB/24/122 CP 2872.
561. Instructed by H. O'Brien Moran of Limerick.
562. The account of this trial is taken from the *Limerick Leader*, 18 and 20 May and *Limerick Chronicle*, 19 May 1921. Material reproduced is by courtesy of the *Limerick Leader* and the National Library of Ireland.
563. WO/83/41, p.15. The circumstances of the arrest are also described in the BMH statement of Morgan Portley, no. 1559, at p.28. It is clear that the arrestees were subjected to a sustained beating with ash branches and rifle butts.
564. *Circular Memoranda on Martial Law*, Regulation 17.
565. The record of his trial can be found at PRO/WO/35/98, and see PRO/CO/904/201.
566. PRO/WO/35/208.
567. PRO/WO/83/41, p.15.
568. *Cork Examiner*, 10 June 1921.
569. *Limerick Leader*, 10 June 1921.
570. T. Toomey, *The War of Independence in Limerick, 1912–1921* (Limerick: privately published, 2010), p.575.

CHAPTER 30

571. Most of the case papers at the Public Record Office do not survive. A section of the record survives because it became mixed up in the papers relating to the two prisoners captured at Mitchelstown; Clifford and Sullivan: PRO/WO/71/382. The account of this trial is taken in the main from the Public Record Office at Kew and also the *Limerick Leader*, 23 May 1921. Material reproduced is by courtesy of the *Limerick Leader* and the National Library of Ireland.
572. Instructed by H. O'Brien Moran. Patrick Kelly was profiled in Healy, *The Old Munster Circuit*, pp.48–51.
573. Reproduced by permission of the *Limerick Leader* and courtesy of the National Library of Ireland.
574. PRO/WO/35/208.
575. PRO/CAB/24/125 CP 3003, Cabinet Report Week Ending 28 May 1921.

CHAPTER 31

576. R.J. Kinahan instructed by H. O'Brien Moran.
577. PRO/WO/35/208.
578. PRO/WO/83/41, p.14.
579. PRO/WO/35/208.

CHAPTER 32

580. The account of the trial is drawn from the *Cork Examiner*, 28 May 1921.
581. *Cork Examiner*, 28 May 1921. Reproduced courtesy of the *Irish Examiner* and the National Library of Ireland.
582. Ibid.
583. R v Ibrahim 1914 AC 599.
584. PRO/WO/35/208.

CHAPTER 33

585. Willis and Bolster, joint BMH witness statement no. 808, p.9. The third man was Patrick McCarthy.
586. O'Malley, *On Another Man's Wound*, p.213; see also Moylan, BMH witness statement no. 838, p.103 and P. O'Brien, BMH witness statement no. 764, p.22.
587. Moylan, BMH witness statement no. 838, p.95.
588. Summary of Evidence, third witness.
589. George Power, BMH witness statement no. 451, p.12.
590. Sergeant Gibbs joined the army in 1914 and served in France from 1915 to 1918. He was invalided home twice. Regimental records show that he was a respected and well-liked NCO.
591. Annie Barrett, BMH witness statement no. 1133, pp.4–6.
592. *History of the 17th Lancers*, p.143.
593. *New York Times*, 29 September 1921 and the *Cork Examiner*, 29 September 1921.
594. Diary of Sir Henry Wilson, Chief of the Imperial Defence Staff, 29 September 1920 (IWM).
595. *House of Commons Debates*, 20 October 1920, col. 931. The report refers to the search for a man named Wills. There seems little doubt that this is a reference to Willis. The information was supplied by telegraph by Art O'Brien, formerly a member of the House.
596. PRO/WO/35/103.
597. Lieutenant McCreery was killed in ambush at Gort. Robert Bruce McCreery was twenty-two years of age at the time of his death. He was buried at Sherborne, Dorset.
598. The account of this trial is taken from the *Cork Constitution*, the *Cork Examiner* and the *Limerick Leader*; the affidavit of Barry Sullivan sworn in the case of Buckley v Major General E.P. Strickland and the Attorney General for Ireland, unreported and the petition for clemency to the Lord Lieutenant and Governor General.
599. PRO/WO/83/40, Minute Book of the Judge Advocate General, 1921.
600. An ROIA court martial trying a case carrying the death penalty was required to have a legal member certified by the Lord Chief Justice to be a person of legal knowledge. ROIA, Section 1(2).
601. Albert Wood KC represented Barter, McCarthy, Harold and Murphy. His instructing solicitor was Barry Sullivan. John Bourke represented Breen, and Patrick Lynch KC with Joseph McCarthy, instructed by Denis Boudren, represented David Buckley.
602. The petition drafted after conviction indicated that the summary of evidence had been discarded. It appears never to have been served on the defence.
603. Affidavit, Barry Sullivan in the case of Buckley v Major General Strickland and the Attorney General for Ireland, Unreported.
604. Harold, BMH witness statement no. 991.
605. *Cork Examiner*, 24 May 1921.
606. Ibid.
607. *Limerick Leader*, 25 & 27 May 1921.
608. Petition for clemency drafted by Albert Wood KC.
609. Petition for clemency, and see also *Cork Examiner*, 30 May 1921.
610. Although there was a degree of tension between the military and civilian authority over who had the power to exercise clemency. In the case of Joseph Murphy, convicted of the

murder of Private Squibs, the decision on clemency was pending before the Lord Lieutenant and Governor General, when General Macready stepped in and commuted sentence.

611. PRO/WO/83/41, p.220.
612. John Murphy, BMH witness statement no. 1217, p.8.
613. It was later said by Sullivan that the Sixth Division legal officer, H.M. Meyler, was recalled to London as a result of his representations about bias. This is contradicted by other evidence which clearly shows Lieutenant Colonel Meyler retired from his post in 1922, after which he was elected to parliament and awarded the CBE.
614. *Record of the Rebellion. Vol. 3: Law*, p.37.
615. Strickland Papers, IWM. See 'Notes on the Organisation and Methods of Sinn Féin'.
616. BMH witness statement no. 217, pp.4–5.
617. See, for instance, George Power, BMH witness statement no. 451, p.12 and P. O'Brien, BMH witness statement no. 764, p.22.
618. BMH witness statement no. 991, pp.11–12.

CHAPTER 34

619. Tried under the name John Moylan.
620. Grazebrook wrote an account of his service in Ireland and this engagement, which was probably the best account of this conflict written by a serving British soldier: The Grazebrook Diary, Soldiers of the Gloucestershire Museum.
621. Moylan, BMH witness statement no. 838, p.254.
622. Ibid., p.255.
623. *Record of the Rebellion. Vol. 3: Law*, p.4.
624. *Grazebrook Diary*, p.40.
625. Moylan, BMH witness statement no. 838, p.252.
626. Ibid.
627. Ibid.
628. *Manual of Military Law* (6th edn), Rules of Procedure, r 34.
629. The account is taken from the *Cork Examiner*. Material is reproduced courtesy of the *Irish Examiner*. This account of the trial is also taken in part from records held by the Soldiers of the Gloucestershire Museum and I acknowledge permission to quote material. For another account of this trial see A. Carroll, *Seán Moylan* (Cork: Mercier Press, 2010).
630. *House of Commons Debates*, 1 June 1921, vol. 142, cols 1047–8.
631. PRO/WO/35/103.
632. *Freeman's Journal*, 6 June 1921.
633. *The Times*, 6 June 1921.
634. Albert Wood KC appeared with SC Porter. Sergeant Hanna KC and Lipsett KC appeared for the Crown.
635. *Cork Examiner*, 10 June 1921.
636. Moylan, BMH witness statement no. 838, p.254.

CHAPTER 35

637. This account is drawn from the *Cork Examiner*, 3 June 1921 and permission given by the *Irish Examiner* is acknowledged. Material reproduced is also courtesy of the National Library of Ireland, who permitted access to the archive.
638. PRO/WO/35/208.
639. PRO/WO/83/41, Minute Book of the Judge Advocate General, 8 June 1921.
640. Loughlin was released on 12 January 1922.

CHAPTER 36

641. This account is taken from the *Cork Examiner*, 9 June 1921 and all quotations are courtesy of the *Irish Examiner* and the National Library of Ireland, who gave access to the archive.
642. PRO/WO/35/208.
643. Abbott, *Police Casualties in Ireland*, p.239.

CHAPTER 37

644. *Sixth Division Record of the Rebellion*, p.38.
645. See Chapter 51 this volume.
646. In the space of a few weeks there were similar incidents at Father Murphy's Bridge near Banteer and Clonfert Bridge. See also Michael O'Sullivan, BMH witness statement no. 1186, p.13.
647. PRO/CAB/24/121 CP 2527.
648. The account of this trial is drawn from the *Cork Examiner*, 14 June 1921. Material reproduced is by permission of the *Irish Examiner* and courtesy of the National Library of Ireland.
649. Instructed by Denis Boudren, solicitor, Cork city.
650. PRO/WO/35/208.
651. WO/83/41, p.104.
652. It has been asserted elsewhere that the decision not to execute these men had more to do with the fact that Lord Bandon had been kidnapped to secure the safety of Daly. See L. Deasy, *Towards Ireland Free* (Dublin and Cork: Mercier Press, 1973), p.294. This is unlikely, since the army had ignored other instances of hostage taking, notably Mary Lindsay, her butler and Major Compton-Smith. In any event the convention not to permit executions pending an appeal to the Lords was long standing. It should, however, be acknowledged that it is likely that the Cabinet at Westminster welcomed a pretext that might avoid further executions while the peace process gathered pace.

CHAPTER 38

653. Census 1911.
654. General Macready, Cabinet Weekly Summary, PRO/CAB/24/121, CP 2757.
655. The account of this trial comes from the *Waterford News and Star*, 17 June 1921. Material reproduced is by consent of the *Waterford News and Star* and courtesy of the National Library of Ireland.
656. Instructed by P.R. Buggy of Waterford. Patrick Lynch KC was later Attorney General. J.J. Mooney became Judge Advocate General.
657. Under Proclamation No. 2, home owners were required to keep a list of residents fixed to their front door.
658. PRO/WO/35/208.
659. *Irish Law Times*, 10 July 1921.
660. Ned Aylward, BMH statement no. 980, pp.13–16.

CHAPTER 39

661. General Macready, Weekly Cabinet Survey, week ending 12 March, CAB/24/121 CP 2757.
662. This account is taken from the *Cork Examiner*, 17 June 1921. Material reproduced is courtesy of the *Irish Examiner* and the National Library of Ireland.
663. Instructed by James F. d'Arcy, solicitor, of Tipperary.
664. The preamble to the Treason Act 1795 required proof of treason 'upon the oath of two lawful and credible witnesses'.
665. *Circular Memoranda on Martial Law*, Reg. 66.
666. Census 1901 and 1911.

CHAPTER 40

667. Instructed by William Barry of Midleton.
668. The account of this trial comes from the *Cork Constitution*, 22 & 23 June 1921. Material reproduced is courtesy of the National Library of Ireland.
669. See BMH, statement no. 1476, in which Higgins sets out a full account of the siege.
670. WO/83/41, p.157.

CHAPTER 41

671. The account of the trial is taken from the *Cork Examiner*, 25 June 1921. Material reproduced is courtesy of the *Irish Examiner* and the National Library of Ireland.

672. Instructed by H. O'Brien Moran, solicitor.
673. P. O'Brien, BMH statement no. 764, p.32.
674. O'Donoghue, *No Other Law*, p.107.
675. PRO/WO/35/208.

CHAPTER 42

676. The account of this trial is drawn from the *Waterford News and Star*, 1 July 1921. Material reproduced is courtesy of the *Waterford News and Star* and also the National Library of Ireland, who granted access to the newspaper archive.
677. Later Attorney General, 1924–6, a judge of the High Court, 1926–40 when he was appointed to the Supreme Court. O'Byrne was instructed by Mr O'Connor, solicitor, of Wexford.
678. PRO/WO/35/208.

CHAPTER 43

679. This account is taken, unless otherwise stated, from the *Clonmel Chronicle*, 2 July 1921. Material reproduced is courtesy of the National Library of Ireland.
680. Instructed by W.D. Mockler.
681. *Cork Examiner*, 2 July 1921.
682. PRO/WO/35/208.
683. PRO/WO/83/41, 15 July 1921.
684. *Circular Memoranda on Martial Law*, PRO/WO/35/66.

CHAPTER 44

685. The spelling is taken from the 1911 Census. The trial record and the Register, PRO/WO/35/208, shows Kildrina.
686. Ned Aylward, BMH statement no. 980, p.18.
687. PRO/CAB/24/123 (CP 2948).
688. See Nicolas Carroll, BMH witness statement no. 1705, p.5. The men who died were very probably Patrick Walsh and Seán Quinn.
689. This account of the trial is drawn from the *Cork Examiner*, 2 July 1921. Reproduction of material is by consent of the *Irish Examiner* and courtesy of the National Library of Ireland.
690. PRO/WO/35/208.

CHAPTER 45

691. This account is taken from the *Limerick Leader*, 1 July 1921. Material reproduced is courtesy of the *Limerick Leader* and the National Library of Ireland, who provided access to the archive.
692. Instructed by J.H. Moran, solicitor.
693. *Irish Law Times*, 23 July 1921, p.182.

CHAPTER 46

694. *Manchester Regiment Record of Service in Ireland, 1921*, p.43.
695. *Sixth Division Record of the Rebellion*, p.123.
696. Evidence from the Court of Inquiry into the death of Walter Leo Murphy, PRO/WO/35/155B.
697. Evidence of Lt Colonel Evans, Court of Inquiry into the death of Walter Leo Murphy. PRO/WO/35/155B.
698. Walter Leo Murphy was wanted in connection with the death of Captain Thompson, an intelligence officer with the Manchester Regiment. He was also sought in connection with the shooting of Sergeant Henry Bloxham, RIC: see Adams, *Police Casualties in Ireland*, p.187.
699. Dublin Castle press release, 28 June 1921; *Cork Examiner*, 29 June 1921.
700. The circumstances in which Daly met his death are outside the scope of this book. The incident is dealt with by Hart, *The IRA and Its Enemies*, p.96. See also report of the Military Court of Inquiry, *Cork Examiner*, 1 July 1921.

701. The account of this trial is taken from the *Cork Examiner*. Material is reproduced courtesy of the *Irish Examiner* and the National Library of Ireland.
702. J.F. Bourke appeared for John Ryan, James Murphy, John Driscoll, Patrick McAuliffe, Patrick Lane, Dan Forde, George Murphy, Denis Lane, John Finn, Jeremiah Forde and John Dineen. Joseph McCarthy acted for Murray, O'Keefe, Desmond, Collins, Sullivan, Patrick Dwyer, William Dwyer, Thomas Riordan and John Horgan. W.C. Hungerford acted for Tim Healy and Eugene Riordan.
703. The sentence of death by shooting is taken from PRO/WO/35/208, although the press report, *Cork Examiner*, 5 July 1921, implies that Murray was acquitted of the more serious charge of improper possession of arms and ammunition. The Register may be taken as correct.
704. The BMH statement of Dan Forde, no. 810, suggests that Forde was sentenced to fifteen years' imprisonment. That is incorrect. He was sentenced to one year's imprisonment.
705. Herlihy, BMH witness statement no. 810, p.20.
706. Herlihy, BMH witness statement no. 810, p.14 suggests that only a few of the convicted men were Volunteers. Forde, who contributed to witness statement no. 810, does not make that suggestion.
707. PRO/WO/83/41 JAG Minute Book, 18/7/21.
708. PRO/WO/35/208.
709. *Cork Examiner*, 5 July 1921. The Register, PRO/WO/35/208, is ambiguous on this point.

CHAPTER 47

710. This account of the trial is drawn from the *Cork Examiner*, 7 July 1921; material is reproduced courtesy of the *Irish Examiner* and National Library of Ireland.
711. Instructed by Maurice McCartie of Killarney.
712. PRO/WO/35/208.
713. JAG Minute Book PRO/WO/83/41, 15 July 1921, p.260.
714. The prisoner was released on 12 January 1922.

CHAPTER 48

715. Fossa Historical Society online archive.
716. Regimental archive, the Royal Fusiliers.
717. Fossa Historical Society online archive.
718. Instructed by Maurice McCartie, solicitor, of Killarney.
719. Also instructed by Maurice McCartie.
720. It is likely that this means the court assigned an officer to watch his interests in accordance with Reg. 19 of the *Circular Memoranda*.
721. This account is taken from the *Cork Constitution*, 7 July 1921. All material reproduced is courtesy of the National Library of Ireland.
722. Firearms Act 1920 10 &11 Geo 5 Ch 43. The Act increased penalties for unlawful possession of a firearm: two years' imprisonment was the new maximum.
723. PRO/WO/83/41, JAG Minute Book 1921.
724. PRO/WO/35/208. We are entirely reliant on the accuracy of the Register, although there is no reason to doubt the reliability of this document.
725. Fossa Historical Society online archive.
726. The identity of this man is uncertain. It is likely that he was Frank Morgan from Nenagh. He was then thirty-four years old, a former railway worker. Census 1911.

CHAPTER 49

727. Instructed by H. O'Brien Moran, solicitor. McGelligott later became one of the first batch of circuit judges appointed by the Irish Free State.
728. This account is taken from the *Clonmel Chronicle*, 9 July 1921. Material is reproduced courtesy of the National Library of Ireland.

CHAPTER 50

729. This account is taken from the *Cork Examiner*, 8 July 1921. Material reproduced is by consent of the *Irish Examiner* and courtesy of the National Library of Ireland.

730. Instructed by Mr E. Hunt.
731. PRO/WO/35/208.

CHAPTER 51

732. Unless otherwise stated, the account of this trial comes from the *Limerick Leader*, 1 July 1921, and such material that is reproduced is by permission of the *Limerick Leader* and courtesy of the National Library of Ireland.
733. *Limerick Leader*, 1 July 1921.
734. PRO/WO/35/208.
735. See Chapter 37 this volume.
736. Proclamation No. 1 required all civilians to obey orders given by or on behalf of the military: 'All persons will render obedience to their orders in all matters whatsoever.' See Appendix 2, this volume.
737. 17th Infantry Brigade, *Summary of Important Instructions*, PRO/WO/35/66.
738. See the *Diary of Lieutenant Grazebrook*, p.25. Similar tactics were employed outside the Martial Law Area: see proclamations contained in PRO/WO/35/66. For further detail on this aspect of the conflict, see O'Callaghan, *Revolutionary Limerick*, p.151.
739. *Diary of Lieutenant Grazebrook*, p.18.
740. T.P. Coogan, *Michael Collins* (London: Hutchinson, 1990), p.178.
741. Percival Lectures, Lieutenant General A.E. Percival. See also the trial of John O'Sullivan, chapter 30 this volume.
742. Grazebrook Diary, p.18.
743. Cork Examiner 22 February 1921.

CHAPTER 52

744. Sentence of death was commuted in respect of Denis Murphy, Timothy Murphy, Edward Punch, Diarmuid O'Leary and Patrick Casey (Milford).
745. John Egan and Patrick Higgins.
746. The following prisoners remained under sentence of death until 1922: John O'Sullivan, Michael O'Keefe, Jack Shine, Patrick Loughlin, Thomas Murray, William Daly, Timothy Keohane, John Driscoll, Cornelius Driscoll, Thomas Looby, Denis Driscoll, Peter O'Connor, Frank Morgan, John O'Connor, Patrick Clifford and Michael O'Sullivan.
747. PRO/WO/35/208.
748. Jack Shine and John Duane.
749. Campbell, *Emergency Legislation in Ireland, 1918–25*, p.78.
750. See, for instance, R v Cornelius Murphy PRO/WO/71/376.
751. *Circular Memoranda on Martial Law*, PRO/WO/35/66.
752. S1 (2) (b) Restoration of Order Act 1920.
753. See, for instance, Babington, *For the Sake of Example*.
754. *Record of the Rebellion. Vol. 3: Law*, p.14.
755. Minute Book of the JAG, PRO/WO/83/40, p.554.
756. R v Murphy [1921] 2 IR 190. This was a court martial under the Restoration of Order in Ireland Act 1920 but the principle is of general application because the officers trying this court martial were drawn from the same pool as those trying cases in the Military Court. It should be noted that the JAG reviewed this conviction and concluded that the inconsistencies were insignificant. JAG Register of Opinions 451–600 at p.37. General Macready commuted the sentence to life.
757. R v Mulcahy and Ronayne, PRO/WO/71/386.
758. PRO/WO/71/380, trial transcript, p.109.
759. The trial of the men concerned in the Mallow Barracks raid was conducted under the ROIA in the last week of May 1921. See, for instance, *Cork Examiner*, 24–30 May 1921.
760. PRO/WO/71/386.
761. This offer was made in the case of Daniel O'Brien, Cornelius Murphy, Frank Morgan and John Moylan. Each of these prisoners declined representation. Patrick Casey (Ballybricken) accepted the offer of assistance.
762. *Circular Memoranda on Martial Law*, WO/35/66, Regulations 19–22.
763. Notably Denis Boudren and C.K. Murphy in Cork, Barry Sullivan in Mallow, William Barry in Midleton, P.R. Buggy in Waterford and H. O'Brien Moran in Limerick.

764. Foxton, *Revolutionary Lawyers*, p.231.
765. Denis Boudren and Barry Sullivan are two examples.
766. Patrick Casey, PRO/WO/71/381.
767. Patrick Casey (Ballybricken) is one; John O'Sullivan, where a request for an adjournment to secure the attendance of witnesses was overruled; Thomas Looby, where a request for an adjournment of some days was refused; and Cunningham, where counsel complained that he had only been instructed over the weekend.
768. One was John Allen, the other was John Moylan.
769. The best-known example is the Caherguillamore raid, Bruff, east Limerick on 27 December 1920. And see also the BMH witness statement of Denis Mulchinock 1074.
770. See Moylan, BMH statement 838, p.248; and O Maoileoin, BMH statement 845, pp.71–5.
771. PRO/WO/71/386.
772. A voire dire: a trial within a trial to determine the admissibility of evidence.
773. Michael O'Callaghan, Emly.
774. Minute Book of the Judge Advocate General, PRO/WO 83/41, p.15.
775. See the influential Devlin Report: *Report of the Committee on Evidence of Identification*, 1976, Cmnd 338.
776. These cases included that of Adolf Beck and George Edalji. See also W. Wills, *Circumstantial Evidence*, 6th edn (London: Butterworths, 1912). The Criminal Division of the Court of Appeal was set up in 1907.
777. This perception appears to have been heightened by an intelligence briefing circulated to all officers which made this point graphically. See 'Notes on the Organisation and Methods of Sinn Féin', Strickland Papers, IWM; and see Minute Book of the Judge Advocate General, 1921, PRO/WO/83/40.
778. Grazebrook Diary, p.25.
779. *Record of the Rebellion. Vol. 3: Law*, p.37, which sets out a letter written by Bryan Kelly, a prisoner from Mallow who tried to set up a false alibi for one of the men tried for the Mallow Barracks raid.
780. Macready, *Annals of an Active Life*, vol. 2; see also O'Callaghan, *Execution*, p.170.
781. See, for instance, MacNamara, Punch and Murphy; and Malone, BMH witness statement no. 845, pp.76–8.
782. Deasy, *Towards Ireland Free*, Appendix D, p.340.
783. See Campbell, *Emergency Legislation In Ireland, 1918–23*, p.96.
784. The prisoner who purported to witness the imposition of the sentence of death on Higgins did so by reference to his own release on 10 May. But it is a matter of record that Higgins was not tried until 21 June. It is likely that what the prisoner saw was a pre-trial hearing relating to the taking of a summary of evidence.
785. See, for instance, Keane, PRO/WO/71/384. The handwritten annotations pencilled into the record by the President of the court confirm this analysis.
786. Regulation 66.
787. An example is Harty in the Clonmult case and the trial of James O'Connell.
788. See the trial of Adam Jones, Wexford, 29 June 1921.
789. Thomas Looby, tried 30 June 1921.
790. Affidavit of Barry Sullivan, solicitor for prisoners tried in respect of the Mallow Barracks raid.
791. Interview with General Strickland, *Evening Standard*, 25 January 1921.
792. PRO/W0/71/376.
793. See Moylan, BMH statement no. 838, p.253. And see Vincent Rice, witness statement no. 843, p.4.
794. Comyn, *Their Friends at Court*, p.50.
795. See, for instance, John Moylan, 30 May 1921.
796. An example might be the disclosure issue which arose in the Rahanisky House trial and also the case of Malone.
797. John Moylan, Thomas Malone, Patrick Clifford, William McNamara, Patrick Higgins, Diarmuid O'Leary, Dan Forde and Michael O'Sullivan.
798. O Maoileoin, BMH witness statement no. 845, pp.76–8.
799. Cornelius Murphy, Michael Sullivan and Patrick Clifford.
800. The same cannot be said of courts martial under the ROIA. See, for instance, the trial arising out of the Mallow Barracks raid.
801. O Maoileoin, BMH witness statement no. 845.

802. Daniel O'Callaghan. See PRO/WO/71/378, General Strickland recommended clemency on the ground that there was some doubt about O'Callaghan's involvement.
803. Strickland Papers, IWM, Memo to all units dated 19 January 1921: 'In awarding punishment it is desirable to draw a distinction between loyalists and those known to be disaffected.'
804. *Sixth Division Record of the Rebellion*, p.77. 'The failure to execute these desperados ... had the worst possible effect.'
805. Babington, *For the Sake of Example*, p.15.
806. PRO/WO/71/377, Memo General Strickland to General Macready, 20 January 1921.
807. PRO/WO/71/384, Memo Brigadier Cameron to General Macready, 19 May 1921.
808. PRO/WO/71/382, Memo General Strickland to General Macready, 8 May 1921.
809. With the exceptions of Patrick Casey and Daniel O'Brien, who were executed without their case being reviewed by the Judge Advocate General.
810. See the Waterfall trial and WO/83/41, JAG Minute Book 1921, entry 19 July.
811. Macready, *Annals of an Active Life*, vol. 2, p.518.
812. E. O'Malley, *On Another Man's Wound*, p.350.

CHAPTER 53

813. Archives, Camberley Staff College, lecture to junior officers, November 1923 by Lieutenant Colonel J.S. Drew.
814. Healy, *The Old Munster Circuit*, pp.149–51.
815. See P. Mackenzie, *Lawful Occasions* (Cork: Mercier Press, 1991), p.7.
816. Ex parte DF Marais [1902] AC 109.
817. R v Allen [1921] 2 IR 241.
818. R (Childers) v Adjutant General of the Provisional Forces [1923] 1 IR 5.
819. Ex parte Milligan 71 US 2 (1866).

APPENDIX 2

820. Reproduced courtesy of the Council of Law Reporting for Ireland.
821. First Schedule: The Generals or Other Officers Commanding 6th Division, 16th, 17th, 18th, and Kerry Infantry Brigades.
822. Second Schedule: To a Military or Police Officer at any Military or Police Barracks, or to a Priest or Other Minister of Religion who Will at Once Arrange for their Delivery to the Nearest Military or Police Barracks.

Index

A

Allen, John 53, 54, 55, 56, 57, 58, 59, 62, 69, 70, 87, 88, 89, 101,102,112, 115, 126, 187,241, 243, 257, 268, 271, 279, 280, 282, 285, 296, 297
Anderson, Sir John 22
Armley, Lieutenant 92, 93, 94

B

Barrett, Annie 290
Barrett, James 61, 62, 280
Barry, William 205, 292, 295
Barter, Denis 171, 176, 177, 179, 181, 290
Baylor, Michael (aka Fitzgerald) 128, 129, 130, 131,132, 133, 268, 286,
Baynham, Hubert, RIC. 195, 200
Bell, Alan 21
Blackburn, Mr Justice 14, 273
Blood – Smyth, Arthur 128, 138
Boland, William 262
Boudren, Denis 53, 126, 287, 290, 292, 295, 296
Bourke, John, F. 53, 55, 74, 76, 174, 184, 279, 280, 286, 287, 290, 294
Bowles, Michael 128, 132, 286
Branston, Captain 242, 243, 249
Breen, Timothy 174, 178, 179, 290
Brown, Herbert 262, 276
Buckley, David 174, 175, 176, 177, 178, 179, 181, 290
Buckley, John 262

C

Callaghan, Jeremiah 60, 61, 63, 66, 67, 68, 139, 280
Cameron, Brigadier General 106, 113, 114, 253, 297
Carey, James 128, 129, 130, 132, 286
Casey, Michael 159, 160, 240
Casey, Patrick (Ballybricken) 92, 93, 94, 95, 96, 240, 243, 244, 254, 271, 282, 295, 296, 297
Casey, Patrick (Milford) 206, 207, 209, 295
Cassel, Sir Felix, 23, 27, 47,48,49,50, 51, 69, 78, 86, 106, 167, 279, 280, 283, 284
Chapman, Spencer, ADRIC, 26, 27, 30, 31, 33
Childers, Erskine 257, 282, 297,
Churchill, Winston 22, 23, 25, 275
Clarke, James 69, 70
Clifford, Patrick 55,87, 95, 100, 101, 103, 104, 110, 112, 113, 114,115, 119,120, 167, 183, 184, 187, 193, 229,240, 241, 244, 253, 271, 272, 283, 285, 289, 295, 296
Coakley, Patrick 140, 141, 142, 143, 144
Cockburn, Lord Chief Justice 13, 14, 16, 264, 272, 273
Cohalan, The Most Reverend, Bishop of Cork, 26, 287
Colbert 145, 146
Colis, Captain, 104
Collins, John 217, 294
Compton-Smith, Major, 86, 90, 282, 292
Comyn, Michael 80, 83, 84, 85, 86, 87, 88, 89, 101, 102, 115, 141, 142, 250, 256, 257, 283, 284
Conroy, Cornelius, 128, 129, 130, 131, 132, 286
Coote, Patrick 148, 149, 151, 152, 283
Costello, John 112, 205
Creedon, Michael 72, 74, 75, 76, 77, 78
Cregan, Patrick 169, 170, 245
Cronin, Patrick 189, 190, 272

Crowley, Tadhg 27, 29, 31, 277
Cunningham, Cornelius 154, 155, 156, 157, 158, 246, 247, 248, 289, 296

Daly, George 204
Daly, William 191, 192, 292, 295
Darling, Mister Justice, 47
Dennehy, Jeremiah 128, 132, 286
Dennehy, Timothy 154, 155, 156, 157, 158, 246, 247, 248, 289
Desmond, Tim 217, 294
Dineen, John 217, 294
Dodds, Mr Justice, 88
Dove, Lieutenant, 82, 83, 129
Driscoll, Cornelius 191, 295
Driscoll, Denis 222, 223
Driscoll John (Waterfall) 217, 220, 294
Driscoll, John (Jones Bridge) 191, 295
Driscoll, Lawrence 128, 132
Duane, John 153, 271, 295
Duane, Michael 262
Dwyer, Patrick 217, 294
Dwyer, William 217, 220, 294

E

Edgell, Inspector RIC 30
Egan, John Joseph 81, 108, 109, 111, 112, 113, 114, 115, 117, 119, 120, 205, 229, 239, 246, 254, 271, 285, 295
Evans, Lieutenant Colonel, 60, 62, 63, 138, 217, 218, 219
Eyre, Edward John 12, 13, 14, 111

F

Fenton, Mamie 126
Finn, John 217, 294
FitzAlan, Viscount, 109, 179
Fitzgerald, J.F. 280
Fitzgerald, Michael (see Baylor)
Flavin, Thomas 262
Foley, Major, Provost Marshal 50
Forde, Dan 217, 271, 294, 296
Forde, Liam 92, 282
Forde, Jeremiah 217, 294

G

Gabbett, William 126, 127, 252
Garde, William 80, 82, 86, 90, 111
Gardiner Wallis 65, 280, 286
Gibbs, Sergeant, 17th Lancers 171, 172, 174, 176, 177, 290
Giffard, Hardinge QC (See Lord Halsbury)
Goodbody, James 106
Gordon, George 12, 13, 14
Gover, Major 62, 80, 128, 131, 133, 138, 243
Grazebrook, Robert Michael, Captain 155, 158, 182, 183, 247, 276, 288, 289, 291, 295, 296
Greenwood, Sir Hamar 22, 24, 33, 71, 91, 117, 186, 280, 281, 285

H

Halsbury, Lord (see Giffard) 14, 17, 56
Hammond, Lieutenant 82, 83, 90, 91
Hanna, Henry 55, 57, 87, 102, 112, 113, 186, 256, 265, 284, 291
Harold, Owen 174, 176, 177, 179, 180, 181, 290
Hart, Vernon 4, 27, 28, 29, 30, 31, 32, 33, 241, 257,276, 277
Harty, John 80, 82, 86, 88, 90, 296,
Hassett, John 148,149, 151,152, 251
Hayes, Jack 262
Healy, Tim 217, 294
Healy, Tim 56, 57, 58, 256, 279,280
Henry, Sir Denis K.C. M.P. 22, 57, 95
Higgins, Patrick 80, 82, 112, 114, 115, 120, 204, 205, 247, 248,271,281, 292, 295, 296
Holmes, Philip Armstrong, Divisional Commissioner, RIC 186,277
Hooper, Patrick, J. 3, 272
Horgan, John 217, 294
Hunt, Hanley 231, 232, 252

J

Jones, Adam 81, 208, 210, 243, 296

K

Keane, Thomas 104, 105, 106, 107, 108, 109, 186, 251, 253, 254, 271, 284, 296
Kearney, John 148, 149, 151, 152, 288
Kelleher, Michael 137
Kelly, Bryan 180
Kelly, Patrick 165, 289

Kennedy, Hugh 110,, 114, 116,, 159, 205, 284
Kenworthy, Commander, M.P. 179, 231, 232
Keogh, James 137
Keohane, Timothy 191,295
Kinahan, Robert, J. 161, 169, 201, 206,215, 216
Koe, Lieutenant, 82

L

Lane, Patrick 217, 219, 294
Lane, Denis 217, 294
Langtry, Eugene 60, 61, 62, 63, 65, 66, 68, 280
Latimer, Colonel, ADRIC, 26
Lavery, Alexander 263
Lemon, George 262, 276
Lendrum, Alan 21
Lindsay, Mary, 60, 68, 69, 70, 71,281, 292
Lloyd George, David, 4, 22, 23, 24, 25, 52, 87,111,116,117, 173,232, 274
Longworth, Ernest Victor, Lieutenant Colonel
Looby, Thomas 211, 212, 295, 296
Looney, Michael 74, 76
Loreburn, Lord Chancellor. 16
Loughlin, Patrick 188, 291, 295
Luttrell, James 194, 197, 200
Luttrell, John 194, 195, 196, 197, 198, 199
Luttrell, Patrick 194, 196, 198, 199, 200
Luttrell, Thomas 194, 196, 198,200
Lynch, John, B. 148
Lynch, Patrick 57, 81, 104, 108, 109, 110, 113, 148, 149, 150,, 161, 163, 174, 195, 205, 256, 265, 280, 283, 290, 292
Lyons, John 60, 61, 63, 65, 67, 68, 69, 271, 280

M

MacCartie, Maurice, 294
Macready, General, Sir CFN. 2,3, 22, 23, 25, 27,28, 43, 47, 48, 49, 50, 57, 58, 59, 64, 69, 70, 71, 78, 86, 88, 89, 90, 91, 94, 95, 102, 106, 110, 111, 112, 113, 114, 115, 117, 118, 119, 120, 164, 167, 179, 187, 188, 205, 212, 221, 229, 239, 259, 260, 261,266, 268, 271, 275, 276, 277, 278, 279,281, 283, 286, 287, 291, 292, 295, 296, 297
MacNamara, Fr, 106
MacNamara, William 148, 149, 150, 151, 152,271, 288,296
MacSwiney, Seán 128, 129, 130, 131, 132, 133, 286
Magner, Canon Thomas J. 27, 29, 31, 32, 277
Malone, Thomas 123, 124,125, 250, 251, 286, 296
Marshall, Kenneth 174, 178
Maxwell, Patrick 262,
McAuliffe, Patrick 217, 220, 294
McBride, John 134, 135
McCarthy, Daniel 174, 176, 177, 178, 179
McCarthy, Joseph 74, 80, 100, 137,141,153,155,189,191,211, 222,225, 256, 283, 290, 294
McCarthy, Tim 60, 61, 62, 65, 68, 69, 271, 280
McCreery, Robert Bruce, Lieutenant, 17th Lancers 171, 172, 174, 176, 290
McGelligott, Edward, 229
McKay, Bridie, 128, 129, 130, 132, 133, 286
McKenna, James 194, 196, 197, 198, 199, 200
Meagher, James, F. 201, 202, 286
Medlar, Laurence 145, 146, 147, 288
Meyler, Lieutenant Colonel, Border Regiment 35, 36, 74, 97, 174, 180, 242, 256, 277, 281, 291
Milling 21
Molony, Lord Chief Justice, 54, 57, 70, 87, 88, 89 279
Montgomery, B.L. 36, 234, 265
Moore, Maurice 80, 83, 85, 86, 89, 90, 271
Morgan, Frank 224, 225, 227, 228, 294, 295
Morrison, Captain 92
Moylan, Seán 172, 182, 183, 184, 185, 186, 187, 264, 271, 276, 279, 280, 286, 290, 291, 295, 296
Mulcahy, Cornelius 72, 74, 75, 76, 78
Mulcahy, Thomas 72, 74, 75, 76,77,78,89, 90, 172, 243, 244, 245, 271, 278, 281
Murphy, Charles, K. 155, 188, 281, 288, 295

Murphy, Cornelius 47, 48, 49, 51, 53, 126, 271, 295, 296
Murphy, Denis 61,138, 139, 252, 295
Murphy, George 217, 294
Murphy, James 217, 294
Murphy, John 174, 177, 179, 180, 291
Murphy, Joseph 69, 243, 290
Murphy Timothy (Pigott's Lane Limerick) 161, 162, 163, 164,295
Murphy, Timothy (Rahanisky House) 128
Murphy, Walter Leo, 217, 218, 219, 220, 293
Murray, Thomas 217,218, 219 220, 221 254, 294, 295

N

Nolan, James 262
Noonan, Reverend James 233, 234, 235

O

O'Brien, Daniel 96, 97, 98, 99, 254, 271, 295, 297
O'Brien Moran, H. 159, 289, 290, 292, 294, 295
O'Brien, Thomas 60, 61, 62, 65, 67, 68, 69, 271, 280
O'Byrne, John 81, 208, 210
O' Callaghan, Daniel 60, 62, 65, 66, 68, 69, 251, 252, 271, 280, 297
O'Callaghan, Michael 215, 216, 246
O'Connell, James 201, 203, 278, 296
O'Connell, Michael 169
O'Conner, Sir Charles, 2, 102, 110, 111, 112, 113, 114, 115, 120, 205, 259, 284,
O'Connor Peter 224, 225, 226, 227, 228, 251, 295
O'Connor, John 224, 225, 226, 227, 228, 251, 295
O'Connor, Martin 225
O'Connor, Maurice 281
O'Connor, Thomas 224, 225, 226, 227, 228
O'Keefe, Daniel 217, 220, 294
O'Keefe, John 228, 132, 286
O'Keefe, Michael 263, 295
O'Leary, Diarmuid 37, 80, 82, 85, 86, 89, 90,254, 271, 277, 281, 282, 287, 295, 296
O'Loughlin, Maurice 263
O'Mahony, Patrick 60, 61, 62, 68
O'Malley, Ernie 106, 172, 174, 180, 254, 276, 282, 284, 290, 297,
O'Sullivan, John 165, 166, 167, 251, 254, 295, 296
Orgill, Lieutenant, Manchester Regiment 63, 72
Otter, F.E. 174

P

Portly, Morgan 283, 289
Powell Mister Justice, 102 183, 186, 187
Punch, Edward 161, 162, 163, 164, 246, 254, 272, 295, 296
Purcell, Michael 213

R

Reardon, James 29, 286
Reilly, John 159, 160
Renehan, Michael 128, 129, 130, 132, 286
Riordan, Bart 74
Riordan, Eugene 217, 219, 220, 294
Riordan, Thomas 217, 294
Ronayne, Patrick 88, 89, 90, 102, 172, 243, 244, 271, 278, 281, 282, 295
Ryan, John 217, 294
Ryan, Michael 263
Ryan, William 229

S

Sealy, James 201, 202, 203
Sheehan, Denis 60, 61, 62, 63, 65, 66, 68, 280
Shiels, Dan, 281
Shine, Jack, John 168, 251 271, 295
Shinnick, Fr Ned, 60
Simon Sir John 52, 52, 87, 102, 279, 283, 284,
Skinner J.G. 101, 283
Staveley – Dale, Captain, 97
Strickland, Major General Sir E. P. 25, 26, 28, 36, 39, 49, 68, 69, 70, 78, 86, 88, 89, 92, 94, 96, 98, 100, 101, 102, 113, 114, 183, 227, 241, 249, 251, 253, 256, 275
Sturgis, Mark 70, 90
Sullivan, Barry 78, 90, 172, 175, 179, 183, 186, 282, 290, 295

Sullivan, Christopher 262
Sullivan, Michael 100, 101, 103, 104, 110, 113, 114, 115, 119, 120, 183, 187, 193, 229, 244, 253, 283, 289, 292, 295, 296
Sullivan, Patrick 80, 83, 85, 86, 90
Sullivan, Tim 217, 294
Sumner, Lord 119, 120

T

Tapling, Captain 108,
Terry, Edmund 80, 82, 86, 90
Thompson, James 128, 132, 286
Tone, Theobald Wolfe 9, 10, 48, 274
Toogood, Alex, Lieutenant, 107
Twomey, Cornelius 128, 132, 286
Twomey, John 128, 132

V

Vandeleur, Lieutenant Colonel, 38, 40, 48, 74, 80, 97, 100, 128, 242, 256

W

Walsh, David 91
Walsh, Robert 80, 86, 90
Wedgwood–Benn, Captain, M.P 179, 186.
Willis, Colonel 51, 89, 282
Wilson, Sir Henry, 24, 26, 173
Wood, Albert 179, 183, 184, 290, 291
Wood, Mackenzie M.P. 95
Woodley, Major Richard, 67, 139
Wylie, William 17, 24, 114, 274, 275

Y

Young, F.E. Captain 35, 36, 53, 74, 77, 80, 92, 100, 128, 174, 175, 242, 243, 244